Continued from front flap]

also meets the minstrels of the countryside and the great exponents of their art, dancers, composers, legendary fiddlers and others who have left their mark and recollections of so many glittering occasions. The story is taken through the eighteenth and nineteenth centuries to the present day.

An analysis is attempted, for the first time, of the elements or characteristics of the traditional idioms of Scottish dance music. This is followed by a description of the instruments associated with the music from early times. Over a hundred examples of dance tunes are provided and there is a bibliography of printed works containing significant numbers of Scottish airs, covering the period from 1670 to 1900. Also included are John Glen's index of dance tunes which were published in the late eighteenth-century collections, and the contents of the principal manuscript collections. There is a general index and a separate music index.

Rantin' Pipe and Tremblin' String

A HISTORY OF SCOTTISH DANCE MUSIC

Rantin' Pipe and Tremblin' String

A HISTORY OF SCOTTISH DANCE MUSIC

GEORGE S. EMMERSON

*with 35 illustrations in plates and
104 music examples in the text*

McGILL – QUEEN'S UNIVERSITY PRESS

MONTREAL

1971

Made in Great Britain at the
Aldine Press · Letchworth · Herts

ISBN 0 7735 0116 9

72.5-741
Library of Congress Catalog Card No. 70-150061

This book is published in Great Britain
by J. M. Dent & Sons Limited

This book has sprung from the interaction of a love of the dance, music, literature and social history of Scotland, nurtured by the author over many years. It owes its existence to the fact that although there have been two excellent books on Scottish music published in the past thirty years—those of Henry George Farmer and Francis Collinson respectively—there has not yet been a book devoted to Scottish music from the point of view of dance and the dancer. This is the first.

When I say that this is not a book for the musicologist, I do not mean to imply that its concerns have been treated with indifference to scholarship; but to serve the needs of the layman as well as the scholar judicious compromise is necessary, and an attempt has been made to achieve this.

Fifty years ago it would have been predicted that a book on Scottish dance music in the second half of the century could have little interest for any but the musical antiquarian. Such were the signs of the times, and not even the most sanguine could have dared imagine the amazing resurgence of the love of Scottish traditional dance and music which we have seen in the past twenty years; and which bids fair to persist as long as Scottish cultural identity is cherished by the Scots and their multitude of descendants in all parts of the world.

In this connection one must reserve a special word of acknowledgment for the Royal Scottish Country Dance Society whose work has been prodigious. The many Highland dance associations have also played their part, a role which began with the desire of the Highland émigrés of Glasgow and London, one hundred and fifty years ago, to ensure the preservation of their cherished music and dance. To these must be added the simple fact that the Scots have been attached to their dance and its music for many centuries, with a devotion that defies time.

The aim of this book is to contribute discernment and understanding to existing enthusiasm, and to furnish the information which shall enable both musicians and dancers to treat their great inheritance with comprehension and fidelity. Happily, there is romance in the tale. It has links with the actors and events which make up Scotland's colourful story; we are taken 'ben the hoose' into cottage and castle, along the ringing causies to the assembly hall and by shade of elm and hawthorn to the village inn. We look in on bridals, fairs, harvest homes and supper parties, and meet the minstrels of the countryside and the distinguished exponents, composers and publishers who have left their mark and enduring fame.

There is something said, too, of the favourite musical instruments which have exerted their influence on Scottish dance music and an effort has been made to explain the tonality of the music in a simple way.

This, then, is the inspiration and outline of the scope and purpose of the book. It was not completed without the benefit of comment, guidance, clerical assistance and the availability of library resources.

I gratefully acknowledge the invaluable suggestions and criticism of Hugh Foss of Castle Douglas, an enthusiast for the Scottish Country Dance and its music. I also benefited from some conversations with the late Henry George Farmer, Keeper of the Manuscripts, Glasgow University, whose authority in the music of the Scots, no less than that of the Arabs, was formidable. John Junner of Banchory gladly placed his knowledge of Scottish fiddle music at my service, and was most helpful.

I am happy to acknowledge my considerable debt to my fruitful association with J. Stanley Hamilton, formerly of Ayr and now Toronto, a peerless exponent of Scottish dance music on the piano; Niel Gow himself could not have inspired dancers more. Also to the members of his band. I now formally thank Frances Wilson of Barrie, Ontario, whose musical accomplishments and interest in Scottish Country Dance made her the ideal reader of this book and hence gave special importance to her perceptive observations. Miss Frances Henderson of London, Ontario, was also most helpful, and Miss Marion Burke of Ancaster, Ontario, typed and typed with devotion and enthusiasm, while Marie Wynne was an ever obliging secretary. I am most grateful to them.

Much of the research associated with this work was made possible by a grant from the Canada Council. Thus does the new country contribute to the repayment of its debt to one of its most important founding cultures, and I am most sensible of the honour and most grateful.

The sources of this work are many and various, but no one can refer to Scottish traditional music without leaning heavily on the collectors and scholarly annotators of the eighteenth and nineteenth and early twentieth centuries—Burns, Johnson, Stenhouse, Graham, Laing, Glen, Dick, Cook and Gilchrist, to name the most important.

I would like to acknowledge, also, the great value of the contribution made by the resources of the following libraries and my appreciation of the never failing courtesy and assistance I have enjoyed at the hands of their officers: the Lawson Library, University of Western Ontario (with special recognition of the late J. Davis Barnett, engineer and bibliophile, whose collection has been of crucial importance to me); the Mitchell Library, Glasgow; the British Museum; Glasgow University; the

National Library of Scotland; Harvard College Library; Toronto Public Library; Edinburgh Public Library; Edinburgh University; University of California, Berkeley; New York Public Library.

I have taken my wife, Catherine, and children Mark and Rosslyn, for granted, yet they, too, have sacrificed something that this book should be; it will embarrass them that I should mention it.

In conclusion I wish to thank the publishers for their painstaking editorial assistance from which this book has greatly benefited.

London, Ontario, 1971   GEORGE S. EMMERSON

CONTENTS

ILLUSTRATIONS

Music examples in the text

The superior numerals in the text indicate bibliographical and other notes at the end of the book, pages 213 to 222. Music examples in the text are indicated by numerals in square brackets.

Types of *dances* and the names of individual dances are printed in the text proper with capital letters, e.g. Reels, Jigs *and* Reel of Tulloch, Haymakers' Jig. Types of *tunes* are printed without capitals, e.g. Scottish measure, strathspey; and titles of individual tunes (unless in headings or tabulated matter), and songs and poems, with capitals and quotation marks, e.g. 'Monymusk' and 'Watson's Scottish Measure'.

CHAPTER I

The Dawn over Alba

n the southern shore of the lovely island of Iona is a small bay called Port-
a-Curaich, the Cove of the Coracle, so called, it is said, from Columba's
anding there in 563. Columba, venerated saint of the early Irish church,
xiled himself from his native Antrim to continue his monastic calling on
he island fringe of his people's growing settlement in Argyll. He climbed
a nearby hill, thereafter known as Carn-cul-ri-Erin, the Cairn of the Back
urned to Ireland, from which he assured himself that the long blue line of
his homeland could no longer be seen on the horizon, for he could not
ear to rest within sight of it. 'Farewell land of song', he said, 'where
birds sing so sweetly' and 'where clerics sing like birds' . . . 'there is a grey
ye that looks back upon Erin'.

He gazed over the face of the ocean and doubtless picked out the
scattered, froth-rimmed rocks, topped in green, and slender strands of the
Hebrides:

> Delightful would it be to me to be in Uchd Ailuinn
>   On the pinnacle of a rock,
> That I might often see
>   The face of the ocean;
> That I might see its heaving waves
>   Over the wide ocean,
> When they chant music to their Father
>   Upon the world's course;
> That I might see its level sparkling strand,
>   It would be no cause of sorrow
> That I might hear the song of the wonderful birds,
>   Source of happiness;
> That I might hear the thunder of the crowding waves
>   Upon the rocks;
> That I might hear the roar by the side of the church
>   Of the surrounding sea;
> That I might see its noble flocks
>   Over the watery ocean.[1]

Here was the great music indeed, the high-toned sounds, so dear to the inhabitants of the Isles, of 'the salt main on which the seagulls cry' echoed in Hebridean song. But no trace, in this windswept, treeless place, of the 'sounds of the winds in the elms, like the strings of a harp being played' which he had known in Antrim. Yet here would his race cultivate a new land of song, of the sweet sounds of *cruit* and *tiompan*, which even at this time distinguished the Irish homeland.

Stepping into our tale in the sixth century, it is right that we should place ourselves with Columba, as representative of that cultural force which has so impressed itself on the traditional arts in Scotland and which supported the lamp of learning when Europe was without light.

On the mainland, amid the Grampian forests and fertile straths and carses of Alba, was the kingdom of the Picts, and on the braes and howes of the Lowlands south of the Highland Line, the kingdom of the Britons reaching far into England; and by the salty links bordering the German Sea and in the North and in the Outer Hebrides, the Germanic infiltrations—Danes, Norse, Angles, Frisians.[3] The Vikings were yet to come in force, as were the Norman barons, some four centuries later.

Such were the ethnical bricks of modern Scotland which in course of time were to be bound together with the cement of nationhood, each contributing something of its own. Yet so much was already shared.

In these early times, when written record is so sparse, we look hopefully to the Irish scribes and the relics of the bards, to tell us of music and dance. We catch a glimpse of great fairs and of the Feis of Tara, where bards foregathered with their people to chant their heroic tales to the accompaniment of the *chrotta*, and minstrels played trumpets, 'wide-mouthed horns', pipes, fiddles and *tiompan*.[4] But curiously there is no word of dance. Erse poets sing of the 'strings of melody' and 'where many were our *cruits* and *clarsachs*' (*Am bu lìonmhor cruit is clar*) and of the many 'new songs which were sung together', ('*S dana nua' ga luadh le cheil*),[5] and even among the barbarian Angles 'the merry harp was plucked and many a lay recited'[6] but, apparently, the dance was not danced!

Dance-song

It is strange that there is no mention of dance, especially when the prominent place of dance in pre-Christian festivals is so well confirmed by its survival into medieval times.

There are, however, some illustrations of figures dancing to instrumental music among the illuminations of certain early eighteenth-century Anglo-Saxon manuscript psalters. These designs were obviously suggested by such passages as one in 2 Samuel 6: 'And as the ark of the Lord came into the city of David, Michal, Saul's daughter, looked through a window, and saw king David leaping and dancing before the Lord.'

There is a figure of a bearded man dancing to music provided by a young boy with a harp in the tenth century Psalter (Harleian MS 603, British Museum). This could more reasonably be Saul dancing to the young David, an interesting interpretation of the incident related in 1 Samuel 16: 'And it came to pass, when the evil spirit from God was upon Saul, that David took an harp, and played with his hand: so Saul was refreshed, and was well, and the evil spirit departed from him.'

Another illustration of dancing is the frontispiece to the Anglo-Saxon Canterbury Psalter (Cotton Collection, British Museum) dated *c.* 700, which shows David sitting on a throne playing a nordic lyre, surmounting two hunkered dancers clapping hands, with horn and trumpet players in support.[7] Psalm 150 refers to instruments:

Praise him with the sound of the trumpet.
Praise him with the psaltery and harp.
Praise him with the timbrel and *dance.*

Percussion and reed instruments, apparently closely associated with pagan cults, were banned from the language of religious symbolism at this early time,[8] so we must not depend too heavily on psalter illuminations as sources of musical information. Since, however, the artist saw scriptural life in terms of his own, they can tell us much about Anglo-Saxon life. Later medieval sources of the kind embrace illustrations of a wider range of popular activities including dancing to the bagpipe; but by that time there are a greater number of literary sources to help. European society then comes into clearer view, and we can see in the customs of medieval seasonal festivals and holy-days the vestiges of pagan ritual and play. The communal dances long associated with these were of the ring and processional kind performed to the singing of the dancers.

The communal dance-song—carol or ballad—has taken its place in the literature of the British Isles, but in medieval times and earlier it was a normal part of social life. The ring was formed, often round a tree or object of veneration.

The leader then began a song, such as the following from Scotland, the rest joining in with the chorus as they danced: 'there were twa sisters lived in a bower'. Then the ring moved round and responded, '*Binnorie, O Binnorie!*' The leader again sang: 'There cam a knight tae be their wooer'; and the response: *By the bonnie mill-dams o' Binnorie!*
Or perhaps:

> There were three ladies lived in a bower,
> *Eh, wow bonnie,*
> *And they went out tae pu' a flower,*
> On the bonnie banks o' Fordie

Here the verses unfold a narrative, usually one of tragedy and the supernatural. This style of dance-song in Scotland belongs to the Germanic tongue, although ring dances accompanied by vocal solo and response were, as we would expect, familiar in the Gaelic-speaking region also, judging from survivals such as the *Danssa Mór* of the Isle of Eigg.

The particular way in which the narrative is presented in startling flashes of image and dialogue distinguishes ballads of the class of 'Binnorie', and a whole literature of them survived in the Scottish Border hills and the north-east, or Buchan region, to be preserved by scholars and collectors in recent times. Many, such as the historical ballads, belong rather to the category of romance and minstrelsy than to dance-song. The form has sprung from the dance and perhaps also from the communal work song, which had an identical basic structure and rhythmical purpose. It would be difficult to say which is the more ancient.

It is exciting today in Scotland to encounter children 'carolling' in the street or in the playground, all dancing in a ring, singing:

> *Here we go round the mulberry bush,*
> *The mulberry bush, the mulberry bush,*
> *Here we go round the mulberry bush,*
> *Aroon aboot the merry-ma-tanzie.*

This fragment of dance song is to be encountered in every English speaking nursery, but 'the merry-ma-tanzie' is a tantalizing phrase which is thrown into almost every chorus of the kind in Scotland, a phrase which itself reaches into the past, whether it means 'the merry May dance' or 'the Mary matins say'.

John Barbour (*d.* 1395) in his *Bruce* (Book II) refers to such a carol thus:

> *For quhasa likis, thai may heir*
> *Young wemen, quhen thai will play,*
> *Syng it e-mang thame ilke day.*

Dance and song and drama were thought of together in medieval society and there is no reason to suspect that it had ever been otherwise. The habit of associating song with dance was a long time in dying out. Even in the supremely formal sixteenth-century court dance, some of the slower airs provided the framework of songs which it was customary to sing during the dance.[9] In the case of what we would call theatrical dance—the dancing of professionals for entertainment—and solo dancing, it is evident that some kind of instrumental accompaniment was usual. In Anglo-Saxon society, what we would call acrobatics fell under this head. We read of jugglers, 'tumblers' and 'posture-makers' and we see drawings of them in the illuminations of medieval MSS., some as early as the ninth century, along with drawings of warriors going through the actions of combat, if not actually fighting, with sword and shield, to the music of horn and bagpipe. Examples of these are reproduced in Joseph Strutt's *Sports and Pastimes of the English People*, London, 1801.

Instrumental social dance

The purely instrumental social dance emerged with the more complicated forms of dance for two or three dancers performing as a unit. Where the movement was not energetic, and where it was simple and uniform, the participants could sing together, otherwise it would be the onlookers who sang. The assistance of musical instruments was introduced at this stage. In terms of dates, this development became most marked in Europe in the fourteenth century although it had its beginnings much earlier

A translation of a passage from Froissart (fourteenth century) illuminates this.[10]

> *Here are all the minstrels rare*
> *Who now acquit themselves so fair*
> *In playing on their pipes whate'er*
> *The dances be that one may do*
> *So soon as they have glided through*
> *The estampies of this sort*
> *Youths and maidens who disport*
> *Themselves in dancing now begin*
> *With scarce a wait to join hands in*
> *The choral.*

Here the instrumental and choral dance forms run one into the other.

Then in a French poem from about 1375, *Eches amoureux*,[11] we have social dancers calling for loud music from trumpet, tabor, drum and bell, cymbals, cornemuse (the bagpipe?) and chalumeau (the hornpipe?).

The reels of the Scottish Gaelic tradition have been performed to vocal music into our own times: *puirt-a-beul* *—'port' or dance-music of the mouth—the so-called mouth music, rendered the instrumental social dance in vocal form. The term mouth music is not used of song; it has the meaning of instrumental music made by the mouth and thus would appear to date from a period after the introduction of instrumental music. Ethno-musicologists tell us that most primitive peoples seem to conceive of the words and melody of a song as an indivisible unit, are rarely able to differentiate between them and cannot ordinarily give either text or music alone without difficulty.[12]

It is illuminating in this connection to note Margaret Fay Shaw's experience in South Uist in the nineteen-forties.[13] 'I never heard my friends in Glendale hum or sing an old tune without words. To them the words and the air were inseparable. I once mentioned that I thought a neighbour had the air of a song, and the reply was, "How could she have the air and not the words?".'

Puirt-a-beul, then, is the product of a primitive impulse to associate all

* Pronounced *poort-a-beeul.*

music with words, or rather, with uttered syllables, whether they make
sense or not. The use of meaningless syllables in song texts, sometimes
comprising the complete text, is encountered in the music-making of
primitive societies, particularly of the North American Indians.[14] Thus
puirt-a-beul is compatible with a very ancient origin, even pre-dating
instrumental music, although it is now most obviously tied to instrumental dance music.

We shall return to puirt-a-beul shortly. Meantime, looking at the
Scottish Lowlands and England, we see evidence as early as the fifteenth
century of the development of a variety of communal dances involving
simple figures being performed to instruments playing the tunes of popular
songs. These were the rural dances which came to be called 'country'
dances in sixteenth-century England. The Scots and Irish are later seen to
call their social dances 'reels'.

The English writer Sir Thomas Elyot in a work first published in 1531
states in a much-quoted remark that the names of certain dances were
'taken as they be nowe . . . of the first words of the dittie, which the song
comprehendeth whereof the daunse was made'.[15] In other words, the
name of such a dance was taken from the first line of the verses—or, as in
Scotland, the chorus—set to its tune.

The English Country Dances became very popular, even in court
circles, in the seventeenth century, and new dances were devised in their
form, which caused Charles Butler to remark in 1636 on 'the infinite
multitude of Ballads (set to sundry pleasant and delightful tunes, by
cunning and witty composers), with country dances fitted unto them'.[16]

The tradition of instrumental music among the Gaels is strong, and is
marked by the great number of verses which have been set to tunes already
in existence. Some even deriving from pibroch (Gaelic *piobaireachd*)
themes, and pibroch, of course, was an instrumental art form tracing its
lineage to the early Celtic harp tradition. This also relates us to the dance
rhythms—notably jig—to which the triple-time *port* of the Irish harp and
some elements of pibroch lend themselves. We shall have occasion to refer
to this again.

Puirt-a-beul and work-song

Puirt-a-beul usually comprises a jumble of meaningless syllables and
sundry comic phrases. The following are typical examples from Margaret
Fay Shaw's *Folksongs and Folklore of South Uist* and K. N. MacDonald's
Puirt-A-Beul.

Danns' a bhrigi, danns' a bhocai,	Dance the breeks, dance the bucks
Danns' a bhrigi, a chait bhàin!	Dance the breeks, white cat!
Danns'a bhrigi, danns' a bhocai,	Dance the breeks, dance the bucks
Bha thr'n raoir an taigh Ian Bhàin!	Last evening you were at fair John's house

Danns' a bhrigi, danns' a bhocai,	*Dance the breeks, dance the bucks*
Danns' a bhrigi, a chait bhàin!	*Dance the breeks, white cat!*
Ù a hu a, ù a hu a,	*Ù a hu a, ù a hu a,*
'S geal do shuilean, a chait bhàin!	*Bright are your eyes, white cat!*
Danns' a bhrigi, danns' a bhocai,	*Dance the breeks, dance the bucks*
Danns' a bhrigi, a chait bhàin!	*Dance the breeks, white cat!*
Danns' a bhrigi, danns' a bhocai,	*Dance the breeks, dance the bucks*
Bidh thu nochd an taigh Ian Bhàin!	*To-night you will be at fair John's house* [17]

and from *Puirt-A-Beul*, 'An Doctair Leodach', 'The Macleod Doctor',

At you! at you! bo, bo, bo!	*See on his belt, with rags and dust,*
Take care what may become of you,	*The dirk with all the rust of it,*
The doctor with his dirk may go,	*'twould kill a man with sheer disgust*
And take the head off some of you.	*If he should get a thrust of it.*

—and here is a verse of the familiar Highland sword dance, *Gille Callum*:

Gille Callum da pheighinn	*Gille Callum two pennies*
Gille Callum da pheighinn,	*Gille Callum two pennies,*
Da pheighinn, da pheighinn,	*Two pennies, two pennies,*
Gille Callum bonn-a-sia!	*Gille Callum 'coin of six'.* [18]

The coin of six is the Scots copper coin, one 'bodle', equal to about one-sixth of an English penny.

Numerous reels and strathspeys known to the Lowlander as purely instrumental tunes have puirt-a-beul renderings, as a glance at MacDonald's book will show.

Although puirt-a-beul is used for dancing, it also finds application as work-song. The functions and purposes of work-song are very much the same as those of the dance song and it is not surprising that they bear many similarities. In tasks requiring the co-ordination of a number of workers, the work-song is of inestimable practical help, as the familiar sea shanty testifies. These songs used in the Hebrides in the 'waulking' or 'fulling' of new-woven cloth follow the pattern of the Lowland ballad, with the narrative lines interspersed with chorus lines. The *ioram* (boat song) was rarely far from the lips of oarsmen, and indeed there are songs for every task, such as spinning, herding, milking. Sometimes, as in the case of the milking song, the song takes the form of an incantation propitiating the presiding spirits which also of course soothes the cow, with beneficial results:

> *Come, Mary, and milk my cow,*
> *Come, Bride, and encompass her,*
> *Come, Columba the benign,*
> *And twine thine arms around my cow*

Ho my heifer, ho my gentle heifer . . .
My heifer dear, generous and kind,
For the sake of the High King take to thy calf.[19]

Gerald De Barri (*c.* 1147–1220), a Welsh monk usually referred to by his latinized name *Giraldus Cambrensis*, writing in Latin of his visit to Ireland makes some general remarks on music in which he includes an observation on work-song: 'Music also alleviates toil, and in labour of various kinds the fatigue is cheered by sounds uttered in measured time. Hence artificers of all sorts relieve the weariness of their tasks by songs.'[20]

The work-song in the British Isles has survived longest in the Gaelic-speaking communities, and there is no doubt that the Celtic tradition fosters this as it does singing of all kinds at every opportunity. This distinction with the Germanic strain was noticed before industrialization exerted much effect on the habits of the Lowland people. In 1815, the anonymous editor of Dr Alexander Pennecuik's works wrote: '. . . from a band of Tweed-dale shearers a song is scarcely ever to be heard; . . . a ploughman seldom enlivens his horse by whistling a tune, . . . the sound of a pipe, or flute, or cowhorn, or stock-in-horn, or even of a jew's harp is a rare occurrence in travelling through . . .', contrasted with 'the brave lively sociable and hardy western highlander, . . . an enthusiast both in poetry and music . . . The horse is fired by the sound of the trumpet or the drum, and derives pleasure even from the ploughman's whistle . . .'[21]

It is surprising to read of 'trumpet' or 'drum' in this context, when we know that the bagpipe was used in like fashion, even in the Lowland province of Renfrew at the village of Kilbarchan. Here, in the early years of the seventeenth century, Habbie Simpson led the shearers with his pipes: [22] he is referred to further on pages 17, 27 and 33.

Erse musical tradition

We have mentioned the tradition of instrumental music among the Gaels. Even if no evidence of the existence of such a tradition were available from medieval times, there are numerous indications of it much closer to us—the great line of Irish clarsairs of so recent a date and the great bagpipers in Ireland, too. It is true that the English had many folk musicians of distinction, but they had no tradition of the kind prevailing in Ireland and Scotland or, for that matter, Wales. The folk musicians of Ireland and the Scottish Highlands produced such instrumental art forms as the *port* and the *pibroch*, and this is a unique achievement in the province of folk art. Perhaps it is not correct to use the word 'folk' in this context at all.

This tradition of instrumental music was, however, noted by several people in the twelfth century, and particularly by Giraldus, who was enraptured by Irish music and music-making. Indeed, he tells us, the Irish expended no comparable effort on any other activity. Here is a translation of his words:

> The only thing to which I find this people apply a commendable industry is playing upon musical instruments; in which they are incomparably more skilled than any other nation I have ever seen. For their modulation on these instruments, unlike that of the Welsh to which I am accustomed, is not slow and harsh but lively and rapid, while the harmony is both sweet and gay. It is surprising that in so complex and rapid a movement of the fingers, the musical proportions can be preserved, and that throughout the difficult modulations on their various instruments, the harmony is completed with such a sweet velocity, so unequal an equality, so discordant a concord, as if the chords sounded together fourths or fifths. They always begin from B flat, and return to the same, that the whole may be completed under the sweetness of a pleasing sound. They enter into a movement and conclude it in so delicate a manner, and play the little notes so sportively under the blunter sounds of the bass strings, enlivening with wanton levity, or communicating a deeper internal sensation of pleasure so that the perfection of their art appears in the concealment of it . . .
>
> From this cause, those very strains which afford deep and unspeakable mental delight to those who have skilfully penetrated into the mysteries of the art, fatigue rather than gratify the ears of others, who seeing do not perceive, and hearing do not understand; and by whom the finest music is esteemed no better than a confused and disorderly noise, and will be heard with unwillingness and disgust.[23]

There is a suggestion here that some of the music created by these highly practised exponents was a little over the heads of many of their auditors, which does seem to indicate that it was not dance music. The value of these celebrated remarks, however, is greatly enhanced by the fact that Giraldus was born of a Norman father and a Welsh mother, both of high birth; that he studied and lectured in Paris, and became Court Chaplain to Henry II in 1184.

Therefore, we can be sure, he was conversant with the music of the church and of the people of Europe and England.

Irish instrumental music was thus unique, melodically and tonally, in the time of Giraldus. Even more arresting is another passage:

> It must be remarked, however, that both Scotland and Wales strive to rival Ireland in the art of music; the former from its community of race, the latter from its contiguity and facility of communication . . . Scotland at the present day, in the opinion of many persons, is not only the equal to Ireland, her teacher, in musical skill, but excels her; so that they now look to that country as the fountainhead of this science.

This is not Giraldus's opinion—he had not visited Scotland—but, as he says, the opinion of others, presumably some of those very instrumentalists he admired so much. His statement here, therefore commands our acceptance. He also seems to tell us that the Scots shared the Irish inheritance of music-making, while the Welsh came under Irish influence through an easy commerce between the two peoples brought about by their 'contiguity'.

The Welsh, however, were Giraldus's own people, and had certain musical characteristics peculiar to themselves, particularly in vocal music, which they liked to sing in concert and in parts. This propensity remains with them as it does with the English of Yorkshire to whom Giraldus refers in like fashion in his *Itinerarium Kambriae et Descriptio Kambriae*.

The growth of instrumental music of another kind was emerging at the time of Giraldus from the monasteries in England and France, and from the tradition which gave rise to the peculiar phenomenon of the Goliards—poetic but often ribald clerics and scholars—and the troubadours. These latter were cultivated noblemen who devoted themselves to the composition of love poems, music and dance. They were a glamorous element in medieval chivalry, and Provence, their locale, became in consequence the cradle of secular Renaissance music, poetry and romance. The form of much of their poetry owes something to the form of the dance song, as is evinced by the names of *ballade, rondelle, carolle* and *pastourelle*.

It is strange that although the culture of the Norman kings of England was French, the art of the troubadour and the rhetorical tradition from which he sprung does not seem to have thrived in England; this despite the fact that Henry II of England married Eleanor of Aquitaine, granddaughter of the first-known troubadour and a patroness of troubadours.

The Anglo-Norman baron enjoyed the troubadour lyrics and music, he spoke French as his native tongue, he employed French musicians, and he enjoyed French romances; but he probably had too much hunting and jousting on his hands and not enough learning, and was surrounded by an environment of Anglo-Saxon yeomanry on whom the tradition of scop and gleeman had so strong a hold that it found its way within the castle walls. As for the Anglo-Norman barons in Scotland, they were even more exposed to the native traditions from the fact that the Royal House itself was native.

It is to the troubadours that we must attribute the new class of courtly dances for couples and for one gentleman and two ladies which now emerged, the *Estampies* and *Stantipedes*.[24] Three two-part instrumental compositions for the latter are contained in the early thirteenth-century Reading Abbey MS. which enjoys much celebrity in the history of music because it contains also a dance tune 'Sumer is icumen in' set as a four-part round (*rota*) on the secular theme of the awakening of spring and, in addition, set to verses in the English vernacular.

Little is known about the musical tradition of the Celtic Church, but some scholars have contended that its music was of Oriental foundation, in which case the 'harp' or rote (or *crwth*) (plate 6) had a place in it, for, as Henry Farmer has pointed out [25] the Byzantine churches used the *kithara, aulos* and cymbals in accord with the psalmist David of old. The word psalm itself is derived from the Greek *psalmos*—a song sung to a stringed instrument. Psalms were certainly employed in worship in the Celtic church; Columba himself, according to Adamnan, his biographer, chanted psalms with a loud voice.[26] As for the harp, both Bede and Giraldus testify to its use by the clergy.

From all this, we can see that the characteristic native music of the constituent parts of the British Isles was well established by the twelfth century. The music of the Irish and the Scottish Gaels was conspicuous for its liveliness—'lively and rapid' says Giraldus—a liveliness which has survived to this day. None of this music was written down, but it was stored in the popular memory and perpetuated by oral transmission.

'Bare names' from the Middle Ages

A system of notation which could indicate time intervals as well as tonal intervals—essential for the writing of 'measurable' music—was not invented until about the twelfth century, and because educated musicians had no occasion to note down the native airs, it is not surprising that so few examples of the native music of the British folk are to be found in the repositories of medieval music. Not until the late sixteenth century, when a number of cultivated amateur musicians began compiling music to play on lute or virginals, and some professionals exercised themselves in composing harmonic arrangements of them, do we find written examples of song and dance tunes of the folk in any quantity. The earliest of these surviving private collections of Scottish music is the Skene MS. *c.* 1620.

The first Scottish publications of traditional music did not appear until the eighteenth century, although Scottish tunes are included in earlier English publications. The great treasury of instrumental dance tunes of the Gael only began to appear in print in the seventeen-fifties under the stimulus of the great vogue of the Country Dance and 'Highland Reel' in the growing enthusiasm for public dance assemblies.

This, as it happened, coincided with a considerable increase in antiquarian interest in music and song and it perplexed the principal eighteenth-century writers on Scottish music, Joseph Ritson,[27] William Tytler[28] and John Pinkerton[29] that there was no reference even to 'the bare name of a song or dance tune in use before the year 1500', as Ritson put it.

Their attention had not been drawn to the extensive list of song and dance titles in the poem 'Colkelbie's Sow', *c.* 1450, contained in the Bannatyne MS.,[30] a collection of the national poetry of the fifteenth and

sixteenth centuries compiled by George Bannatyne (1545-1609) 'in tym
of pest' in the year 1568. But nevertheless, to the modern student, the
seem to have given altogether too little thought to the persistence of a
wholly oral musical tradition.

As far as written records go, 'Colkelbie's Sow' is the earliest, and
occasional song titles appear in later literary works, particularly in the two
anonymous poems in the same boisterous Colkelbie tradition—'Peblis to
the Play'[31] and 'Christ's Kirk',[32] both dating from the early sixteenth
century—and that curious prose record of Scottish sixteenth-century life
and thought, *The Complaynt of Scotland*, of uncertain authorship, published
in 1549.[33]

Dance tunes then, as in more recent times, customarily assumed the
name of the songs to which they were set. Certainly, in 'Colkelbie', and
to a greater extent in *The Complaynt,* there are some titles referred to a
dances and others as songs; but we cannot ignore the fact that the ring
dances and simple figured dances—what are later seen to be called 'country
hornpipe rounds' or jigs, or reels (in Scotland and Ireland), or country
dances (in Elizabethan England)—were performed to tunes set to words
Thus a song title is a potential dance title.

At the time these early works were written, some of the dances in
vogue in French and Italian court circles were being adopted in the
Scottish and English courts—*basse dances* and *branles* (English, brawl),
and even the Italian *contrapassi* which latter were very similar to the long-
wise country dances we regard as peculiarly British—and some of these
are mentioned in 'Colkelbie' and *The Complaynt*. There are no allusions
to any dances, or dance tunes, called reels or strathspeys or highland flings,
in these or any other literary works until the eighteenth century. The word
'reel' is used to describe an interlacing figure in Gavin Douglas's translation of the *Aeneid*, in the sixteenth century, and also in its sense of social
dancing or revelling—'sic reeland and sic riot whill near day'.[34]

About the same period William Dunbar (1465?-1530?) refers to a
piper's playing a 'spring' and another poet, Alexander Scott (1530?-
1584?), refers to the jig as a dance; but not until the end of the century do
we come across an allusion to a 'reel' as a dance tune, nor do we encounter
it again until a hundred years later in Henry Playford's publication of
Scottish tunes.[35] This is not to say that the music we would call 'reel'
music' did not exist among the song tunes referred to in the above
literature. But we have no definite record of these tunes, and only through
the survival of the verse structure of a song here and there can we obtain
any hint of what may have been the character of some of the tunes, and
their probable identity.

This is easier where we have complete verses. The most valuable work
in this respect, is the collection of 'prophaine sangs' converted into 'gude
and godlie ballates' by the brothers Wedderburn, ministers in Dundee,

nd published in 1570 for the use of those who would keep their minds
ff temptations of the flesh. The original 'prophaine' verses show through
heir ludicrous disguise, enabling us to identify them and their probable
urvivors in more recent times. Unfortunately songs are often set to more
han one tune in their history; but surely if verse-forms survived, so also
lid the tunes associated with them, even if we cannot identify them.

It has been well known for some time that the texts of the traditional
•allads can be classified under certain families, and recent scholarship
uggests that it may be possible to set up a canon of germinal melodic
Jeas from which all genuine folk-song derives. Indeed, B. H. Bronson
uggests in his edition of Child's *English and Scottish Ballads*, 1857–9,[36]
hat such a canon would not be as large as that of the text families. How-
ver this may be, something of the kind can be seen in Scottish traditional
nstrumental dance music as well as in the traditional song, and perhaps
ve can describe the process as the continuous creation and regeneration
f tunes, through the centuries, developing from some fundamental
melodic protoplasm peculiar to each given race.

Early traces of Scottish dance tunes

n the British Isles, the Celtic and Germanic traditions widely intermingle
1 varying proportions although the two cultural streams are discernible.
n Scotland, this is often over-simplified as a distinction between 'High-
ind' and 'Lowland'.

Of the songs in the *Gude and Godlie Ballates*, 'John, come kiss me now',
Huntis Up', 'Hay now the day daws' and 'Hay trix trim go trix' are of
nost interest to us from the point of view of dance. It is suggested that
John come kiss me now' survives today in the second strain of the well
mown country dance jig, 'The New Rigg'd Ship' [1]. Certainly it fits
ne words admirably in form and spirit, although if we compare it to the
ommon-time tune [2], no. 305 in James Johnson's *Scots Musical
Museum*,[37] it would seem to be better described as a 'set of the old air'.
lurns referred Johnson to McGibbon's *Scots Tunes*, 1768, for this tune,
lthough it is to be found in other sources, including English sources, such
s Playford's *Introduction to the Skill of Music*, 1654, and the *Fitzwilliam
Virginal Book* [*c.* 1650] which contains a set of fifteen variations by Byrd
n the theme. The latter is close to what must be the earliest version [3],
hat preserved in a MS book of *Airs and Sonnets* (F.S. 13, pp. 55 and 56) at
Trinity College, Dublin, in which it is accompanied by a full set of
rerses in sixteenth-century Scots.[38]

The Dublin version reminds one of the tune of 'Hey Jock m'Cuddie',
with its boisterous refrain—'Hullibaloo baloo, hullibaloo balae'—sung to
ring dance by myself and many of my contemporaries at picnics in
icotland as recently as the nineteen-thirties. Doubtless we are here

[1] THE NEW RIGG'D SHIP
Niel Gow's *Second Collection*, 2nd edn, 1803

[2] JOHN, COME KISS ME NOW
Johnson's *Scots Musical Museum*, no. 305, iv, 1792

[3] Earliest version
MS, Airs and Sonnets, Trinity College, Dublin

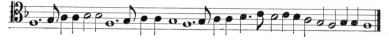

ouching on a case of traditional tunes deriving from a common germinal melodic idea.

Judging by the number of times it is mentioned, 'John, come kiss me now' was very popular as a tune and as a Country Dance in England in the late sixteenth and in the seventeenth century; * yet no verses of known English origin survive.

'Huntis Up' and 'Hay now the day daws' were tunes in the repertoire of Habbie Simpson, the piper of Kilbarchan in the early seventeenth century—

> Now who shall play ' The day it daws',
> Or ' Hunt's up when the cock he craws'? [39]

'The day it daws' is mentioned over a hundred years before this by William Dunbar in 'Satire on Edinburgh' as one of the tunes of Edinburgh's 'common minstrellis', and not much later Gavin Douglas [40] describes minstrels welcoming a June morning with 'The joly day now dawis'. Alexander Montgomerie (*c.* 1556–1610) wrote elegant verses to it which are rarely omitted from anthologies of old Scots poetry, and William Chappell has pointed out English verses on the same theme in the Fayrfax MS.[41]

The subject of the song seems to be the lovers' night visit, a very ancient custom, and perhaps this is why it does not seem to have survived the Reformation. Most curious of all, however, is that this tune, well established in the repertoire of the community, used as a reveille by town pipers for several centuries, apparently disappeared from ken by the eighteenth century. It is improbable that such a tune disappeared altogether, and thus it is with great interest that one turns to the suggestion first made by Stenhouse,[42] that the missing tune is none other than that best known in the eighteenth century as 'Hey Tuttie Taiti' [4], here reproduced from J. Oswald's *Caledonian Pocket Companion*, iii, *c.* 1751. This, of course, is the tune (played slowly) used by Burns for 'Scots wha hae'. It was reputedly a very old tune in his day, and he accepted a tradition held 'widely in Scotland', as he wrote, that it was played at Bannockburn. It was best known in the eighteenth century as a Jacobite carousing song, 'Fill up your bumpers high', but Kirkpatrick Sharpe (*c.* 1830), collected a song in Annandale, 'Bridekirk's Hunting', which was set to it, and which hints at the theme of 'The Day Daws', also in a bacchanalian vein:

> The cock's at the crawing,
> The day's at the dawing,
> The cock's at the crawing,
> We're ower lang here.[43]

* In Thomas Heywood's *A Woman killed with kindness*, 1600, Sisley says, 'I love no dance so well as *John, come kiss me now*; and in Samuel Rowlands's *'Tis Merry when Gossips Meet*, 1609, we read 'Not an old daunce, but *John, come kisse me now*', etc. J. C. Dick. *The Songs of Robert Burns*, 1903.

It seems most probable that Tuttie Taiti was pronounced with the firs syllables of the words rhyming with 'but' and 'gate'. It has been sug gested that the second syllable should be stressed, the more closely t approximate to the sound of the trumpet which the words 'tuttie taiti reputedly imitate. The tune, however, does not lend itself to this theory nor is it a trumpet tune, although it seems likely that it is based on common trumpet motif.

[4] HEY TUTTIE TAITI
Oswald's *Caledonian Pocket Companion*, iii. *c.* 1751

The antiquity of 'Hey Tuttie Taiti' is of consequence to us because it i of the character of a strathspey, and therefore may be the earliest exampl of that class of Scottish dance tune of which we have record. In support o tradition, Stenhouse offers the satirical rhyme quoted by Fabyan,[44] mad in derision of the English at the time of the marriage of Bruce's son, David to the English king's sister in 1328:

> *Long berdys, hartless*
> *Paynted hoodyes, witles*
> *Gay cotis, graceless*
> *Maketh England Thryftles*

The tune fits the verse; but how can one prove such a hypothesis? How ever, Oliver Brown has very kindly drawn my attention to the followin reference to 'Hey Tuttie Taiti' included in a programme issued by th Town Council of Orleans, on the occasion of their annual Joan of Ar memorial celebrations: 'Marche des Soldats de R. Bruce—D'origin écossaise, elle fut introduite en France au XIVe siècle. C'est au son de cett marche que Jeanne d'Arc fit son entrée à Orleans le 29 Avril 142 (d'après un manuscrit du Château Royal de Blois).'
Is this the evidence we are looking for? It certainly supports the traditior of which Burns speaks, although it does not confirm that 'The Day daws

vas the same tune as 'Hey Tuttie Taiti', however likely this may be. A ine entitled 'The day dawes' in no way resembling 'Hey Tuttie Taiti', vas included in the Straloch MS. lute book (early seventeenth century); but his is not particularly Scottish in character and may possibly be the English version referred to in several sixteenth-century English sources.

Turning to 'Hunts Up', here also we have a tune used by town minstrels s a reveille in the sixteenth century. It is also listed among the dances in ie *Complaynt*, and is first mentioned in England, not long before, as the ine of a political parody.[45] The first mention in Scotland is earlier still— The Cadzear sang Hunts up, up on hie'—in Robert Henryson's fable The Wolf, the Foxe and the Cadzear'.

It appears that any tune used as a reveille or 'morning music', was alled a *hunt's up*, and even as recently as the nineteenth century in Cumerland, a custom of traversing the town on Christmas morning playing n instruments and shouting greetings was called 'hun-sopping', i.e. hunt's up-ing'.[46] This generic use of the term 'hunt's up' should prepare is to accept a number of different tunes bearing this title; but that quoted 5] by Chappell [45] from Jane Pickering's *Lute Book* of 1615 (British Museum, Eng. MSS. 2046), judging from its words, is probably close to the ine associated with the *Gude and Godlie Ballates*, and hence with Scotland. t is a jig.

[5] HUNT'S UP
Jane Pickering's *Lute Book*, 1615

The remaining early dance tune title which we have selected for notice, Hay, trix trim go trix', has more the character of a ring-dance refrain, as n—'Hay, trix trim go trix under the greenwood tree'—Hence, perhaps, he meaning of *Trixie* in Sempill's elegy [47] on Habbie Simpson to which ve have already referred:

> *Kilbarchan now may say alas!*
> *For she hath lost her game and grace,*
> *Both Trixie and the Maiden-Trace.*

Perhaps this survives in some children's game. Games of this kind are lluded to in 'Colkelbie's Sow' when processions of shepherds, swine-

herds and cowherds, led respectively by a minstrel playing a flute, bagpipe
and hornpipe, assembled 'to-dance merrily'. This account, it may be
remembered, comes from the fifteenth century; it is the earliest that we
have on this subject.[30]

The master swineherd and his cousin led the dance, attired in bells in
the manner, presumably, of the Morris dancer, accompanied by the
minstrels in concert. 'Play us Joly Lemmane (Jolly sweetheart)' they say
then performed some steps and some of the following dances: Basse
Dance, 'Perdony', 'Trolly lolly', 'Cock craw thou whill day', 'Tays-
bank' (known as a song), 'Terway', 'Lincolne', 'Lindsay', 'Joly
Lemman dawis it not day' (same as above, 'Joly Lemmane'; and same as
'Day Daws'?), 'Most mak revell', 'Symon sonis of Whynfell' and
'Maister Pier de Couyate'.

Some 'bekkit' (bowed), some 'bingit' (lunged), some 'crakkit'
(presumably snapped their fingers), some cringed, and altogether there
was considerable variety of style. Others, however, the poet tells us, had
more 'consate' (conceit) and 'at leisure drest to dance' some more courtly
dances (although the basse dance is already mentioned) of which we have
but a slight idea, musically or choreographically, viz. 'some Ourfute
some Orliance some Rusty bully with a beck and every note in others
nek'. 'Orliance' is doubtless the basse dance, 'Orlyons' (Orleans)
mentioned by Toulouze in his fifteenth-century dance book (*Sur l'Art et
instruction de bien dancer, c.* 1496), and 'Rusty bully'—the Italian figured
dance 'Roti Bolli' described in the same dance book.[48]

Others, again, danced the dances of various parts of Europe (including
'Ireland and Argyle'), then all arrayed in a ring danced 'My deir darling',
which title we cannot relate to any surviving tune or verses.

The mention of Argyle confirms, if confirmation were necessary, that
the foregoing dances to the native airs were of a Lowland variety. There is
nothing in the titles to suggest otherwise, and it is to be expected that they
would be rudimentary Country Dances. What the *Complaynt* later
referred to as 'licht' dances, the most complicated figure of which was
undoubtedly the *hey* or, what Scottish dancers call the 'reel'. The 'hey
[reel] of three' is mentioned by John Skelton, the English poet, in his
Against Venemous Tongues, lines 45–6, 1529. Judging from the examples of
sixteenth-century country dance tunes (English, Scots and Irish) collected
by Chappell,[45] the prevailing folk dance rhythm, at least south of the
Highland Line and, of course, in Ireland, was 6/8 and 9/8, generally 6/8
jig and 3/2 hornpipe, and mostly jig.

It is striking that the written and printed sources of the sixteenth
century, and even later, do not present us with many songs to triple-time
hornpipes. The impression left by allusions in literature, and the hornpipe's
association with shepherds, is that it was predominantly an instrumental
dance form. But, like the jig, one can feel sure that it pre-dates the six-

eenth century. Hugh Aston, a musician of Henry VIII's time, composed
a salon piece (British Museum MSS. Reg. Appendix 58) for a keyboard
instrument, running to about eighty bars, in triple-time hornpipe rhythm,
of which Chappell [45] reproduces a substantial part. This is the earliest
recorded example of the form. One jig which achieved well-deserved fame
in England and Scotland appears as 'A new Northern Dittye' in the
Registers of the Stationers' Company, as recently as September 1580; in
this context, 'Northern' refers to the territory north of the English Mid-
lands, mainly Northumberland and Scotland. Its name—'Greensleeves'.
Its popularity was immense, and it remains with us today, although,
except in Scottish Country Dance circles (where it is sometimes heard in
its original form) it survives in the sedate guise of an affecting slow air
associated with Christmas, an association which scarcely predates the
nineteen-forties. Shakespeare testifies to the original jolly character of the
tune when he has Mrs Ford in the *Merry Wives of Windsor* contrast it with
the Hundredth Psalm—'they do no more keep pace together, than the
Hundredth Psalm to the tune of *Green Sleeves*'.

Although John Playford did not publish a Country Dance to the tune
[6] until the 1686 edition of *The Dancing Master*,[49] it certainly was the
vehicle of a Country Dance shortly after its vogue began in England, as
we gather from its being mentioned by Nashe among a number of
Country Dances in his play *Have with you to Saffron-Walden*, in 1596.
Like many a dance air of this popular character, it was set to many
verses, some very coarse (*cf.* Herd), and some of the nature of mild
parodies. 'Old Kingsburgh', in the far-off Isle of Skye, habitually sang
the following when he was merry over a glass, as Boswell tells us in his
Journal of a Tour to the Hebrides:

> *Green sleeves and pudding pies,*
> *Tell me where my true love lies,*
> *And I'll be with her before she rise,*
> *Fiddle and aw' together.*

The first line of this is identical with the title of Playford's dance and
doubtless was to the same two-strain version of the tune, a version which is
almost identical with that [7] set to words by Burns for Johnson's *Scots
Musical Museum* (no. 388).

Although Greensleeves was a 'Northern' air, it is not here claimed for
Scotland. One reason is that the jig is not regarded as a characteristic
Scottish dance rhythm, even if many jigs are certainly Scottish in origin
and one form is commonly described as 'Scottish-Jig' in eighteenth-
century music publications. The Irish inheritance of the Scottish Western
seaboard would lead one to expect a preponderance of jigs in that part of
the country. There is certainly a considerable store of triple-time tunes in
the islands, but there is no peculiar attachment to the Jig.

[6] and [7] GREENSLEEVES
Playford's *Dancing Master*, 1686

[7] Another version
Johnson's *Scots Musical Museum*, iv, no. 388, 1792

The Scottish jig of Elizabethan literature, which Morley [50] described a
a class of tune most difficult to imitate, is something of a mystery to which
we shall return when we look more closely at the Scottish dance rhythms
It is clear, however, that by the latter half of the seventeenth century, wha
we now call the Scottish measure—in quadruple rhythm—was regarded
in England as the characteristically Scottish kind of tune. There is no hin
of this style of tune in the sixteenth-century remnants we have been dis
cussing, we have to wait for the seventeenth-century manuscript collec
tions of Skene, Mure of Rowallan and others. The jig, however, is the

most widespread of British dance rhythms, even if the Irish have made it their own and may even have created it. The triple-time hornpipe, on the other hand, is early associated with the pastoral regions of England, although by the early eighteenth century it is seen to be very much at home in Northumberland and the adjacent Scottish border country.

So much, then, for our earliest evidence of Scottish dance music. Just a few 'bare names', a hint here and there, a few identifiable jigs, a tantalizing possibility of 'Hey Tuttie Taiti' as our earliest suggestion of strathspey rhythm and the assurance of Giraldus that in his time the Scots and Irish shared a unique tradition of instrumental music, which later history confirms.

CHAPTER 2

Coming of Age
from medieval times to the eighteenth century

As we have mentioned, the herdsmen so graphically described in th fifteenth-century tale of Colkelbie's lost sow danced to bagpipe, stock and-horn (hornpipe) and flute. The cow-horn with its single note simpl added noise to the mêlée. In 'Peblis to the Play' and 'Christ's Kirk o the Green', two other poems in the same boisterous tradition, and probabl from the same period, the minstrel plays the bagpipe for the danc Instrumental social dance seems indeed to have been well established a the folk level at this time.

Nearly a century later, in 1549, *The Complaynt of Scotland* was pub lished. Here we read of eight shepherds, allegorical shepherds one surmise and their female partners, disporting themselves in recreation, singing an dancing. Each shepherd plays in turn a different instrument for th dancing of the others. These instruments are: 'ane drone bag pipe'; 'an pipe maid of ane bleddir and of ane reid'; 'ane trump'; 'ane corne pipe' 'ane pipe maid of ane gait horne'; 'ane recordar'; 'ane fiddil' and 'an quihissil (whistle)'.[1]

The pipe made of a bladder and reed was the bagpipe without a drone the trump was what goes by the name of Jew's Harp today; the corn pip was the hornpipe; and the 'gait' horn was, of course, a goat horn. Th fact that it was called a pipe suggests that it had a reed in it.

These, then, were the popular instruments of rural society, and ther was little of any other kind of society in these times. They provided th music for dances going under such names as 'The North of Scotland' 'Hunt's Up', 'Robin Hood', 'Friars all', 'The Gossips' Dance' and s on; some of them like the last named were probably entertainment dance for one or two performers, others doubtless figure dances and one at least Basse Dance—'Bace of Voragon' (Basse of Aragonne).

Music of court and countryside

The fiddle and recorder were requisite for the basse dance, we can be sur of that, but it was soft music for the outdoors. The early crouds (crwyth cruit), rebecs (rybid, rybybe) (plates 6, 7) and fiddles (fydils) and thei kindred were not very loud, and it is not surprising that the evidence indisputably proclaims that no instrument surpassed the bagpipe in popularity for dancing on the green, at fair, bridal, harvest or simple country hop, during the period we are considering. Nor was this popularity peculiar to Scotland; it was true of England, of the Low Countries, as a glance at some Brueghel paintings shows, and even of Italy and Germany, as many an example from literature suggests. The bagpipe was a universal folk instrument in medieval Europe, particularly among herdsmen, for goats and sheep supplied the material from which bagpipes were made.

Bagpipes varied greatly in design, and even as late as the eighteenth century there were at least four types of bagpipe to be found in Scotland: the Piob Mór or Great Highland Bagpipe as we call it today (plate 11), the Border Pipes, and the bellows-blown large and small pipes (plate 14). It is very uncertain, at times, which class of bagpipe is being referred to in contemporary allusions.

In the early years of the sixteenth century, the record of payments to minstrels who performed for the king reveals a considerable variety of musical instruments—'shawmeris, trumpetis, taubroneris, fithelaris, lutaris, harparis, clarscharis and piparis'. The early Stewart kings were nearly all enthusiastic musicians and James IV and James V in particular had a ready ear for the music of their people, as well as for the courtly airs of their luters and violers. James I, who reigned from 1424 to 1437, was, as Bellenden in his translation of Boece puts it, 'wele lernyt . . . to syng and dance . . . richt crafty in playing baith lute and harp and sindry uther instrumentis of musick'.[2] Among the last, in his continuance of Fordun's *Scotichronicon*, the contemporary historian Walter Bower or Bowmaker included the bagpipe.

James IV was especially skilled on the lute and clavichord. His granddaughter (who was to become Queen of Scots), excelled on the lute and virginals, and Mary's father, James V, went through a considerable number of lute strings, judging from the purchases recorded in the Lord High Treasurer's accounts.[3] His scribe, Maister Bellenden, whom we have quoted above, disapproved of this activity, claiming that 'syngyng, fydlyng and piping' were unsuitable for men of honour or of 'hye estate' as, unlike the martial trumpet, they made men 'soft'.[4]

Apart from the diverse minstrels who converged on the palaces of Holyrood, Falkland or Linlithgow according to the season, the monarch maintained his own musicians. Some of them were French, Italian or English (the Scottish Stuart queens being English or French) but most were Scots, even if a few had to 'leir their craft' in foreign 'airts'. Thus we notice Wardlow, Lindores, Rankine, Boyd, Bennet, Widderspune (fiddlers); Hume and Adeson (lutes); Feldie, Dow and Hay (violars) and so on.[5] It was common for these musicians to raise their sons to the calling, and thus we have several generations of Feldies, Dows and Hays minstrelling at court in the late sixteenth century.

The dancing at court at this time, as remarked earlier, was confined to Basse Dances, Pavans and Branles, with new versions of these being imported from France from time to time. There is no record of the native 'licht' dances of the countryside (with the exception of 'rounds') being performed, but can one doubt that Widderspune *et al* indulged in their native music on occasion? Surely any king such as James v who could even be suspected of writing 'Christ's Kirk' or 'The Gaberlunzie Man' and who enjoyed 'Gynkertoun', a favourite tune of his infancy,[6] must be expected to have had an ear and a heart for the airs of his native earth.

His grandson, James vi, who as James i became King of England in 1603, may not have inherited the romantic charm of his forefathers, nor could he dance, but he is credited with the authorship of the tune, 'The Beggar's Meal Pokes' [8] doubtless on the authority of Oswald' *Caledonian Pocket Companion*, ix, 1758. One suspects confusion with his ancestor James i who was the reputed author of the verses 'The Jolly Beggar' associated with this tune. It is a slow tune of the character of a strathspey.

[8] THE BEGGAR'S MEAL POKES

'Composed by King James the 6th'. Oswald's *Caledonian Pocket Companion*, ix, 1758

The court, of course, was the centre of artistic patronage in Scotland as elsewhere, and its removal to England at the end of the sixteenth century was as serious a blow to the arts in Scotland as was the loss of James iv and the flower of Scottish courtiers at Flodden at the beginning of the century. Yet nothing so drastically affected the everyday life of all walks of society as the success of the Reformation in mid-century, and the establishment of a new theocracy. Here was an event which exerted an influence on every aspect of daily life.

It was at the dawn of this period that the young Mary, Queen of Scots, arrived at Holyrood to claim her own on a dismal overcast day in August

561. There she was serenaded by an assembly of five or six hundred 'ragamuffins', according to Brantôme,[7] or 'a company of the most honest' according to John Knox,[8] with 'instruments of music'. Brantôme described them doubtless more accurately, as 'the vilest fiddles and little rebecs, which are as bad as they can be in that country, and accompanied them with singing psalms, but so wretchedly out of tune and concord that nothing could be worse'.

Whatever this says about quality, there is no doubt about the quantity. A corresponding concourse today would be of the order of five thousand. Surely all the mendicant minstrels and householding amateurs for miles round converged on Edinburgh for the occasion. Yet Knox calls them a 'company of the most honest' which seems to preclude the vagrant 'gut-scrapers' who were a familiar feature of contemporary life. Where, too, were the pipers, with schawm, flute or bagpipe? We can be sure they were there also, though probably near the warmth of the welcoming bon-fires and not very sober. There were to be fewer holidays now, for the saints' days were to be severely proscribed, and in particular the 'super-stitious' time of Yule and the May games. Yet even these did not com-pletely succumb until nearer the end of the century, and not entirely so even then, for the kirk was still battling with the remnants of the Yule festival well into the seventeenth century.

As Spalding tells us, not even the Rev. Andrew Cant and his fellow-ministers in Aberdeen, 'great railers out of pulpit', could suppress the old practices at Yule in 1642. For all the threatenings of the ministers 'the people made good cheer and banqueting, according to their estates, and past their times'.[9]

It is assumed by many that dance and music became anathema to Church and society under the discipline of the reformed church. This is not so. Certainly there were attempts from time to time to suppress the traditional occasions of dance and music, particularly—apart from the former holy days—penny weddings, baptisms and wakes; measures which seemed to reach a climax about the time of the episode of Cant and Yule at Aberdeen, which I have just described, a century after the establishment of the reformed Kirk!

'Minstrelles and pipers at brydells'

The objection to the celebrations attending bridals arose from the Kirk's uneasiness about what it called 'superfluous banquetting'. It was usual for bridal festivities to extend over a period of three days, keeping labourers and servants from their gainful employ. The first step taken by kirk sessions to alter this was to limit the number of people who could attend a wedding. This, depending on the parish, was usually fixed at fifteen or twenty people 'from each side', and the bridal pair were required to

deliver a deposit of money in earnest of serious intention and satisfactor
conduct. This, however, was not enough. The next step was not, as on
may expect, to ban the drinking or dancing, but in fact to ban the music

A typical example from the kirk session records of Galston, Ayrshire
dated 1635, squarely places on 'the minstrells and pipers who is a
brydells' the responsibility for being 'oftymes the cause of fyghting an
jarres—falling out amongst the people', for which reason the Kirl
Session 'concludit that all pypers, fidlers and uther minstrells be dis
chargeit frae brydells in tyme coming'.

One of the earliest examples of this kind of proscription which I hav
come across is in the kirk session records of Perth, dated 1592; but mos
occur in the period 1630–60. They all read very much alike, whethe
they be from the village of Ashkirk in the Borders where the town piper
Adam Moffat, was placed under penalty for 'pyping at bridals' in 1638
or from Stirling at the gateway to the Central Highlands (1648).

The persistent appearance of offenders in subsequent records tells it
own story, and it remained possible for the English traveller, Thoma
Morer, who visited Scotland as late as 1687, to write in his *Short Accoun
of Scotland*, 1702, that the bagpipe was 'the chief delight at marriages' in
Scotland.

All of this evidence testifies to the continued prominent social place c
the bagpiper in Lowland society, a fact which is borne out by severa
verses dating from the seventeenth century.[10]

Now when their dinner they had done, Then Jock himsell began t'advance;
He bad the piper play up soon, For, be his troth, he wou'd gae dance.
The piper piped till's wyme gripped, And a' the rout began to revel . . .
                                                       'COUNTRY WEDDING'

The dinner, the piper, and priest shall be ready.
                                                       'BOB OF DUMBLANE'

Then to his bags he flew wi' speed,* About the drone he twisted;
Meg up and wallop'd o'er the green, For brawly could she frisk it.
Weel done, quoth he, play up, quoth she, Weel bob'd, quoth Rob the Ranter,
'Tis worth my while to play indeed, When I hae sick a dancer.
                                                       'MAGGIE LAUDER'

Sae Tam the piper did play, And ilka ane danc'd that was willing,
And a' the lavr they ranked through, And they held the wee stoupy ay filling.
                                                       'PATIE'S WEDDING'

There is a perplexing dearth of similar material from Gaelic sources; bu
this tells us nothing except that the Gaels have fewer written records from
this period.

* The piper here was 'Rob the Ranter', a famous border piper.

Some of the lines referring to pipers at bridals and festivities allude to some features of their instruments from which we can deduce their character. The 'elegy of Habbie Simpson' reveals his bagpipe to have one drone. *The Poetical Museum* (Hawick, 1784) prints an 'elegy on John Hastie' (*d.* 1700), town piper of Jedburgh which suggests a bellows-blown instrument:

> *John, whan he play'd, ne'er threw his face,*
> *Like a' the girning piper race:*

The allusion here is to the facial expression of the 'bellows' piper.

William Hamilton of Bangour (1704–50) in his poem 'The Maid of Gallowshiels' celebrates the piper of that town accompanying a rural reel:

> *There in the humbler mood of peace, he stands;*
> *Before him, pleas'd, are seen the dancing bands.*
> *In mazy roads the flying ring they blend,*
> *So lively frame'd they seem from earth t'ascent*
> *Four gilded straps the artist's arm surround;*
> *Two knit by clasps, and two by buckles bound.*
> *His artful elbow now the youth essays,*
> *A tuneful squeeze to wake the sleeping lays.*
> *With labouring bellows thus the smith inspires—*
> *To frame the polished lock, the forge's fires.*

There is no doubt here; the bagpipe was of the Lowland bellows type (plate 14).

Of course, people danced to whatever instrumental accompaniment was available. The bagpipe, apparently, was preferred, at least in the Lowlands and by the common people. In the Highlands, General Stewart of Garth tells us, although not until the early nineteenth century, that 'playing the bagpipes within doors is a Lowland and English custom. In the Highlands the piper is always in the open air; and when people wish to dance to his music, it is on the green, if the weather permits; nothing but necessity makes them attempt a pipe dance in the house.' [11]

Dancing and piping 'in time of prayers'

Joseph MacDonald, writing about 1760,[12] tells us that a smaller version of the Great Pipe (plate 11) was used throughout the Highlands for dancing. In general, however, the fiddler ruled supreme indoors, and there is no reason to believe that he had only recently attained to that position. It is well supported by literary allusions that he was as much involved in playing dance music from the sixteenth century onwards as was the bagpiper; but the latter enjoyed the incontestible advantage for the noisy occasion—loudness!

It was undoubtedly this very characteristic which led to the more frequent tangles of players 'upon the Great Pipe' with the burgh and kirk authorities, as evidenced by records. There was such a thing as 'time and place' in the seventeenth century, as there is today, but in the earlier period one of the forbidden times was 'tyme of preaching or prayers'. Normally this encompassed a considerable part of Sunday, and since Sunday was for most the only day available for recreation, one can sympathize with the piper's predicament. It was evidently an unending task for the kirk elders to clear people from the tavern, stop domestic strife, stop the packman travelling, and stop the playing of the pipes 'in time of sermon'.

The wonder is that anyone dared to contravene these regulations, yet kirk and burgh records testify to the carelessness of pipers in this matter. There is frequent censure of the kind—'That na personis passtyme or dans, or reill with dansing and pyping thru the toun on Sunday, the tyme of preching or prayers' (Kirkcaldy); and what about the bold citizen at Neilsoun, Stirlingshire in 1580, who brought with him 'intil the kirkyaird twa or thri pypers, and therby drew in a grit nowmer of people to dans befoir the kirk dur, in tyme of prayeris'? [13]

This kind of outrage at sermon time was not unknown in England, where an even more intense pursuit of sabbatarian legislation is in evidence before and after the Reformation. King James (VI and I) felt obliged by the extreme restrictiveness of Sunday observance in certain parts of England to proclaim the idea that recreation was proper and desirable on Sunday provided divine service had first been attended.[14]

In reaction to this spirit, the Roundheads imposed legislation (1644, 1650 and 1657) which more or less restrained every kind of secular use of Sunday. The whole day was to be 'celebrated as holy to the Lord, both in publique and private'.[15] One could not even travel on a Sunday for any purpose other than attending church.

Similar measures were certainly attempted by many Scottish presbyteries; but they did not have the totality of these English laws during the Commonwealth. In Glasgow, in the year 1594, an attempt was made to prohibit piping between sunrise and sunset on Sundays,[16] but this is exceptional; it was apparently sufficient in general that people should not 'pass tyme or dans during tyme of preaching or prayers', nor create any disturbance after the ten-hour bell in the evenings, or after the town piper had passed on his sunset duty with 'tuik of drum' through the alleys of the town.

There is no evidence whatever of any serious effort by the Scottish Kirk to drive the traditional music 'underground'. Certainly there was a decided aversion to instrumental music in worship, an aversion shared by the Puritans in England and, as Percy Scholes points out, by the puritans —such as Thomas Aquinas—within the old church. We have seen, too, that an effort was made to convert 'prophaine sangs' into 'Gude and

Godlie ballates' for the solace of the devout. Of such, no doubt, was Alexander, one of the lairds of Brodie, who never mentions music or dance in his sombre diary entries of 1617–80 (Spalding Club, 1863). But a letter from the Earl of Lothian to the Earl of Ancrum in February 1641 records that the Covenanting army, then at the height of its solemn undertaking to defy the authority of the king, was 'well provided of pypers' and not a 'sober fiddler' could be found among a number serving, although one of them did play 'exceeding well'.

The organs, after standing unused, were removed from the churches and sold to private citizens for the benefit of the poor,[17] and at the same time attempts to restore something of the burgh and cathedral *sang skuils* for the better psalmody of the church were encouraged. These schools, which had been well established by the time of the Reformation, had been disrupted and their musicians dispersed. Nothing so drastic occurred in England, although Cromwell also removed the organs from the churches, taking care to appropriate one for his own use, and leaving the rest to find their way into taverns; taverns which soon acquired the name of 'music houses'. There, in the words of John Hawkins, music was provided by

'. . . Fidlers and others, hired by the master of the house; such as in the night season were wont to parade the city and suburbs under the title of Waits . . . Half a dozen of fidlers would scrape "Sellenger's Round", or "John, Come Kiss Me", or "Old Simon the King" with divisions, till themselves and their audience were tired, after which as many players on the hautboy would in the most harsh and discordant tones grate forth "Greensleeves", "Yellow Stockings", "Gillean of Croydon", or some such common dance tune, and the people thought it fine music.'[18]

The English Puritans carried on a long campaign of most voluble invective along the lines of Northbrooke's *Treatise against Dicing, Dancing, Plays and Interludes*, 1577, from well before the death of Elizabeth, Northbrooke thought it 'a hell to see' how 'grave women' would 'swing, leape and turne when the pypers and crowders' began to play. And Philip Stubbes a short time later reprehended all public music-making that was not 'to the praise and glory of God'.[19]

There were undoubtedly many divines in Scotland who echoed the words of the English Puritans, but they were not apparently of a significant number. Their energies in any case were diverted by the constant struggle against the monarch's repeated attempts to reduce the autonomy of the Kirk, and by the need, as they felt it, to preserve the reformed religion. Their anxieties about the sending of sons to France and the Low Countries to finish their education, extensively practised by the Scottish upper classes, was not a fear that the new generation would cultivate an interest in the arts and what were regarded as courtly attributes—which they did—

but that they would be exposed to 'superstitious and heretical errors of doctrine' procuring the 'growth and increase of papists'. Hence they demanded that the 'pedagogues' who accompanied students on their sojourn on the Continent should be 'of godly and of good religion, learned and instructed in the same'.[20] Defence of the Reformation was a concern which distinguished the Scottish kirkmen from their English brethren and transcended the pursuit of Puritan ideals.

The first Scottish collections

Many a lute, viol and virginal 'whispered softness in the chambers' of the Scottish gentry through the turbulent years. Many an educated hand inscribed favourite airs in French or Italian tablature in manuscript tune books. Some of these books, of great interest today, have been preserved: we have the compilations of Sir William Mure of Rowallan; John Skene of Hallhills; Robert Gordon of Straloch (lost, but copied); Rev. Robert Edwards, minister of Murroes Parish near Dundee; Alexander Forbes of Tolquhan; William Stirling of Ardoch; William Ker of Newbattles; and the Rev. James Guthrie.

Of these, the Rowallan (*c.* 1612–28), the Skene (1615–20) and the Straloch (1627), are the earliest. They are for the lute and contain many Scottish airs, the earliest forms indeed of some tunes current in later years, such as 'Flowers o' the Forest', 'John Anderson my Jo', 'Adieu Dundee', 'Good Night and God be with You', 'My Jo Janet' and 'Green Grow the Rashes'. The Rowallan contains also a tune entitled 'Ane Scottis Dance', and the Stirling (sometimes called the Leyden) 'New Hilland Ladie'.

James Guthrie of Stirling was a covenanting minister who was executed in 1670 for writing a 'seditious' pamphlet in support of his cause, yet he left a manuscript containing about forty tunes, at least a large proportion of which were popular Scottish tunes.

Another important manuscript from the seventeenth century is named *Blaikie* after its owner, a Paisley bookseller. There were two volumes dated 1683 and 1692 respectively. The first of these had been lost, but the contents of the other are listed by William Dauney.[21] These are mostly popular Scottish airs set for viola da gamba.

There was but one book of music printed and published in Scotland in the seventeenth century, the celebrated *Cantus* by John Forbes, printer in Aberdeen which appeared in 1662 and ran to two further editions (1666 and 1682). This was a compilation of English lute songs, madrigal and continental pieces. Henry Farmer suggests that this represents turning away from the traditional airs on the part of serious music amateurs in Scotland [22]; but it is probably simply evidence of a broadening

musical interest. The lute, virginals and viol had a literature which
.eir exponents had much occasion to study, and the inventories of the
fects in many of the Scottish noble houses at this time frequently include
.rginals. It is interesting in this connection that Aberdeen could support
vo virginal manufacturers in 1618; we gather this from the application of
)hn Davidson, son of a local maltman and former student of the 'sang
:uil', for freedom to practise his trade in the burgh:

> The quhilk day, anent the supplicatioun giwen in be John Dauid-
> sone, eldest lauchfull sone to Johne Dauidsone, maltman, burgis of this
> burght, makand mentioun that sen the tyme he come frome the musick
> schoole, he hes bestowit his tyme in service with his maister, Thomas
> Mylne, virginall macker, quhome he hes seruit sein yeiris as prenteis, and
> thrie yeiris sensyne as a feit servand, as his indenture and discharge
> thairwpoun proportis, and now hauing learned the said calling, and
> being purposed (God willing) to duell and mak his residence in this his
> natiue toun, he thairfoir desyrit the counsall to admitt him frieman for
> vsing and exercising his said calling, and to respect his meane estate, in
> that he hes not present moyen to pay for his friedome, as at mair length
> wes contentit in his said supplicatioun, quhairwith the counsell being
> adwyisit, and hauing seine and considderit his maisterstick, exhibite
> befoir thame, to witt, a pair of virginallis, and theirwith considdering
> that the said calling is not vnder a deacone, being bot latlie put in
> practice within this burght be the said Thomas Mylne his maister, quha
> compeirand personallie befoir the counsall, gawe his approbatioun to
> the said maisterstick as sufficient warkmanship, thairfoir the counsall
> hes admittit and resaued the said Johne Dauidsone, frieman of this
> burght, to vse and exerce the said calling, in macking of virginallis
> allanarlie, and na forder, and that *gratis* without payment of any
> compositioun, in respect he is a burges sone, not hauen moyen to pay
> for his friedome, and the said Johne gawe his aythe according to the
> forme.[23] [Council Register of Burgh of Aberdeen, 11th March 1618.]

Of course, the Aberdeen Sang Skuil was a going concern at this time,
nd it surely tells us something about Kirk attitudes that this could be the
ise in the city of Andrew Cant in a century of theological strife. The
urgh sang skuils were for young boys and usually gave a general educa-
on as well as a musical one. Edinburgh, Glasgow, Dundee, Leith and
naller towns such as Montrose, Cupar and Dunbar all exerted them-
·lves to improve their sang skuils during the seventeenth century, but
Aberdeen became famous for its psalmody and musical interests. Whether
iis had anything to do with it, or not, the Aberdeen Town Council, in
630, 'for dyvers respectis and considerationis moving thame, dischargeit
·homas Wobstar, thair common Pyper, of all goeing throw the towne at
icht, or in the morning, in tym coming with his pyp; *as being ane incivill*

forme to be usit within sic a famous burghe, and being often fund fault with als wei be sundrie nichtbouris of the toun as be strangeris'.[24]

The burgh minstrels

It is difficult to understand why such a well-established institution as th town minstrel should be found fault with so early. Perhaps we have a hir of explanation in the Glasgow records for 1600, in which the burg minstrels are enjoined 'to pas throw the haill towne fra thai beggy quhill thai end, and to leiff af thair extraordiner drinking sua that th; may pas honestlie throw the towne in thair service . . .'[25] These an other records show quite clearly that inebriation was the occupation; disease of professional pipers and fiddlers.

It is evident that burgh authorities were concerned that their 'commo minstrels', as they called them, should conduct themselves in a wa becoming their responsibility. The Glasgow Kirk Session for instance, i 1587, took exception to 'Jarvie', the town piper, playing in the Sal market to the 'glaiking and dancing', as they phrased it, of his nephev and one Martha McClelland, and referred his conduct to the attention c the bailies. Then over a hundred years later, in Hawick, we find 'Jafra th piper' being summoned 'for a relapse in drunkeness and rambling in th streets occasioning the school boyes to follow after him through the tour (23rd June 1717). And a year later being censured for playing befor William Whaton, the fiddler, who was dressed in 'a military posture with boots, spurs and red clothes, and mounted on a horse, in a rambl through the town. This was apparently instigated by the 'schollars' an inspired by the prospect of 'a pint of brandie and a gallon of ale', great fu but indecorous for the holder of distinguished office.

The official burgh minstrels were rarely more than two in number. On played the fyfe, or flute or bagpipe, while the other beat the drum (plai 3). Their routine task was to sound the reveille (usually around four in th morning) and the curfew (usually eight in the evening), and to attend a ceremonial occasions, pageants and processions.

The instructions given John Cowpar by the Burgh of Aberdeen i November 1574, are typical:

> John Cowpar to pass every day in the morning at four houris, an everie nicht at viii houris at evyne, through all the rewis of the toun playand upon the almany quhissil, with ane servand with him playan on the tabroune, qhuairby the craftesman thair servandis and a utheris laboriouss folkis being warnit and excitat, may pass to thai labouris and fra thair labouris, in dew and convenient tyme.[26]

By the seventeenth century, the word *swesche* was often used instead c *tabroune*, short for *swesche tabroune* (spelt in various ways) the Swiss side drum then much favoured for military use, and the bagpipe had almost completely displaced the fyfe or flute ('Almany quhissil') in burgh service. The town minstrels were maintained by the burgesses or persons of means' and could expect to have meals at the appropriate times from any freeman on their route, being enjoined to be 'content to sic as salbe presentit to thame'. The arrangements varied a little from burgh to burgh.

If we may take the country town of Kilbarchan, Renfrewshire, as a typical example of its kind, the town piper's tasks included playing for dancing at weddings, leading the bridal procession thrice round the kirk, following the shearers at harvest time and playing before the provost's guard as occasion demanded. He was always in attendance at the various festivals—Beltane, St Barchan's Feast and fairs—the 'clerk plays' and horse races [27]; every public occasion in fact, as one would expect, and not an insignificant range of public occasions for the early seventeenth century.

There are instances in Border towns of the piper being entitled to half of the earnings of the fiddler at penny weddings at which the piper was not required [28]; but this was not a general practice.

The town minstrels enjoyed the protection and status of their livery; the independent professional of the hedgerows was subject to the vagaries of all authority. Some part of their traditional privileges remained, privileges they inherited, no matter how tenuously by the seventeenth century, from the bard and *druth* or *clerwr* of the Celts, or the *scop* and *gleeman* of the Anglo-Saxons. They could thereby expect food and shelter at mansion and farmhouse; but at the same time they were liable to be caught up in the permanent band of hungry, ill-clad, needy poor, among whom were a host of inferior imitators. They began to fall under a cloud when the anti-vagrancy by-laws of Edinburgh (1560) and Glasgow (1574), specifically included 'pipers, fiddlers, and minstrels'. These laws culminated in 1579 in a national anti-vagrancy act which declared all minstrels vagrant who were not in the special service of the Lords of Parliament, or the burghs. This statute was but a copy of that which had been passed in England some years before; but economic conditions being what they were, it was not an easy one to enforce, as we may judge from the following proclamation made in Edinburgh on 17th November 1587:

> chairgeing all menstrallis, pyperis, fidleris, common sangsteris, and specially of badrie and filthy sangs, and siclyke all vagabounds and maisterles persouns quha hes na service nor honest industrie to leif be, remove and depairt furth of this burgh incontinent, and be nocht fund within the samyn heirafter under the payne of imprysonment in the thevis holl and punesing of thair persouns at the will of the magestrats.[29]

There was nothing anti-musical in this. The simple fact was that many beggars, then as in more recent times, counterfeited the musician, and vagrancy posed many problems for towns throughout the later middl ages. They were prepared to look after their own indigents, that is, thos native to the town, but were not so ready to accommodate all who cam their way, especially on the occasion of epidemics, or plague, which wa a great scourge of the period. Thus we read the ordinance at Aberdeen o 15th September 1539—typical of pronouncements made by nearly ever town—that on account of 'the contagius infeckand pest' in 'diverse partis of the country, all 'codderaris, vagaboundis, and puyr boddeis' not nativ to the town were to be branded on the cheek and banished.[30] Th itinerant minstrel was on very shaky ground indeed; better to find a plac in which to settle.

Different circumstances prevailed in the non-burghal part of th country, an extensive part, serrated by glens, mountains, lochs and seas whence, indeed, we must suspect many a travelling minstrel issued fortl into the Lowland towns along the Highland Line. The occasional Iris harper, too, carried his fertilizing influence into Scotland in continuatio of that reciprocal process established long ago and remarked upon b Giraldus. The most distinguished of the Irish harpers to visit Scotland i the seventeenth century was Rory 'Dall' O'Cahan (*c*. 1550–1650), wh was much esteemed in England also, as indeed was his instrument, th *clarsach*, the old Celtic harp (plate 5).

The Country Dance in England

England had a use for these attractive Irish and Scottish airs, particularl the jigs and the jaunty Scottish quadruple-time tunes. I refer to th Country Dance which had become all the rage at Court. John Playford bookseller to the lawyers, responded to the resurgence of interest conse quent on the termination of the Civil War, with a collection of over hundred Country Dances complete with figures and tunes, *The Englis Dancing Master*, 1651.[31] It was the first of eighteen editions (the eighteenth *c*. 1728, contained over 900 dances) and the first of a number of celebrate books of music which Playford and his son Henry compiled an published.

It seems a strange contradiction that it was in the first years of Purita rule that Playford launched his considerable enterprise. In the same yea as the production of his first collection, he produced *A Musical Banquet*, t which, be it noted, a list of twenty-seven London music-teachers wa appended. Then followed the second edition of *The Dancing Master* (th word 'English' being dropped from the title) and *Booke of New Lessons fo the Gittern* in 1652 and *Musick's Recreation* in 1669. This probably testifie to the presence of a considerable market; Samuel Pepys, for instanc records frequenting Playford's shop. More books followed: *An Introduc tion to the Skill of Music* in 1654, *Musick's Delight* in 1666 and furthe

:ditions of *The Dancing Master*. Each edition of the last showed alterations, ιdditions and deletions vis-a-vis its predecessor, and no edition contained ·ess than one hundred dances. Many of the tunes in the Playford books ,vere Scottish and Irish, but it is not likely that this explains his dropping he word 'English' from the title of *The Dancing Master*. Its inclusion in he first place was in contradistinction to the title of a popular play, *The French Dancing Master*.*

This outpouring of books of music in the Commonwealth period in Ξngland, many of them instruction books for beginners, does not signify ι triumph for the Puritan pamphleteers. We conjure up a vision of much lomestic music-making and much dancing of Country Dances in the ·ong galleries of the Great English houses. This dancing was not new, but ?layford's books were greatly to increase the Country Dance repertoire. They were to launch it into its golden age as the darling enjoyment of the ;reat new middle classes of the eighteenth century, in all the centres of ashion in the British Isles and even for a time on the Continent; but not)efore the Commonwealth ended with the restoration of the monarchy in :660, raising hopes in far-off Scotland that a more tolerant era would)egin. The spouts of the Cross at Edinburgh ran with claret, and at night there were bonfires in the streets, and fireworks in the castle till after nidnight.

There were also six viols, three of them base viols, playing there con-tinually. There were also some musicians placed there wha were resolved to act their parts, and were willing and ready, but by reason of the frequent acclamations and cries of the people universally through the haill town, their purpose was interrupted. Bacchus also, being set upon ane puncheon of wine upon the front of the Cross with his cummerholds, was not idle.[32]

Alas, this sanguine beginning was not justified by events, and the Covenanters faced new battles with disputable royal prerogatives. No nore devout men could be found than these, yet several of their leaders layed the native airs along with the psalms. We have already noted James Suthrie's collection (page 30).

Certainly this unsettled time was not a good one for the arts, but it is ·reposterous to suggest that the song and dance of the countryside, Iighland and Lowland, were allowed to decay. The faction of the ·cottish Kirk crystallized as the 'Wee Free' division in the nineteenth entury and which then permeated the Scottish Western Highlands with levastating consequences for the traditional arts and ancient customs, was ιardly discernible in the Scottish Kirk of the first century or so after the

Originally entitled *The Varietie* (*c*. 1660), but renamed from a comic dancing master in the ·ay. Pepys mentions attending a performance in May 1662.

Reformation. Nor do the non-conformist groups who developed with th Industrial Revolution, turning their backs on the world as they did, offe us any reliable analogy to the early Scottish Kirk. It is misleading to judg the one from the other.

The evidence is that the native music and dance were, in general, take: very much for granted—an inevitable part of life. Undoubtedly th increasing enthusiasm for country dancing in England, fostered by th growing fashion for public and private dance assemblies in towns grea and small, and at this or that spa where the fashionable were wont to fore gather in their season to 'take the waters', brought the Scottish tunes t wider notice. At the end of the century, the issue of Episcopacy havin been exchanged for Jacobitism, the corresponding circles in Scotlan succumbed to the social influences of their southern counterparts, and th dawn of a belated renaissance seemed in prospect.

CHAPTER 3

'Their Allegros and a' the rest'*
Scottish music-making in the eighteenth century

The first unmistakable portent of the increasing refinement which was to
distinguish Scottish social life at its upper levels in the eighteenth century
was the 'Grand Concert of Music' presented in Edinburgh on St
Cecilia's Day, 22nd November 1695, by an orchestra of thirty musicians.
The programme included contemporary compositions by Bassani (1657–
1716) and Corelli (1653–1713) and suggests considerable preparation.[1]
Indeed, there is evidence of its having been preceded by possibly less
ambitious concerts from as early as 1693. We gather this from a dispute
which came before the judges of the Court of Session in January 1694,
between one named Beck who, with some associates, had 'erected a
concert of music', and one Maclean, who at that time held the appointment of 'Master of the Revels'. Maclean claimed that it was within the
prerogatives of his office to demand licence payment from Beck. The
judges ruled that Maclean's authority extended only to music 'in connection with plays and puppet shows', and that 'musicians were not
subject to Masters of the Revels abroad', where the office was best known,
and that Maclean only 'used it to drain money from them [the promoters
of the concert] without restraining immoralities, if they paid him'.[2]
    Even allowing that the extent of the suppression of secular music in
Scotland in the seventeenth century has been grossly exaggerated, one's
eyebrows rise at sight of the fact that eleven of the musicians in the
orchestra at that celebrated St Cecilia concert were professional teachers of
music, three of whom have special claim to our notice. Matthew
McGibbon, oboist, and Daniel Thomson, trumpeter, each had a son
who was to publish important collections of Scottish airs and continue
the musical traditions of their families with distinction; and Adam Craig,
violinist, published *A Collection of the Choicest Scots Tunes* [1730].

The Edinburgh Music Club

The remaining nineteen members of the orchestra were amateurs of the
first rank and fashion. This was no doubt the nucleus from which sprang

* The title of this chapter is taken from verses by the Rev. John Skinner (1721–1807) in
defence of native strains against the intrusion of classical music into the musical repertoire of the
middle and upper classes. The verses are printed on page 179.

the Music Club which comes to notice by 1717, meeting weekly at th
Cross Keys Tavern, the proprietor of which, John Steill, was an enthu
siastic musician and an esteemed singer of Scots songs. It is sad to notic
his effects up for auction in 1729 (*Caledonian Mercury*, 26th February)
they included a considerable collection of musical instruments and musi
books.

The Music Club presented concerts to which Allan Ramsay seems t
allude in a poem of 1718:

> *For beaux and belles no city can compare,*
> *Nor show a galaxy so made, so fair,*
> *The ears are charm'd, and ravish'd are the eyes,*
> *When at the concert my fair stars arise.*[3]

The favourite music of these occasions was that of Corelli and Handel
Then in 1723 the Edinburgh Dance Assembly was inaugurated
patterned after those which had long flourished in English centres o
fashion. A directress supervised each weekly evening of dancing durin
the winter season, and the profits were subscribed to the hospital an
poor-house, and occasionally other deserving causes. The dancing bega
with Minuets, and ended with Country Dances. The constitution of th
orchestra in the early years is unknown.

In March 1728, a new music society was formed for the purpose o
presenting weekly concerts in St Mary's Chapel. The original seventy
members of the Society were gentlemen, and hence the name of thei
enterprise, the 'Gentlemen's Concerts'. These were probably the earlies
subscription concerts given this name. Professionals were hired to lead th
orchestra and to reinforce certain departments as necessary.

The Society so prospered that after failing to build a new hall in a join
venture with the Dance Assembly, they built one of their own in 1762, o
the plan of the Grand Opera House at Parma: the celebrated St Cecilia'
Hall, at the foot of Niddry's Wynd. The music at these concerts consiste
of the overtures, concertos, sonatas, symphonies and chamber music
generally, of the composers then most in vogue—Handel, Gluck,
Corelli and Purcell being the best of them. Here Handel's oratorios wer
first performed in Scotland.

The St Cecilia Hall, thought Henry Cockburn, was 'the best and
most beautiful concert hall' he had seen. 'There have myself,' he writes,
'seen most of our literary and fashionable gentlemen predominating in
their side-curls, and frills, and ruffles, and silver buckles; and our stately
matrons stiffened in hoops and gorgeous satin; and our beauties with high-
heeled shoes, powdered and pomatumed hair, and lofty and composite
head-dresses'.[4] With all its memories, it would have been exciting today
to be able to attend a concert there; but it fell into other uses with the
removal of its patrons from the 'old' to the 'new' town. After being long

disused the Hall was restored and reopened in June 1968 to house a collection of harpsichords, etc., bequeathed to Edinburgh University.

In 1721, in a poetic address 'To the Music Club', Allan Ramsay urged the members to show that 'music may have as good fate' in Scotland's glens as in Italy's 'green retreat' and with 'Corelli's soft Italian song Mix "Cowdenknows" and "Winter nights are long".' Nor, he continued, 'should the martial "Pibrough" be despis'd'.

The exhortation was not necessary: devotion to the native airs transcended social class, and throughout the century, as we shall have occasion to notice again, the attachment to the gude Scots songs and to the gude Scots jigs, reels and strathspeys, at dance salon or tavern meeting, actually increased.

The Tea Table Miscellany

It was about the time Ramsay wrote his poem to the Music Club that the fourth edition of Thomas D'Urfey's ribald collection of 'the best merry ballads and songs, old and new', entitled *Wit and Mirth: or Pills to purge melancholy*, appeared in London.[5] This contained some genuine Scottish airs, along with numerous parodies of Scottish songs and some imitations. Perhaps this was what prompted Ramsay to compile something more suitable for the ladies to sing at their afternoon 'teas'. In any event he had a natural desire to introduce his revised and new versions of some of the favourite songs, and this he did in *The Tea Table Miscellany*, as he called it, in *c*. 1724.[6] It cannot always be said, strangely enough, that Ramsay made all the old themes more decorous, or even improved them all; but he had a droll wit and, at his best, a jovial touch. There is every indication, too, that toleration of indelicacy at that time, was greater than it was over a century later. One need only notice some of the titles of the traditional tunes published for that market and consider how they would be received even today: 'Geld him Lasses', 'Piss on the Grass',* 'Maggie's wame is fu' I trow', 'She's sweetest when she's naked' and so on.

In the title of his collection, Ramsay was alluding to the custom of afternoon and evening tea parties enjoyed by the gentlewomen in the capital, a custom which persisted throughout the century. Tea-drinking was too expensive for the lower classes, and when it did begin to make inroads among them towards the end of the century, the more devout were inclined to regard it as one of the signs of growing self-indulgence.[7]

The Edinburgh tea party involved conversation, music on the spinet, some unaccompanied Scots songs, and cards. Anecdotes have come down to us of the beautiful Lady Mary Lilias Scott of Harden, daughter of a beautiful mother remembered as 'the Flower of Yarrow', singing 'with

* In J. Walsh's *Caledonian Country Dances, c.* 1744. The tune is later called 'Nancy Dawson'.

such feeling and effect as to draw tears from those who heard her', and o
Lady Murray of Stanhope, Grizel Baillie's daughter, whose singing wa
no less celebrated at these occasions.

The *Tea Table Miscellany* did not contain any tunes; they were we.
known and the same tune was sometimes used for several lyrics. 'Cowden
knowes', for example, was used four times, 'Yellow-Haired Laddie
thrice. But the music for the songs, set by Alexander Stuart, was pub
lished in 1726 (plate 16), a year after William Thomson published h:
collection of Scots songs—*Orpheus Caledonius*—complete with music, i
London. Thomson dedicated his book to the Princess of Wales, an
republished it, enlarged, in 1733. It is the first of the important Scottis
song publications.

The next collection actually published in Scotland, in 1730, was Ada
Craig's *Choicest Scots Tunes*, already mentioned. It comprised settings f
the harpsichord or spinet (plate 16), and was dedicated to the 'Honourab
Lords and Gentlemen of the Musical Society of St Mary's Chapel
Meantime, two more collections containing Scottish tunes had appeare
in London—*The Musical Miscellany* by John Watts, 1729, and *Aria
Camera*, c. 1730, with some original compositions *inter alia* by 'M
Alexander Urquahart of Edinburgh'.*

John Gay's *Beggar's Opera* with its considerable body of Scottis
traditional tunes was now at the height of its popularity. This wor
which set the fashion for ballad opera in England, was first produced
the Haymarket Theatre, London, in 1728, amid scenes of much contro
versy and enthusiasm. It was a satire on the manners of the time and o
the Italian opera which enjoyed a tremendous vogue during the ear.
decades of the century.

Allan Ramsay wrote the first of the ballad operas, *The Gentle Shepher
published in 1725, three years before Gay's masterpiece, although it w.
not performed until some time after 1729. It is strange that there is no cle
record of the first performance.† It was a development of an earlier work
Ramsay's entitled *Patie and Roger*, and it was under this name that it w
performed at various times in London between 1750 and 1775 with
substantially Scottish cast, also in Philadelphia and New York.

* Davidson Cook procured one of the two known copies and reviewed it in *The Scott
Musical Magazine*, 1921.
† The tunes used by Ramsay in this celebrated pastoral were 'The wauking of the faulds', 'F
gar rub her ower wi stra', 'Polwart on the Green', 'O dear Mother, what shall I do?', 'Ho
can I be sad on my wedding-day', 'Nancy's to the green-wood gane', 'Cauld Kale
Aberdeen', 'Mucking of Geordie's byre', 'Carle an the King come', 'Winter was caul
and my claithing was thin', 'Leith Wynd', 'Oer Bogie, Kirk wad let me be', 'Tweedsid
'Bush abune Traquair', and 'Corn Rigs are Bonny'. Other songs mentioned in the text a
'Broom of Cowdenknows', 'Milking of the Ewes', 'Jenny Nettles', 'Maggie Lauder', 'T
Boatman' and 'The Lass of Patie's Mill', which last was Ramsay's own work.

Unlike *The Beggar's Opera*, there is no satire of manners or of Italian opera in this work. The shepherd falls in love with the country lass and when it is revealed that he is, after all, of gentle blood, there is danger of broken hearts until it is likewise revealed that the country lass has a similar lineage. The good and the true and the beautiful are here extolled with much pathos and humour. A scene from *The Gentle Shepherd* is the subject of a painting by Sir David Wilkie; it shows the shepherd playing his stock and horn (plate 2).

Scots tunes and ballad operas

The Beggar's Opera in contrast had considerable satirical bite. The hero, for instance, is a highwayman (Macheath), and one outrageous implication in the play is that the ways and honour of a highwayman were little different from those of a gentleman! As Mrs Peacham asks: 'What business hath he (Macheath) to keep company with Lords and Gentlemen? He should leave them to prey upon one another' . . . 'Why must our Polly differ from her sex and love only her husband?' . . . 'she loves to imitate fine ladies, and she may allow the Captain (Macheath) liberties in the view of interest.'

Nevertheless, if Polly must be married, could she not introduce into her family someone other than a highwayman? 'Why you foolish jade, thou wilt be as ill-used, and as much neglected, as if thou hadst married a Lord!' To all this, Polly replies that she did not marry for honour or money, but for love; at which her mother holds up her hands in horror that her daughter should show herself so 'ill-bred'.

So runs the argument. Some thought it an incitement to crime, an immoral influence. Others, like Samuel Johnson and Sir Walter Scott at a later date, thought it all very witty and not in the least immoral. The success of the work was immediate and resounding, and it was frequently presented throughout the century and in all the principal towns, though not in Scotland until the Edinburgh Company of Players presented it there in June 1733.

The song 'Lumps o' Pudding' has a tune claimed by both England and Scotland, an excellent jig which serves for the finale of the opera and gave rise to Handel's wry observation that his operas had been driven off the stage in 1728 by 'lumps of pudding'.*

The lampooning of the Italian opera was no doubt particularly relished by many. The 'Italianate' music, as it was called, was not accessible to the lower classes, except, perhaps, in London where certain pleasure gardens,

---

* Other Scottish songs parodied in *The Beggar's Opera* are: 'Cold and Raw', 'Over the Hills and far away', 'Gin Thou wert mine ain thing', 'The Lass of Patie's Mill', 'O Bessy Bell', 'The Last time I came o'er the Moor' and 'Bonny Dundee'.

such as Lambeth Wells and Sadler's Wells Music House, presented concerts of current favourites at popular prices. Even in 1738, one London coffee house correspondent complained of the excessive cost of attending the performance of a Handel oratorio—'everybody knows', he writes, 'his entertainments are calculated for the Quality only'.

Nor, in Scotland, did the population at large hear much of the music played at the Gentlemen's Concerts, or on the spinet (plate 16) or harpsichord here and there in the aristocratic houses or in the houses of the city merchants. But even in the highest society, the native lyrics of the countryside were the most cherished of music. A remarkable number of the Scottish gentry turned their hands to the composition of new verses for existing tunes, and, as we shall see, to the composing of reels and strathspeys for the dance.

The best known of the aristocratic song writers, each commemorated by at least one masterpiece in the traditional style are: Lady Grizel Baillie ('Were na my hert licht'); Jane Elliot ('The Floo'ers o' the Forest'); Lady Nairne ('The Auld Hoose', 'Rowan Tree'); Lady Barnard ('Auld Robin Gray'); the Duke of Gordon ('Cauld Kail'); Sir Alexander Boswell ('Jenny Dang the Weaver').

This was their own music, it surrounded them from the cradle, and they never tired of it. In the seventeen-seventies, Captain Edward Topham, an Englishman, tells us:

> After supper is removed, and they are tired of conversing they vary the scene by singing, in which many of the Scots excell . . . There is a plaintive simplicity in the generality of their songs, which from the mouth of a pretty Scotch girl is inconceivably attractive . . . The eye, the whole countenance speak frequently as much as the voice.[8]

This was not a local phenomenon, it was a custom and habit of Scotsmen everywhere, from the Hebridean croft to the music room of the Lowland mansion. Members of the Musical Society at Aberdeen found it objectionable that the Scots songs should be relegated to the close of the programme, since some members had to leave early or were then anxious about the hour.

Gay wrote a sequel to his brilliant satire and others were quick to turn their hands to the ballad opera form. One, *The Highland Fair, or Union of the Clans*, by Joseph Mitchell, D.L., 1731, holds some obvious interest for us. It was styled 'A Scots Opera' and was claimed wholly to consist of 'Select Scots Tunes'—fifty-one of them! It was not produced in Scotland, however, and the Scots who attended it in London were said to have been greatly diverted by the Scots accents affected by the performers.*

The ballad operas and the repertoire of singers who performed before

---

* Attempts have been made in Scotland in recent years to revive this work.

onsiderable audiences at Vauxhall, Ranelagh and Marylebone, the ravourite London pleasure gardens, bear ample testimony to the popularity of Scottish airs in England. We read in the *Gentleman's Magazine* for 750 that 'The Highland Laddie written long since by Allan Ramsay, nd now sung at Ranelagh and all the other gardens; often fondly encor'd, nd sometimes ridiculously hiss'd'—for the 'Forty-Five rising was still 'esh in memory. The authentic vied with numerous imitations of which Within A Mile of Edinburgh Town' has come down to us as the most accessful, with the tune by James Hook (1746–1827), a prolific composer of ballads and catches.

Country Dances and music making

'he publication of Country Dances begun by Playford with such access in the seventeenth century now flourished beyond all imagining. }y the middle of the century, every music publisher of note was issuing ets of *Country Dances*, many of them annually, running into hundreds. Walsh, the most prolific publisher during the first half of the century, arned to Scottish sources and produced his *Caledonian Country Dances* in everal editions in the seventeen-forties. Then Bremner some twenty years ter drew upon the unexploited field of the instrumental reels and strathpeys of the Highlands for the same purposes. Others followed. The cotch reel in both allegro and strathspey forms soon followed their music nto the ballrooms of the South.

At a time when the fashionable Scottish poet James Thomson was vriting the words of 'Rule, Britannia' and Thomas Arne was setting it to music, other Scots were planning the restoration of the Stuart Dynasty. Matters came to a startling head in 1745 with the muster round Prince Charles Edward at Glenfinnan, and thus began a process which was to ead to the disruption of Highland society and to profound repercussions n the history of Scotland and the British Empire. When Wolfe assailed Quebec and Clive subjugated India, Highland soldiers were in the van rith them. The inspiring naval victories of 1759 led Garrick to write the ousing song 'Hearts of Oak'; while romantic Scots toasted the 'King wer the Watter' and sang with feeling, if with little expectation, 'Will ye o' come back again?' It was of Scotland they were thinking. Scotland, a ation now only in the cultural sense, but a nation very much aware of self, was poised to make immense contributions to the realm of ideas and ractical science, poised to build new nations, poised to spread her music nd dance to the most distant outposts of empire. The Scot Tobias mollett has Humphry Clinker write from Edinburgh: 'The Scots are l Musicians. Every man you meet plays on the flute, the violin, or ioloncello.'[2] He was referring, of course, to his gentlemen friends in

Edinburgh, some of whom were members of the orchestra. He allud
also to a 'nobleman, whose compositions are universally admired
undoubtedly Thomas Alexander Erskine, sixth earl of Kellie (1723–81
who wrote several overtures, symphonies and songs in the classical style (
the time, and who was especially renowned for his Minuets.

Although Smollett refers only to the men, women were no less activ
Some played the flute (like the young Susannah Kennedy, later Counte
of Eglinton), or even the violin (like Suphy Johnston), and of course tl
spinet or virginals and harpsichord. But the pear-shaped 'Englis
Guitar' was very fashionable with young ladies at this time *; tl
Spanish 'guittar' is also mentioned, Daniel Dow advertising to teach i

Twenty years later, Edward Topham wrote from Edinburgh in son
perplexity: 'The degree of attachment which is shown to music in gener
in this country exceeds belief. It is not only the principal entertainmen
but the constant topic of every conversation; and it is necessary not only (
be a lover of it, but to be possessed of a knowledge of the science, to mal
yourself agreeable to society.' [10]

Now music-making at the 'concerts', the taverns, the Theatre Roy.
and St Andrew's Chapel, and in the 'chaumers' of the gentry, reached
notable peak of intensity, not only in Edinburgh, although Edinburgh .
this date led in all these matters, but also in Glasgow and Aberdeen i
particular.

The reigning beauties of the time were as likely to be encountered at tl
concert as they were at the dance assembly. Robert Chambers [11] tells ho
old George Thomson (1757–1851), exalted by association with Burns i
the compiling of A Select Collection of Original Scottish Airs, recalle
seeing the 'lovely faces' of many of the belles of Edinburgh at the concer
in the seventeen-eighties, notable among them being Lucy Johnston (
Hilton (plate 21); Jane Maxwell, Duchess of Gordon; Elizabet
Burnett and Euphemia Murray of Lintrose, all celebrated by Burn
These ladies were even more familiar with the strathspeys and reels (
Niel Gow and William Marshall than they were with the concerti (
Corelli and Pergolesi.

Lord Drummore (1690–1755), who was governor of the Musi
Society around the mid-century, was an enthusiastic performer on tl
Border pipes and the employer of the celebrated border piper Geord
Sime. The two musical interests were not mutually exclusive in Scottis
upper-class life.

* Such is the instrument held by Lady Caroline, fourth Marchioness of Lothian, in tl
portrait of her by Allan Ramsay, son of the poet. The vogue of the English guitar about 177
was so great that harpsichord and spinet makers faced economic difficulties. It is said that or
of the Kirkmans, English harpsichord makers, broke the vogue by supplying cheap guitars
milliner girls and street ballad singers whom he taught to accompany themselves. G. Jon(
article 'Music' in Encyclopedia Londinensis, 1810–29.

At the concert

A considerable run of Italian violinists led the orchestra from about Drummore's time to the end of the century, and several other continental instrumentalists strengthened the string and wind departments. These performers were frequently in demand for teaching and private entertainment as well as for engagements with the music societies of Glasgow and Aberdeen, and certainly exerted an influence on Scottish music-making at the upper levels.

Singing, however, was especially popular. Purely instrumental music which was not used for dancing was more demanding of the undeveloped powers of abstract musical thought than was vocal music. The Italian singers of the London stage appeared in the provinces on concert tours. Mazzanti, Domenico Corri, Valentino Urbani (Valentini) and Giusto Tenducci are among the names that found greatest favour in Scotland and we shall have occasion to refer to them again. It is easy to understand how the formal art of music came to be called 'Italian Music' by the populace in general at this time.

In his recollections of the Gentlemen's Concerts, Henry Mackenzie writes:

. . . the first leader whom I remember was Arrigoni, who was also a teacher of the violin,—a firm, ready and true performer on that instrument. After him Puppo * filled that situation, a clever and acute man, with great taste and delightful tone; lastly Stabilini, who was a violin player of considerable eminence, but indolent and indifferent about the performance except his own solos.[12]

'Stab' as he was familiarly called, fell a victim to dissipation in 1815, and was the author of the deathless lines:

A piece ov toarkey for a hungree bellee
Is moatch supeerior to Corelli [13]

—another Edinburgh character in a great age of characters.

George Thomson tells us that the most accomplished violinist to visit Edinburgh in his time was Giovanni Giornovichi, known as Jarnovick, whom he ranked close to the celebrated Pagnanini of later date. Doubtless this was the person who was the inspiration or composer of 'Jarnovichi's Hornpipe' in the Gow (4th) Collection.

In 1772, when the noted Scottish publisher Robert Bremner was residing in London, he was asked by the Edinburgh concert society to engage a violoncellist on their behalf. As a result of this commission a

---

* A portrait of Puppo published by H. M. Humphrey, London, 27th November 1781, bears the imprint, 'Signor Puppy, First Catgut Scraper' (see no. 7, plate 171, Percy A. Scholes, The Oxford Companion to Music, London, 1939). He retired from Edinburgh in 1782.

young Austro-Hungarian, Christoff Schetky, rode into Edinburgh la
on a cold February afternoon in 1773, accompanied by his brother Kar
After eating at Peter Ramsay's Inn in St Mary's Wynd, they found the
way to St Cecilia Hall where a concert was about to be held. There the
were introduced to Joseph Reinagle, a fellow countryman and trumpet
in the orchestra, who took them in charge. Reinagle had been a memb
of the entourage of the Old Pretender in 1715, but had not long befo
moved to Edinburgh from Portsmouth. His wife's name, Anne Lauri
suggests that she was a Scot.

Like Stabilini, Schetky and Reinagle found Edinburgh society ver
much to their taste, and Schetky, especially, became well integrated int
its colourful eccentricities, so much so, indeed, that it is easy to forget h
Hungarian origin. He composed various song and dance tunes after th
Scottish traditional style and was acquainted with Robert Burns throug
the latter's visits to the capital. He apparently enjoyed jovial company, an
in 1787 established the Boar Club at his favourite howff—Hogg's Taven
All the members were 'bores'; their talk 'grunting', their room the 'sty
and the jar provided for a collection of 'fines', of course, the 'pig'—the ol
name for an earthenware crock. One of the founder members was Rober
Aldridge, whom Chambers describes as 'a famous pantomimist an
dancing master'.[14] If this is correct, then surely he was the celebrated Iris
dancer who was a familiar entr'acte performer in London and Dubli
theatres in the seventeen-sixties and seventies, and the source (at least of th
title) of 'Aldridge's Hornpipe' [92].

Schetky's daughter remarks in her biography of her father:

> Was it not strange that, after being flattered and admired at foreig
> Courts, and meeting with so much prosperity everywhere, he should a
> last settle down in a small place such as Edinburgh then was, in th
> remote country of Scotland? But I have sometimes imagined that thi
> country then must have been more like an old Continental city than i
> its present stage of progress. There were all the nobility of the countr
> assembled from their ancient fastnesses in the north—the courts of law—
> the university—the little exiled Court of France at Holyrood, where m
> father often appeared—those splendid St Cecilia concerts (the audienc
> composed exclusively of aristocracy) combining so much talent—ad
> to this, the easy access a well-educated and accomplished foreigne
> found to the best society,—these things must, I think, have combined t
> make him like the place.[15]

Joseph Reinagle's son, also Joseph, studied the cello with Schetky and
was sufficiently accomplished on the viola and violin to lead the orchestra
for a time, before moving to Oxford. Another son, Alexander (1756–
1809), emigrated to America in 1786, and as a conductor and manager
became a leading figure in the musical and theatrical life of Philadelphia.

e was later joined there by his nephew, Schetky's son Johann (1776–
31)—for Schetky married father Reinagle's daughter Maria in 1774.
oth Alexander Reinagle and young Schetky published collections of
cottish tunes in Philadelphia; Reinagle's was entitled *A Collection of the
ost Favourite Scots Tunes*, and Schetky's covered a wider field, including
arl of Moira's Welcome to Scotland or the Countess of Loudon's Strathspey
ranged as a rondo for piano, 1823, and Young Roscius's Strathspey with
riations, etc. All were very typical publications of the period in America,
stifying to the widespread appeal of Scottish national music.

Undoubtedly the best known of the Schetky sons was John, who,
ough a good cellist, forsook music as a profession, and became Marine
ainter in Ordinary to George IV, William IV and Queen Victoria. He
as the intimate of Sir Walter Scott and other celebrities with whom his
ork brought him into frequent contact; and closed with a fitting climax
e Edinburgh episode of the Schetky family.

The concert vocalists

)f the many Italian vocalists who toured the musical centres of eighteenth-
entury Scotland, none was more highly esteemed than Tenducci. His
eatment of Scots songs was widely admired. George Thomson, whom
e have quoted earlier, tells us that Tenducci

. . . made his appearance occasionally when he came to visit the Hopetoun family, his liberal and steady patrons; and while he remained he
generally gave some concert at the Hall, which made quite a sensation
among the musicals. I considered it a jubilee year whenever Tenducci
arrived, as no singer I ever heard, sang with more expressive simplicity
. . . whether he sang the classical songs of Metastasio, or those of Arne's
Artaxerxes, or the simple melodies of Scotland. To the latter he gave
such intensity of interest by his impassioned manner, and by his clear
enunciation of the words, as equally surprised and delighted us.

I can never forget the pathos and touching effect of his 'Gilderoy',
'Lochaber-no-more', 'The Braes of Ballenden', 'I'll never leave thee',
'Roslin Castle'. These with the 'Verdi prati' of Handel, 'Fair
Aurora' from Arne's *Artaxerxes*, and Gluck's 'Che faro', were above all
praise.[16]

Mr and Mrs Domenico Corri and Urbani were also singers. Corri
ved in Edinburgh for eighteen years from 1771 but ended his days in
Iampstead in May 1825, in the seventy-ninth year. His speculative turn
f mind led him into music selling, theatre-management and an attempt
o emulate Vauxhall with his Ranelagh Gardens in 1776, at a site now
ccupied by Queensferry Street and with Comely Garden, 1777; all
pparently of little avail to his economic solvency.

Urbani also adapted himself to the life and culture of the Norther capital, perhaps even more thoroughly than Corri, taking considerabl interest in the native music, especially the songs, which latter he was wot to sing at the concerts. He was one of the contributors to Johnson's *Sco Musical Museum*, 1787, and was a most prominent figure in Scotland musical life as singer, impresario, publisher and 'Director of Oratorio He is noticed preparing a choir for the reintroduction of Handel oratorios in 1803—*Messiah* being performed twice in the most ambitiou presentation to that time, and also *Samson*. Two years later Urba moved to Dublin where he died in 1816.

Urbani not only turned from his 'Italian trills', to sing the ne Burnsian settings of old Scots lyrics, but also joined the ranks of tho collecting the unrecorded songs still to be heard from the lips of tl caddies, servants and tradesmen of the city and countryside. He solicite the help of Robert Burns and even asked the poet to write verses for a Italian air.[17] This is the reverse of Thomson's engaging Haydn an Beethoven, Pleyel and others, to write music for Scots verses.

There is no harm in this, but there is harm in the corruption of trad tional tunes, or tunes in the traditional idiom, which resulted from pressir them into the conventional harmonic mould of the 'Germanic' 'Italianate' music of the period. Alexander ('Sannock') Campbe (1764–1824), an organist and teacher of harpsichord and singing 1 Edinburgh, perceived this at the end of the eighteenth century. 'Ever thing,' he writes, 'that comes through the hands of professed musicia savours strongly of pedantic garnish.'[18] He had in mind particular William McGibbon's *Collection of Scots Tunes*, three volumes publishe in 1742, 1746 and 1755. He thought that McGibbon's German tutela; was evident in these books and opined that the Italian influence 'did le harm to our Scottish melodies'. The Italian influence, presumably, tend more towards melodic embellishment than harmonic convention. The was no checking the vogue in fashionable circles, and it is no surprise read in the programme of an Edinburgh concert in 1755: '"Tweedside newly set in the Italian manner (for the sake of variety) by Signor Pasqual Nevertheless, John Watlen, an English publisher in Edinburgh, prefac his own *Complete Collection of Scots Songs*, 1796, with the remark that I had set the airs—'plain and simple, without being Italianized in tl least', which suggests that many shared Alexander Campbell's view of tl matter. It says a great deal for Francesco Barsanti that his *Collection of O Scots Tunes* dedicated to Lady Erskine and published in [1742], remarkably free from alien influences. Campbell composed the air Robert Tannahill's 'Gloomy Winter's now Awa'', and other pieces the traditional style, but he is best known as the author of *An Introducti to the History of Poetry in Scotland* in which he makes original observatio on the tonality of Scottish music; and for *Albyn's Anthology* (1816–18),

ollection of melodies and Gaelic vocal poetry. Sir Walter Scott—who
as not musically gifted—was one of his poorer pupils. His brother John
Campbell (1750–95) was a particular friend of Robert Burns and a pupil
Tenducci. He was also esteemed for his singing of the native songs.

' Their chief amusement is dancing'

inseparable from the outpouring of Scotland's musical soul at this time
as the passion for dancing. Dance and music probably played a larger
art in the social life of the Scottish people in the eighteenth century than
ver before. Certainly the way of life in the eighteenth century forms a
ramatic contrast to that of the seventeenth in this regard, and just as the
allants at the court of Elizabeth forsook some of the more lusty games for
ne Galliard and Lavolta, so also did the Highlanders of the parish of
Moulin, Perthshire, two centuries later, abandon their customary racing,
rrestling and putting the stone for what their minister called the 'more
egant, though less manly, amusement of dancing, which is become very
ommon, especially on holidays'.[19]
   Now select 'public' dance assemblies and formal balls—those of the
Capillaire Club and Caledonian Hunt in Edinburgh and their counter-
arts in Glasgow and Aberdeen, for instance—and later in the century the
volunteer' balls and King's Birthday balls (attendance at which some-
mes became a test of loyalty, revolution being very much in the air),
nasonic balls and so on, occasions which had no counterparts earlier in
ne century, now crowded the annual calendar.
   Minuet and Country Dances and Highland Reel dominated the ball-
oom, Reels and Country Dances the oyster-cellar parties and the private
ssemblies in Fortune's Tavern. The rural harvest-home of the Lowlands
nd the ball at many a great house of the time—Blair Castle, Hopetoun
House, Dalkeith, Hamilton House, Inverary and Taymouth—differed
ery little in content, if a great deal in deportment and execution. The
Northern Meeting at Aberdeen and Inverness, week-long and formal in
xtreme, drew upon the nobility and quality of the North-East, with the
ndefatigable Duchess of Gordon setting the pace.
   The native music, in this period of Scotland's 'most energetic, peculiar,
nd most various life', was as dear and inspiring to the highest in the land
s to the humblest country fiddler. Browsing through the statistical
ccounts of the various Scottish parishes for this period, one finds time
fter time that 'their chief amusement is dancing'.
   The change in manners and economy in Scotland in the eighteenth
entury was dramatic; but it was still an agrarian community. The
inerant fiddler and piper moved from fair to fair and market to market,
ne dancing master from town to town.
   Roads at the beginning of the century, whenever they existed as more

than mere pony-tracks, were almost impassable to wheeled traffic. In the North-east much culture and brigandage had existed side by side through out the seventeenth century, but in the early years of the eighteenth it wa not unusual to see a group of brawny Highlanders, armed with broad swords, dirks and firelocks, accompanied by a piper, move about the fair at Banff, Elgin and Forres and other places, to note those receiving mone or cattle so that they could be plundered later. By the end of the century th broadswords and dirks and much of the feuding had disappeared, as als had much of the population.

At the Mid-Summer's Eve Fair at Keith in 1700 some members of a particularly troublesome band of 'vagabonds' from Strathspey wer apprehended by Duff, Laird of Braco, and at length brought before th sheriff of Banffshire on a charge of 'keeping the markets in their ordinar manner of thieving and purse cutting . . .'[20] They were also accused o often spending whole nights in dancing and debauchery, to the fiddlin of James Macpherson or Peter Brown. A family of Browns left a consider able fiddling reputation in Kincardineshire and Strathspey to the exten that they were thought by some in these regions to have been the origina tors of the strathspey style of music. Nevertheless, it is James Macpherso who has impressed his name on posterity through the tune reputed to hav been composed by him, and performed by him as he was being led to th place of execution. Burns lent a significant hand to the Highlander's fam with his replacement of the original popular verses by strong and charac teristic lines of his own in the poem 'M'Pherson's Farewell'. The tune i known as 'MacPherson's Rant' [47].

> Farewell, ye dungeons dark and strong,
> The wretch's destinie!
> M'Pherson's time will not be long
> On yonder gallows-tree.
> *Sae rantingly, sae wantonly,*
> *Sae dauntingly gaed he,*
> *He play'd a spring, and danc'd it round*
> *Below the gallows-tree.*

There are several versions of the event. One of the more picturesque i that Macpherson asked the crowd round the gallows, whom he had jus regaled with his playing, if anyone would accept his fiddle in remem brance of him; but finding no one prepared to do so, he broke the instru ment over his knee—or over the executioner's head—and threw himsel indignantly into eternity.

The flower in the bud

At this period, some hundred miles to the south in the old burgh c Kinghorn on the Firth of Forth, another fiddler whose reputation ha come down to us, though rather as a legitimate rogue and character, was busy at his trade. There must have been something very special about any fiddler singled out for literary treatment by Allan Ramsay [21] in a period replete with mendicant fiddlers. Thus Patie Birnie steps into our pages. His face (plate 15), as Robert Chambers expressed it, mingled 'cleverness, drollery, roguery and impudence' [22]; his wit, and his grasp of the strathspey idiom, are exhibited by his song, 'The Auld Man's Mare's Deid' [57]. The other song claimed for him by Allan Ramsay, 'O wiltu, wiltu do't again!' has not been preserved as far as is known.

The occasion of Ramsay's generous verses was Patie's death in 1721 at the age of eighty-six. From these we learn that his life was typical of the fiddler of his time, and not in any serious particular different from that of Habbie Simpson of a century before.

He would keep an eagle eye open for strangers calling at the ale house, then hurriedly entering, he would feign to be out of breath and, craving their pardon for keeping them waiting (thus implying that they had sent for him), would proceed to play them a tune or sing a song. Even if he had never seen the stranger before he would say that he 'weel ken'd his honour's faither, and had been merry with him, and an excellent goodfellow he was'. He would interrupt his songs or tunes with a droll tale or two, then sip his drink and curse 'with birr' the 'cork-headed' loons who ran to Italy to learn the 'ha ha's' of Italian music; music which he thought ill-suited to real men. Thus we learn that the fashion for Italian theatrical music had reached Scotland and was sufficiently evident to come to an old town fiddler's attention. Sometimes a short husky fellow, Johnny Stocks, would dance on a table to Patie's playing and sometimes dance it out with a lass—

> *With cutty steps to ding their striddle,*
> *and gar them fag.*

Patie was thrifty and prudent, did not want, and saved in the Scottish manner for his old age. When illness struck him he promised the minister never to get drunk again; but when health returned he explained: 'Wha' kents what people rave about in a fever?'

Six years after the death of Patie Birnie the celebrated Niel Gow was born in 1727 in the Gaelic-speaking community of Inver by Dunkeld in the county of Perth. The contrast between them, professional fiddlers both, illuminates the contrast between their times and environments. Both impressed their personalities on their contemporaries, both resorted to the local tavern to play for visitors, both played for the dancers at bridal and kirn, the Scottish harvest home; but whereas Birnie was a Lowlander with his share of Lallan coarseness and toughness, an unofficial town minstrel, Gow was the supreme fiddler with the easy manner of a Highlander enjoying the patronage of his laird. Gow takes his place with the

performers, collectors and composers of the eighteenth century, a uniqu
breed living in a culturally enriched environment of a rare age; Pat
Birnie belonged to a century of troubles, great upheavals, inflame
feelings and economic hardship.

Just as 'Lochaber no more' rubbed shoulders with 'Che faro' at tl
concerts, with no sense of incongruity, so also did Reel and Countɪ
Dance with Minuet and Gavotte at the dance assembly. Thus it need nᴇ
surprise us to find 'Mr Reinagle' composing a reel or slow air in tɦ
national idiom (cf. 'Mr Stewart Junr. of Carnock's Reel', and 'Dumfriᴇ
Races', Gow's fifth Collection), or 'Mr William Clarke', following i
the footsteps of his father Stephen, organist of the Episcopal Chapel i
Edinburgh, in harmonizing the airs in Johnson's Museum and composinᴇ
'Mrs Normand Lockhart's Reel' (Gow, Fifth Collection), or 'Mr McIntyrᴇ
dedicating a strathspey to 'Dr Haydn', or Mr Schetky composing the aᴀ
of 'Clarinda' or 'Mary's Dream'.

Thus we see that the general cultural climate was conducive to a greᴀ
flourishing of Scottish dance music. Indeed, the astonishing fecundity ᴏ
the eighteenth century in Scotland with respect to genius and creativ
activity in all walks of life embraced the fiddler and composer of reels an
strathspeys no less than the poet and philosopher. Not only was theɪ
Robert Burns, the consummate writer and restorer of the lyric poetry of tɦ
Lallan tongue; there was also a Marshall, a 'Red Bob' Mackintosh and
Niel and Nathaniel Gow to raise the music of the reel and the strathspe
of the countryside to new heights of expression, in compositions of theɪ
own as well as in peerless execution of the old. It was as though there weɪ
some recognition by nature that an era was ending and that somehow onᴇ
last great effusion was necessary to ensure that some of it would surviv
into the new. Nor were these names the only ones; there were Daniᴇ
Dow, the Cummings of Strathspey, 'King' McGlashan and many morᴇ
as well as itinerants such as Patie Birnie and fiddler-dancing masters lik
Johnny McGill of Girvan, Ayrshire,* born c. 1707, or James Gregg ᴏ
the same county who died in 1817, or that 'red-wud Highlander', ᴀ
Burns called him, John Bruce of Dumfries, who was raised in Braemar iɴ
the early part of the eighteenth century and spent some time as a prisonᴇ
in Edinburgh Castle for being out in the 'Forty-Five'.† Or those brethreɴ
in the tradition of that Macpherson who 'play'd a spring and danc'd ᴀ
round, below the gallows-tree'.

* Robert Riddell of Glenriddell in his Collection of Scotch, Galwegian, and Border Tunes, 179
describes the composer of the tune 'Johnny McGill' as 'Town Piper of Girvan'.

† John Bruce was a composer of the tune to which Burns wrote 'O Whistle and I'll come ᴛ
ye, My Lad' and was reputed, with little foundation, also to have composed 'Whistle o'er tɦ
Lave o't', [136, 371], a set of 'De'il Stick the Minister'.

CHAPTER 4

'Sang abune a' sang'
collections, composers and fiddlers*

The full title of Henry Playford's collection of Scottish tunes published in 1700 is *A Collection of Original Scotch Tunes (Full of the Highland Humours) for the Violin: Being the First of This Kind yet Printed; Most of them being in the Compass of the Flute.*

The phrase 'Highland Humours' alludes perhaps to the characteristic noted by Dryden about this time when, in reference to Chaucer's work, he says '. . . there is the rude Sweetness of a Scotch Tune in it, which is natural and pleasing, though not perfect'.[1] One suspects, however, that it was not only the tonality of the tunes which was remarkable to English ears, but sometimes also their rhythm. The contents are of great interest:

Mr McLaine's Scotch-measure†
Mr McClauklaine's Scotch-measure
I love my Love in seacreit
Madam McKeeny's Scotch-measure
Cronstoune
Keele Cranke
The Berkes of Plunketty
Good night, and God be with you
The Laird of Cockpen's Scotch-measure
My Lord Sefoth's Scotch-measure
Ginleing Georde
The Collier's Lass
Sir William Hope's Scotch-measure
Stir her up, and hold her ganging
Oreck's Scotch-measure

Bess-Bell
Dick a Dollis
A New Scotch-measure
Wappat the Widow my Lady
If Love is the cause of my mourning
The Berks of Abergelde
For old long Gine my Joe
Allen Water
Madam Sefoth's Scotch-measure
Wallis' Humour in Tapping the Ale
The Laird of Cockpen's Scotch-measure
A New Scotch-measure
Widow, gin thou be waking
Aways my Heart that we mun sunder
The Lass of Leving-Stone

* And in some hour there comes delight.
  When thorter's flesh forgets its thrang
  In flight that is abune a' flight
  And sang that is abune a' sang. WILLIAM SOUTAR.
† McLaine's Scots Measure was in Blaikie's MS., 1692.

My Lady Hope's Scotch-measure   I fix my Fancy on her, a Round (
Peggy was the pretiest Lass in aw   Quoth the Master to the Man
  the Town   Cosen Cole's Delight
Bride next   Holy Even, a Scotch-measure
The Comers of Largo, A reell*   The Deal stick the Minister

There are a few obvious mis-spellings, such as 'For old long Gine m
Joe', 'Leving-Stone' and 'Sefoth' for 'Seaforth'. Most of the tunes a
identifiable under the same names later in the eighteenth century, but tl
number of the so-called 'Scotch-measures' is noteworthy. This sugges
that the term had been in existence for some time, although this is its fir
appearance in print; the Scottish Measure is discussed further on page 12:
Excepting the song collections following on the appearance of the tun
for Ramsay's *Tea Table Miscellany* and Thomson's *Orpheus Caledonius*, n
like publication of Scottish tunes appears until Oswald's first *Curio*
Collection of Scots Tunes, c. 1740.

James Oswald is first noticed in an advertisement of 12th August 173
announcing *A Collection of Minuets ... Composed by James Oswald, Dancir
Master*. This collection did not appear until January 1736, by which tim
Oswald had moved from Dunfermline to Edinburgh where he taugl
dancing with one Mr Jones in Skinner's Close. He is particularly famou
for his *Caledonian Pocket Companion*, a collection of 500 Scottish air
including about forty of his own composition, and there are many othe
arranged by him, published in twelve issues or volumes between 1740 an
some time before his death in 1769. Burns possessed this work and s
words to seven of Oswald's airs,† unfortunately with indifferent succes
as their compass is too great for most voices, all the airs in the *Companio*
being set for German flute or violin. By a troublesome error, Oswald wa
commonly credited with the tunes 'Roslin Castle' and 'Tweedside', an
was unfairly charged with palming off some of his own compositions a
David Rizzio's, as the reader may discover if he should pursue this subjec
further (*cf.* John Glen's *Early Scottish Melodies*).

Oswald enjoyed considerable celebrity in London, and was appointe
Chamber Composer to George III, in whose musical education he ha
been said to have had a hand. He composed some art music, notabl
Twelve Songs, c. 1742, *Six Pastoral Solos for a Violin and Violoncello*, c. 174
Airs for Spring, c. 1747 and *Twelve Seranatas* (*sic*) *for Two Violins and*
Violoncello, c. 1765, which, says Farmer, 'reveal an extremely gifte

* This is not what we would classify musically as a reel. It is an odd sort of tune akin to tl
triple-time hornpipe.
† 'It isna, Jean, thy bonny face' ('The Maid's Complaint'); 'Yon wild mossy mountair
('Phoebe'); 'The Lovely Lass of Inverness'; 'If thou shalt ask my love' ('Jamy come tr
me'); 'O were I on Parnassus' Hill' ('My love is lost to me'); 'Go Fetch to me a Pint (
Wine' ('The Stolen Kiss'); and 'Anna, thy charms my bosom fire' ('Bonny Mary').

musician who knew precisely what he wanted to say and could express it convincingly'.[2] Alexander Campbell, whose praise was worth something, expressed the opinion that '. . . had he [Oswald] composed nothing else but 'The Braes of Ballenden' and the air to 'Lovely Nymph', introduced in the burletta of *Midas*, his fame would live as long as a relish exists for genuine Scottish melody'.[3]

The manuscript collections of reel music

The seventeenth-century manuscript collections noticed in chapter 2 were not devoted to Scottish dance music *per se*, but contained song tunes of which some were certainly dance airs. The same is true of Oswald's printed collections.

The earliest manuscript devoted to Scottish instrumental dance tunes is that transcribed by David (A.) Young for the Duke of Perth and dated 1734. This is now called the Drummond Castle MS., and contains the earliest written record of such tunes as the 'Reel o' Tulloch', 'Tulloch-gorum', 'Gille-Callum', 'Caber Feidh', 'Duke of Perth's Reel' and many others; a complete list is given in Appendix A, page 225. The collection is in two sections, one devoted to Highland Reels and the other to Country Dances, including figures to the dances.

Other similar MS. collections of Country Dances, tunes and figures, have come down to us from the same period—the Holmain (*c.* 1710–50), Bodleian (1740), and the Menzies (1749), which contains no tunes, the contents of which are given in Appendix A, pages 223–224, and the Bowman (after 1750).

It is interesting that the Bodleian and Drummond Castle MSS. are from the same hand—that of David Young—as is the McFarlan MS. in the National Library of Scotland. The tunes of the country dances are mostly the vehicles of song, but some are of the category of instrumental reels. The Menzies MS. contains two dances clearly marked 'a strathspey reele'— 'The Montgomeries' rant' and 'Conteraller's rant'—and this seems to be the earliest written allusion to the strathspey as a class of music or dance.

Several MS. fiddle books from this period have survived and are in various hands, but the most comprehensive work of the kind is a manu-script violin tutor of James Gillespie of Perth, dated 1768 (Appendix A, page 226). This contains a large number of tunes which had not appeared in previous collections and some not even in later collections. The tutor is the first of its kind produced in Scotland and came to light only in 1923 when Henry Farmer acquired it from a bookseller in London. It is in four parts listing airs and marches, Scots tunes, minuets and hornpipes, and jigs and reels.

Printed dance music and the currency of tunes

These manuscript compilations testify to a demand for printed publications of Scottish music—particularly dance music—which was not being satisfied. It was not until mid-century that the first publication of a book of Scottish instrumental dance music appeared—Robert Bremner's *Collection of Scots Reels or Country Dances*—produced in fourteen numbers between the years 1751 and 1761. In a second collection, published in 1768, Bremner included the figures of Country Dances which could be performed to the tunes. Most of these tunes were appearing in print for the first time, and many for the first time in written record of any kind.

The first of these publications was followed by Neil Stewart's collection issued in nine numbers beginning in 1761. Stewart opened his business in Edinburgh around 1759, i.e. about five years after Bremner; his shop, or shops, varied in location over the years and became a family concern. He published many notable Scottish dance music collections, such as those of Dow and McGlashan, and the early productions of Marshall and Gow.

Of Bremner little is known until he started business in Edinburgh about 1754 'at the Sign of the Golden Harp opposite to the head of Blackfriars 'Wynd', as publicized in advertisements of 11th and 15th July that year. Not long after this he changed his sign to the 'Harp and Hautboy' and moved his premises to the Cross Well. Music publishing at this time was largely concentrated in London, and doubtless through his inevitable connections with the publishers, Bremner saw an opportunity to develop his business there. In any case, he established a shop in London in 1762 once again 'at the sign of the Harp and Hautboy', opposite Somerset House in the Strand, and rapidly became the most important music publisher of his time. He left his Edinburgh shop in the charge of John Brysson, who continued on his own after Bremner died in 1789.

Three other collections of Scottish instrumental music in the traditional idioms which were published at this time are worthy of our notice for various reasons, although they are not concerned with reels and strathspeys. They are William McGibbon's *Collection of Scots Tunes* in three books, 1742, 1746 and 1755; Barsanti's *Collection of Old Scots Tunes*, 1742; and Francis Peacock's *Fifty Favourite Scotch Airs* [1762]. Peacock was a celebrated dancing master and musician in Aberdeen who, at the end of his career in 1805, published the first book to contain directions for the performance of Reel steps.

The publications of Bremner and Stewart were the forerunners of a veritable spate of collections of reels and strathspeys set for the violin and sometimes also the German flute which was now very popular with bass for the harpsichord or cello. Here *A Collection of Scots Reels or Countr*

Dances with a Bass for the Violoncello or Harpsichord, and there *A Collection . . for the Violin, Harpsichord, Piano Forte or German Flute* poured forth in unprecedented profusion.

These collections were compiled by music-sellers, and amateur as well as professional musicians, most of the latter being noted exponents of the music on the violin. For the most part the collections comprised tunes current in the traditional repertoire of country fiddlers and pipers, but more and more they contained original compositions in the traditional idioms.

Almost every fiddler, or 'musician' in Scotland—and there were hundreds of them—amateur and professional, turned his hand to composing a reel, jig, strathspey, hornpipe or slow air in the lyrical style of the countryside. Was it ever otherwise? There could be nothing new in this. What was new was the possibility of being permanently associated with once's tune in print. With purely oral transmission, the identity of the individual composer was lost. Perhaps tradition would preserve the memory of the composer of a particular tune, especially if the tune and its associations were outstanding. Or, if the musician himself were super-lative, his legend would persist; although it must be said that with the exception of certain Irish harpers and the MacCrimmons of Skye, there is a surprising paucity of examples known to us.

In the oral transmission of a tune, the introduction of variations and embroideries of the original were inevitable. Thus it is no surprise to read the Gows' remark in the introduction to the second part of their *Complete Repository of the Original Scotch Slow Strathspeys and Dances* [1802], that in every part of Scotland where we have occasionally been, and from every observation we were able to make, [we] have not once met with two professional musicians who played the same notes of any tune'.

In this way a tune, even if originating in one creative mind, underwent modifying processes through oral transmission and became in that sense not only the property of the folk but the product of the folk. The habits of musical thought of that folk were brought to bear upon the tune and influenced its cast, whatever its original form; such is 'folk' or 'traditional' music.

When the tune is 'frozen' on the printed page by its creator, it is no longer the property of the folk, nor so violently exposed to the vagaries of oral transmission. It is in a sense no longer a living organism subject to growth or change. Thus, strictly speaking, it is not 'traditional' although it may in every way conform to the traditional pattern and be couched in the traditional idioms. Nevertheless, a Scottish reel like 'Largo's Fairy Dance' [51] seems every bit as much a traditional dance tune as does, say, 'Reel o' Tulloch' [43] or 'Duke of Perth's Reel' [41], although, unlike the last two, its composer (Nathaniel Gow) is known, and it was first presented to the world in the printed page.

The new generation of fiddlers-composers-dancing masters-musi‹
seller-publishers in the eighteenth century was a phenomenon to match th‹
age. Daniel Dow, William Marshall, 'Red Bob' Mackintosh and Nie‹
and Nathaniel Gow—to name only the greatest of the composers—
became names of national celebrity. It is noteworthy that the geographica‹
centre of this talent was the Central Highlands, and in particular th‹
County of Perth.

The fiddler-composers and their collections

The first of the fiddler-composers to compile a collection of his ow‹
compositions of Scottish dance music was John Riddell (1718–95) o‹
Ayr. His collection of Scots reels, etc., was published by Bremner, c. 1766‹
With reference to the tune of 'Finlayston House', Burns wrote that 'thi‹
most beautiful tune is I think the happiest composition of that bard bor‹
genius John Riddell of the family of Glencarnock at Ayr'. 'Stewarto‹
Lassies', the jig 'Dumfries House' and the reel 'The Merry Lads of Ayr‹
are outstanding tunes attributed to him, although the last named i‹
obviously a set of a tune, 'The Lads of Air', which appears in th‹
Bodleian MS., and Burns attributes 'Stewarton Lassies' (which h‹
describes as 'the oldest Ayrshire reel') to Captain Alexander Cuningharr
of Kirktonholm (d. 1770).[4]

The next to produce a collection of his own compositions was Danie‹
Dow (1732–83), who appears to have pursued the profession of music-
teacher in Edinburgh. His is the first collection to include the word
'strathspey' in its title—Thirty-Seven New Reels and Strathspeys—this wa‹
about the time of Edward Topham's visit to Edinburgh, 1775 (page 42).‹
His most celebrated compositions are the immortal strathspey, 'Monymusk', 1631, which he named 'Sir Archibald Grant of Monemusk'‹
Reel', and 'Athol House', 'Bonnie Annie', 'Comely Garden', and‹
'Lady Charlot Murray's Reel'. Some of his tunes appear in other collections under different names. Not much is known about him, except tha‹
he was believed to have been a native of Kirkmichael, Perthshire, and tha‹
he taught the guitar when Charles Kirkpatrick Sharpe's mother was a girl,‹
died of a fever at the untimely age of 51 in January 1783, and was interred‹
in the Canongate Churchyard. He had been in the habit of presenting‹
concerts in St Mary's Hall, Niddry's Wynd, so it seems only right that a‹
benefit concert should have been held there for his widow and four‹
children shortly after his death. His compositions were highly esteemed in‹
their time and still live.

Dow's wife returned to her native Strathardle (Perthshire) with her‹
children and there the third son, John, became a noted fiddler, being‹
compared favourably with Willie Stewart of Dalnacardoch, a blind‹
fiddler of some celebrity in his time.

We have to turn to Glasgow in 1779 for the next collection to appear— *A Collection of the Newest and best Reels and Minuets . . .* by Joshua Camp- bell. Campbell was the leading musician in the Glasgow of his time, supplying an appropriate complement to his brother James, the town's most fashionable teacher of dancing. He appears to have owned a cooperage in a close near the present Stirling Street although by the eighteen-eighties he is styled as a teacher of instrumental music in the Glasgow directories, with addresses on the High Street (Tilloch's Closs and Pipework Closs). His earliest notice appears to be that of 1762— Joshua Campbell Musician proposes to teach the guitar having been at some expense at Edinburgh in perfecting himself with the best masters there. Ladies and Gentlemen that want to be taught the above instru- ment shall be carefully attended by the above person who will be found in the third close above Bell's Wynd Glasgow'.

He published three books of music, two of which are of dance music, including a number of reels of his own composition which he did not identify. Not the least of his distinctions was his being appointed to the office of Bellringer of the Tolbooth Steeple. In the Council Records, 27th July 1791, we read that his duty was to play 'one full hour upon the said bells, from two till three o'clock in the afternoon, each day, Saturdays and Sundays excepted'. The music was mainly 'favourite Scotch Airs'. In addition, however, the bells played a selection every two hours by clockwork. The 'barrel' of the clock was constructed to play 'The Easter Hymn', 'Gilderoy', 'Nancy's to the Green Wood gane', 'Tweedside', 'The Lass o' Patie's Mill', 'The Last time I cam o'er the Moor' and 'Roslin Castle'.[5] These were the days in which it was possible to stand in the broad thoroughfare of the city and savour the associations of the much loved tunes, the musical spirit of Scotland, chiming over the clatter of hooves and the chatter of business. The tolbooth is silent now, but as long as its aged form survives, so also somehow does Glasgow.

The next name to meet our eye is that of Alexander McGlashan, whose elegant carriage and dress acquired for him the sobriquet of 'King'. He appears to have been an excellent violinist, and he led the band at the Edinburgh assemblies for some time in the seventeen-eighties or there- abouts. He conducted business as a teacher of music at various addresses, being first noticed in 1759 in Bailie Fife's Close and lastly in Skinner's Close in 1797. He gave regular annual concerts between the years 1766 and 1799. His first publication was *A Collection of Strathspey Reels* [1780], which he humbly hoped, its being 'so much wanted', would be 'accept- able to the Public', as he flattered himself that 'upon comparing it with others of the kind', it would be found 'preferable to any yet published'.

He published two further collections in 1781 and 1786 which contain much of great interest. John MacGlashan, the piano teacher of 13 Thistle

Street, who also published a collection of Strathspey reels in 1798 m.
have been Alex's brother.

In the same month (March) and year of McGlashan's first collectic
there appeared _A Collection of Strathspeys or Old Highland Reels_ by Ang
Cumming, 'Musician at Grantown in Strathspey'. This collectio:
comprising tunes gathered over many years in Strathspey, is for that reasc
of the greatest interest. The editor was probably related to that family
Cummings who were notable fiddlers in Strathspey in the early eighteen
century, as indeed he seems to tell us when he remarks that he '. . . follow
the profession of his forefathers; who have been for many generatio:
Musicians in Strathspey . . .' Musicians who may have known the piper
the Laird of Grant (plate 1).

It is curious that this collection is the only one to come to us fro:
Strathspey itself, in view of the special position this region has con
manded in Scottish dance and dance music.

Another collection from the North which claims our attention is th
by Patrick Mcdonald [1784], containing eighty-six _Highland Vocal A_:
collected in Sutherland by Patrick's gifted brother Joseph. The Macdona
family, with four sons and seven daughters, was a considerable an
interesting one. The father, Murdo, was ordained minister of Durnes
Sutherland, 28th September 1726, and served through the period of Ro
Don, the celebrated Gaelic bard of Reay, who was a close frienc
Patrick was born on 22nd April 1729 and Joseph on 26th February 173
and both studied the violin with Kenneth Sutherland of Cnocbreac, wh
enjoyed some celebrity.

Although Patrick became sufficiently competent as a violinist to stan
in for Stabilini in the St Cecilia Orchestra on one occasion in later year
he apparently was not in his youth as apt a pupil as Joseph. Their sist
Flora, who married a Dr Touch, minister of St Cuthbert's Chapel
Ease, also acquired distinction as an instrumentalist.

Joseph was sent south to Haddington Grammar School, to finish h
education; but he obviously was very much a product of his nativ
Sutherland, and not merely a skilled performer of the Great Pipe, but
knowledgeable student of its music and character. His treatise on th
theory of the Scots Highland bagpipe is a source book of the greate
importance to all later students of the instrument. Patrick arranged the pul:
lication of this in 1803, for Joseph died of a fever in India in 1762, shortl:
after his arrival to take up an appointment. It was only by good fortur:
that this valuable work was preserved through the interest of Sir Joh:
Murray MacGregor who acquired it in Bengal and passed it on to Patrick:

Patrick finished his education at Aberdeen University and entered th
ministry in the West Highland parish of Kilmore where he remained unt
he died sixty-nine years later in 1824, the father of nine sons and fo:
daughters!

Malcolm McDonald, who published four collections of strathspey reels, etc., was no relation. He appears to have been a native of Inver, the home of Niel Gow, and certainly he played cello to Niel after the death of Niel's older brother Donald. His first publication entirely consists of his own compositions which, Glen remarks, 'are of that strange wild nature so characteristic of the compositions of Daniel Dow'.

Robert Riddell of Glenriddell, whose collections first appear during the time we are considering (*c*. 1787), was Burns's neighbour near Dumfries. His wife Maria enjoyed a correspondence with the poet, whose taste she shared, and her memoir of him is one of the most perceptive and sincere that has been left us. Burns wrote words for three of Riddell's airs—'The Blue-eyed lassie', 'Nithsdale's Welcome Hame' and 'The Day returns, my bosom burns'—but it is not disputed that Riddell had no great musical gifts.

Hey-day of reels and strathspey reels

The publication of reels and strathspey reels, etc., was now at its height; dancing masters, musicians and publishers had never been so active, not only in all the centres of fashion, but also in the countryside at large, in the glens and by the lochs. Most of the collections were published by subscription and distinguished by a dedication to an important patron. The subscription lists serve as compendia of the celebrated names associated with the high social life of the time, including, very often, those of fellow musicians, the directresses of the Assembly, the Grants and Gordons of Strathspey, the law lords and tobacco lords, the landed proprietors and the like, many with names honoured in Scotland's story. We can imagine them, and many others less well known to us, sending for their copy ere the ink was dry, and culling with pride the new tune bearing their name— Miss Drummond's Favourite', or 'Miss Murray's' or 'Mr Grant of Kinaird' or 'Miss Admiral Gordon' [61] or 'The Marquis of Huntly's Farewell' [62] and so on—and setting it on the music-stand before the violin, the harpsichord or spinet.

Even secondary towns—to modern eyes some of them little more than villages—had their musician-dancing masters.

At Montrose, around 1790, was Archibald Duff whose first collection of reels, strathspeys, etc., was published in 1794. Not long after this, however, he moved to Aberdeen where he developed a very successful practice at the Concert Rooms, Broad Street, supported by many of the distinguished families who formerly patronized the celebrated Francis Peacock. He produced another collection of dance tunes in 1811 and 1812, and preceded John Mackenzie, the grandfather of the eminent Scottish composer Sir Alexander C. Mackenzie, as conductor of the Philharmonic Society in Aberdeen.

Archibald Duff's brother Charles settled in Dundee, where he pe formed a similar role in the town's musical and dancing life, althoug apparently more as a musician and music-seller than as a dancing maste He returned for a few years to Montrose, probably on the departure of F brother, between 1798 and 1808. His first collection was published abor 1790, and contains a number of tunes composed by John McDonal dancing master in Dundee, who was Charles Duff's employer for a time Duff's name last appears in the Dundee directory in 1822.

At Banff by the far-off Moray Firth around 1783 Isaac Cooper pr vided for a distinguished clientele in the traditional dual role of musicia and dancing master. In publishing his collection he observes that th public had been 'so much imposed upon by people who have publishe reels, and called them new and at the same time they were only old ree with new names'. He advertised himself as the teacher of an impressiv list of instruments—the harpsichord, violoncello, psaltery (viol), clarione pipe and taberer, German flute, Scots flute, fife 'in the regimental styl and hautboy; and of

'. . . the Irish Organ Pipe, how to make flats and sharps and how t make the proper chords with the brass keys. And the Guitar, after new method of fingering (never taught in this country before) whic facilitates the most intricate passages.'

He begged leave to inform

'all who have a taste for Highland reels, that he has just now compose thirty strathspey reels for the Violin or Harpsichord, with agreeable an easy basses, all in the true Strathspey stile.'

Here Cooper reveals what we may call the illicit traffic in reels whic helped to pad out some collections. How much this was intentional c accidental it is impossible to say. We shall have more to say on this late Returning inland to the 'source of Tay' again, and deliberately leavin the Gows, Marshall and Mackintosh for special treatment later, we mu notice Robert Petrie (1767–1830), born at Dow's reputed home towr Kirkmichael, Perthshire. Petrie left a local reputation of being both profligate and an excellent fiddler, a not uncommon combination as w have seen. Our information, for what it is worth, is that he was awarde the prize of the 'silver bow' at a competition in Edinburgh or a cup at competition in Aberdeen in 1822, or both. If it be true that he is th composer of that excellent strathspey 'The Braes of Tullymet', then hi fame is secure. 'Mrs Garden of Troup' is another of his more successfu compositions. He published no less than four collections between 179 and 1800.

Petrie's name appears with that of McGlashan, Stabilini, Nathanie Gow and some other Edinburgh musicians among the subscribers c aniel McLaren's collection of 1794. McLaren appears to have been a tive of Taymouth, Perthshire, and to have pursued the calling of usician in Edinburgh. He claimed as his own compositions 'Mr acdonald of Staffa's Strathspey', 'Mr Macdonald of Staffa's reel', 'Mr olin Campbell's Strathspey' and 'Mr Colin Campbell's Reel', which ere published together in leaflet form. The first named strathspey is better own as 'Niel Gow's Second Wife', and hence commonly and erneously accepted as one of Gow's compositions. Little more is known McLaren's career.

While referring to natives of Perthshire, it is appropriate to include John lark (of whom little is known) but whose collection comprises some ry good compositions of his own, and John Bowie (1759–1815), usician and music-seller in the Fair City itself. He is first found advertisg in 1785, and his *Collection of Strathspey Reels and Country Dances* 789] is notable in that it is the first Scottish publication since Bremner's 1768 to include the figures of a number of Country Dances. In 1797 he ued a single sheet containing 'Four new Tunes composed by John)wie, Huntingtower, near Perth, one of which is the much admired w Strathspey called the Loyal Farmers, with addition of the Slow set of e Braes of Mar, etc.' Then in 1801 he advertises 'Just published and sold the Music Shops A New Strathspey called the Perthshire Yeomanry d Lady Herriot Hay's Reel composed by John Bowie, Author of Miss urray of Ochtertyre's Strathspey, and others so much danced of late . . .' Successor to Bowie as a music-seller in Perth was a talented fiddler, mson Duncan, who was born at Kinclaven in the same year (1767) as bert Petrie. As a boy, he had regularly walked the many miles from his me to Perth to take lessons from a curious character, Saunders Borlum, cooper to trade, whom he paid in oatmeal (from his father's mill). He er moved to Edinburgh for a time to broaden his musical studies then ok up the appointment of musician to the laird of Aldie at Meiklour ouse, during which time he was often called upon by Niel Gow to join m at some of the larger functions for which Niel was engaged in the incipal towns. He also had the experience of playing with John Gow's nd in London, and even after he married and settled in Perth around 10, he was called upon to reinforce Nathaniel Gow's resources, as at the lls associated with George iv's visit to Edinburgh in 1822. Samson's n, Thomas (b. 1807), became a noted artist.

Dancing-masters and lesser composers

he popularity of the Scotch Reel in the dance assemblies of the South led the emigration of Scots dancing masters as well as musicians. Of these, eorge Jenkins has claim to our attention if for no other reason than that ： was the composer of the 'Marquis of Huntly's Highland Fling' [64]—

the first (and still, so far, the only) use of the term 'Highland Fling' applie
to a tune. He taught Scottish dancing in London about the year 1794 an
died about 1804. Although Jenkins composed a few good reels an
strathspeys, it was Glen's opinion that a number of his tunes did n
possess the true Scottish character. Some of these tunes are contained i
William Campbell's *Country Dances* which came out in twenty-seve
annual numbers from the year 1790.

Another Scot to follow the profession of dancing master in Londo
was Duncan MacIntyre; at least one of whose tunes, that to Tannahill
'Louden's Bonnie Woods' ('The Earl of Moira's Welcome to Sco
land'), may be known to the reader. Several tunes in his collection are n
strictly original, but among the best are the strathspeys 'Mr Moore's
'Miss E. Elphinstone's', 'Miss MacIntyre's', 'Mrs Gow's', and 'Mi
Cumming's' (the original of 'Lord John Campbell's Strathspey' i
Gow), 'Miss Downie's' (called by Petrie 'Garden Shiel') and 'Ni
Gow's' (air of the song 'Kinrara'). The reels include 'Lady Franc
Somerset's' and 'Mrs Davidson's'.[6]

His collection was published in 1795, and there is evidence that I
contributed some of his compositions to William Campbell, mentione
above, and Nathaniel Gow. Clearly he was a good composer of strath
speys. Not much is known about him, except that he spent some years i
India and died about 1806.

Of the remaining secondary editors and composers of Scottish dan
music, we know that Alex. Gibb was a dancing master at Haddingto
and Edinburgh between 1780 and 1810. His school settled in 'a lar
commodious room foot of Skinner's close', as it was described in some
his many advertisements. But the most distinguished dancing master
this period in Edinburgh was David Strange who employed Charl
Stewart, first as musician, then, under the exigencies of bad health, too
him into partnership in 1802. Strange died very shortly after and Stewa
continued on his own.

Stewart's *Collection of Strathspey Reels Giggs, etc.* was published in 177
and his *First Book of Minuets, High Dances, Cotillions, etc, etc. as used by l
late master Mr Strange*, in 1805.

Glen judged some of his dance tunes excellent. A sad comment on th
incapacity of Stewart's last years is offered by the following announc
ment in March, 1812: 'Benefit Ball . . . Mrs Stewart (wife of Mr C
Stewart, late teacher of dancing in Edinburgh) begs leave most respec
fully to inform her friends and the public, that the pressing necessities of
young and helpless family have again induced her humbly to solicit the
countenance and support on the present occasion . . .' Stewart's death wa
announced in June 1818. His son Robert (1804–85) attained tl
position of leader and repetiteur in the orchestra of the Theatre Roya
Edinburgh.

In more obscure by-ways, we have John Anderson, author of two
.llections. If we judge from the dedication to the first, he was associated
one time with the Musical Society of Greenock. John Morison (1772–
.48), Rose Street, Peterhead, was organist of St Peter's Episcopal
hurch, a fiddler, and publisher of two collections (*c.* 1797 and 1800) of
.s own compositions; Alexander Leburn (1767–1836) of Auchter-
uchty; and James Walker of Dysart among the fertile undulations of
.fe.

Leburn's collection (1793) contains thirty-six tunes, all but ten of
hich appear to be of his own composition. One of these is 'Mrs
.uncan's Reel' which is also claimed by Nathaniel Gow. An obituary
. the *Fifeshire Journal* described him as a self-taught philosopher with a
.irst for knowledge.

James Walker (1771–1840) carries us well into the nineteenth century.
.e published two collections and was a kenspeckle figure at fashionable
.ncing parties and assemblies in this region. His great-grandson related
. John Glen the following anecdote as told him by an old gentleman:

'Auld Jeems Walker—I will never forget that man. My father always
invited the band to the big house after the ball was over to perform
there. One named Rattray from Cupar, was playing firsts, and your
ancestor [Auld Jeems] seconds, when suddenly Rattray's first string
snapped, and I expected a collapse, but to my astonishment, the old
man (whom I thought in my ignorance to be asleep, and not able to
sustain the music) was immediately alive to the occasion, and carried
through the piece to its close, after which he was highly complimented
by the audience.'

This anecdote tells us much about the social place of Scottish dance
.usic and the discernment of its auditors at this time in Fife. James
.alker, Junior, was a musician and dancing master, but predeceased his
.ther.

Whether we should include William Shepherd (*d.* 1812) alongside
.hn Watlen, Robert Ross of Edinburgh, and James Aird of Glasgow
.ho were music-sellers and publishers) or among the musicians, is not
.rtain. Shepherd first appeared in Edinburgh directories as a musician
.t was soon classified as a publisher in partnership with Nathaniel Gow.
.hn Glen thought that in some of Shepherd's tunes there was a want of
.iginality, while others show 'considerable excellence and taste'.

One of his lodgers in 1810 in his home at 51 Princess Street was the
.lebrated oboist, Thomas Fraser (*c.* 1760–1825), whose lyrical genius so
.oved Robert Burns, and who must be mentioned in any account of the
.usical celebrities of eighteenth-century Scotland. Burns met Fraser
.hile the latter was instructing a band of Breadalbane's Fencibles quar-
.ed in the vicinity of Dumfries in the summer of 1793. Talking of the

tune 'Saw ye Johnnie Coming?', Burns tells George Thomson in a lett₎
that when Fraser played it 'slow' he made it 'the language of despai₎
Then again, in another letter Burns writes [7]: 'Among many of his airs th₎
please me, there is one, well known as a Reel by the name of "T₎
quaker's wife" & which I remember a grand Aunt of mine used to sin₎
by the name of "Liggeram cosh, my bonie wee lass"—Mr. Fraser plays
slow, & with an expression that quite charms me—I got such an e₎
thusiast in it, that I made a Song for it.' *
    We can see from this how a reel (or jig, for 'The Quaker's Wife' is
jig) could be played andante and made the suitable vehicle of a song, a₎
here indeed is the meeting point of Scotland's song and dance music.
    Fraser's style of playing the melodies of Scotland, writes Willia₎
Stenhouse in 1820, 'is peculiarly chaste and masterly'. He turned ₎
hand to serious music for his instrument and also performed in concerts
Edinburgh, his native town, with great distinction. Perhaps his be₎
known composition is the delightful jig 'The Haddington Assembly' [79
He does not appear to have composed very much and he did not publi₎
a collection, but he was doubtless an outstanding and influential figure
Edinburgh musical life, and worthy to be remembered with the celebrat₎
Mackintosh, Marshall and Gow to whom we now turn.

Robert Mackintosh

Robert Mackintosh was a violinist of some distinction. He taught ₎
instrument in Edinburgh, as first recorded in Williamson's 1773-
directory, as 'Musician Skinner's Close'. Baptie states that he was born
Tullymet around 1745.
    'Red Bob', as he was called, charged one guinea per quarter for t
'public' class and one guinea per month for a 'private hour'. He ga₎
concerts of vocal and instrumental music, in one of which in 1783 ₎
shared the bill with J. P. Salomon, the impresario who brought Haydn
London and who was subsequently immortalized by Haydn's dedicati₎
to him of a series of delightful symphonies. The tickets for this concert, ₎
note, were three shillings, each obtainable at 'Mr Mackintosh's lodgin₎
Advocate's Close'.
    Then he spent three years (1785–8) in Aberdeen where he led ₎
orchestra in the Gentlemen's Concerts, except for a time when he had ₎
take second place to a Mr Thrustans of London. Mackintosh would m₎
Francis Peacock, the eminent Aberdeen dancing master, who played t
cello (and violin) in the orchestra and who published a collection
Scots songs in [1762] and the first Scottish book on dancing in 18₎
Mackintosh, we are told, was of an irascible disposition and readily ga₎
offence to other members of the orchestra. He returned to Edinburgh a₎

* 'Blythe Hae I Been on yon hill'.

practised there until 1803, then moved south to London where he resided in Little Vine Street, Piccadilly, until he died in 1807.

Mackintosh composed 'airs', minuets and gavottes, as well as reels, and these were published in four collections: 1783, 1793, 1796 and 1804. His second collection was dedicated to Mrs Campbell of Lochnell and the third to Mrs Oswald of Auchencruive, the charming Lucy Johnston (plate 21). In 1798 he advertised a ball to be held, in place of a concert, in Bernard's Room, Thistle Street, with tickets 5s. each—no modest price for the period! It was he who composed the settings for Andrew Shirrefs's (1762–1807) 'A Cogie o' Ale' and 'A Pickle Ait-Meal'.

Some of his sons and nephews were also fiddlers or pipers. He had a large family, thirteen in all, the first son being born in 1767. His second son, Abraham, was born in 1769 and lived to follow his father's profession from about 1793, first in Edinburgh (Todrick's Wynd) and after 1797 in Newcastle where he was noted as a dancing master. His first collection, published in 1792, comprised thirty of his own compositions, and he followed this with two more collections and some sheets during his sojourn in Newcastle. One of Abraham's tunes is possibly 'Athole Brose' which is ascribed in his father's third book to 'Mackintosh, Junior'. This tune appears with the sub-title 'Niel Gow's Favourite', in the Third Gow Collection, and consequently is often attributed to Niel Gow.

'Red Bob's' elegant strathspeys certainly warrant their many admirers among connoisseurs; but when strathspeys are mentioned, thoughts understandably turn to Marshall whom Robert Burns described as 'the first composer of strathspeys of the age'.

William Marshall

William Marshall was born at the town of Fochabers, Banffshire, on 27th December 1748, the third son of a large family. His formal education amounted to six months' attendance at a grammar school; nevertheless he managed to obtain enough from his father and by dint of his own efforts to accomplish himself in mechanics, astronomy, architecture and music at various stages in his long life. He died at Newfield Cottage, Dandaleith on 29th May 1833, in his eighty-fifth year.

At the age of twelve he entered the service of the Duke of Gordon, and for thirty years held several posts, including those of butler and factor to His Grace. He married Jane Giles when he was twenty-five and they had five sons who all entered military service, and one daughter. It is said that Marshall was well built and exceeded the average height; he was always dressed neatly and retained his good looks into ripe old age. Some of this can be seen from a portrait by Moir of which an engraving is extant (plate 22). He appears to have been a self-taught violinist and very early

showed a creative propensity for composition in the idioms of the nativ
reel and strathspey, gifts which were highly valued and encouraged by th
Gordon family.

It is difficult to determine how accomplished Marshall was as a per
former, but he was certainly highly esteemed as one, displaying, we ai
told, fine taste and feeling with no superfluous graces or ornamentation
Rather did his strength appear to lie in skilful management of the bov
good tone production ('breadth of intonation') precision and 'splendi
expression'.[8] All of this suggests more than the typical fiddler's equipmen

The nature of his own compositions hints at this; some of his friends
we are told, found his melodies too difficult to play, either on account c
wide intervals or other transitions, or of extensive compass. His answe
was that he did not write for bunglers, and that since his tunes *could* b
played, they should practice more.

Marshall published four collections of his own compositions; the tw
earliest through Neil Stewart, Parliament Square, Edinburgh, in [1781
then another in 1822 dedicated to the Marchioness of Huntly, the copy
right of which was purchased by Alex. Robertson, 47 Princess Street, wh
also published a posthumous edition. On the title-page of the 182
edition it is stated that:

> The author . . . thinks it necessary to mention that several of his strath
> speys and reels have occasionally been published by most of the col
> lectors of Scottish music without his permission; of this, however, h
> does not complain, especially as he had not till now any intention t
> publish them himself. His only complaint is their not mentioning hi
> name along with those reels of his composition they published, whick
> for obvious reasons, were by some neglected, but, in particular, thei
> changing the original names given by him to other names according t
> their own fancy.

Marshall himself changed the names of twenty-seven tunes in the 182
edition and ten tunes in the posthumous edition were renamed by him c
by Robertson.[9] In a letter to his publisher, dated December 1825, h
writes:

> I have copied, and likewise have sent, all I at present remember, but i
> the engraving take care that there be no repetitions, which is an un
> necessary expense, and may be avoided by a careful comparison. I hav
> named some of the tunes which must be attended to, and as to those nc
> named you can use your own discretion.

For a close analysis of the fate of many of Marshall's tunes in his ow
and other collections, the reader should consult Glen's biographica
sketches.[10]

Marshall's compositions have been accounted as 114 strathspeys, 84 reels, 21 jigs, 3 hornpipes, 33 slow airs and 2 marches, a total of 257.

There is no doubt that as far as the idiom of Scottish dance music is concerned, Marshall had all the craftsmanship he required, but the beautiful slow air, or airs, 'Chapel Keithing', amounts to an exasperating still-birth of two beautiful melodies which Haydn, whose name comes to mind when one hears them, could have developed as a masterly adagio in a quartet. Marshall begins very well, but the second tune cries out for further development, and just then, as though caught red-handed, he drops it with a conventional but meaningless run to change key and return to the original. This is where knowledge of the artifice of composition would have enhanced the art.

However, in musical invention and feeling for the strathspey, Marshall is not lacking, even if he ignores, for the most part, the characteristic modes in favour of the ordinary major. His 'Marquis of Huntly's Farewell' [62], 'Miss Admiral Gordon' [61], 'Craigelachie Bridge', 'Duchess of Manchester's Farewell' and 'Knockando House', are particularly celebrated.

The Gow family

Niel Gow was a very different personality, very much of a character in the traditional mould of Scotland's gangrel bodies and yet, through his genius, an aristocrat among them. He enjoyed a dram, as the saying goes, but what was this in a hard-drinking age? He was a youth of twenty-one when Marshall was born, fame already coming his way; and soon he was to be recognized as the greatest fiddler of his time, establishing a celebrity which was to enshrine his name for many generations.

Niel spelled his name with the 'i' before the 'e' in Gaelic fashion. He was born at Inver, Perthshire, in 1727, the son of a plaid weaver, and started fiddling at nine; he taught himself, in the way of fiddlers, until he was about thirteen, when he received some instruction from John Cameron, a servant of Sir George Stewart of Grantully. At eighteen, he was persuaded to enter a fiddling competition which he won, we are told by a contemporary report, 'with the cheerful consent of the other competitors'.[11] Yet, John Glen tells us, there is no indication that Gow's fame extended beyond Perth, his native county, previous to the publication of his *First Collection . . . dedicated to Her Grace the Duchess of Athole*, 1784.

Thus it was not until Niel was nearly sixty years of age that his fame began to spread; but it was to be of an enduring kind. Testifying to this, though perhaps as much to his personality as his skill, is the fact that no less than four portraits of him were painted by Sir Henry Raeburn. One is in the Scottish National Portrait Gallery (plate 18) and two replicas of it are in the hands of the Duke of Athole and Perth County respectively; the others, including one originally given by Raeburn to Gow, are now in private collections. The names of Lord Gray and Maule of Panmure were originally associated with these, though I am not certain of their history. In addition to this, of course, Niel's likeness appears in such paintings as Sir David Wilkie's 'Penny Wedding' * and David Allan's 'Penny Wedding' and his 'Highland Dance' (plate 17); in the last he is playing on the fiddle, and his older brother Donald is at the cello. He appears in the title-page engraving of Captain Simon Fraser's collection, and doubtless in other engravings.

It is true that these portraits show the great fiddler, possessing, in the words of one of the numerous memorial eulogies,

> . . . an open, honest, and pleasing countenance, and a homely, easy and unaffected manner, accompanied by an acute penetration into the character and peculiarities of others, strong good sense, and considerable quaintness and humour, and above all, by a perfect honesty and integrity of thought and action, placing him on a footing of familiarity and independence in the presence of the proudest of the land, which, perhaps, no one in his situation ever attained either before or since.[12]

The impression Niel has left for posterity is a happy one. Many humorous anecdotes about him gained currency, although most of them can be shown to be spurious. True or not, they bear testimony to his reputation; myths are the stuff of heroes, not of lesser men.

A characteristic tale is that of his being asked on one occasion how he had managed to get home to Dunkeld from Perth one night after playing for a ball in Perth. He replied that he 'didna mind the length o' the road; it was the *breadth* o't that he cast oot wi'!' [13]

Murray of Abercairney, 'Auld Abercairney', was one of those numerous products of the Scottish aristocracy in the eighteenth century who retained the common touch; just the kind of man to find a kindred spirit in Niel Gow, who often spent days on end at Abercairney's house playing for the laird and his guests. Many a jovial time they had together, from all accounts. On one occasion, the story goes, Abercairney gave Niel a loan of five pounds on the undertaking that it was to be repaid in music. Some time afterwards, at a party held in Dunkeld House, Abercairney laid a wager with the Duke of Atholl, that he could embarrass Niel. At a suitable pause in the evening's entertainment, Abercairney, in front of the whole company, demanded of Niel his reason for not repaying the five pounds he had borrowed. ''deed, Abercairney', replied Niel, 'if you had ha'en sense to have held your ain tongue, I would have been the last man to have spoken about it.' [14]

---

* Wilkie's painting was made in the eighteen-twenties, long after Niel's death.

Abercairney doubtless paid up with pleasure. The riposte is very characteristic and sufficiently ingenious to be authentic.

It is said that in 1745, when Niel was a lad of eighteen, he followed Lord George Murray and Prince Charlie as far as Perth, and it was generally believed by Niel's intimate friends that he composed his popular strathspey 'The Lass of Luncarty' at this time, on the occasion of the Highland army's passing through Luncarty. Niel's attachment to the cause was not sufficiently strong to draw him further from his native airt.

Niel, with his brother Donald on the cello, now came into great demand at balls and bridals in their native county. Donald had a sensitive style, to the inspiration of which Niel attributed much of the fire and enthusiasm of his own performance when they were playing together.

Niel was associated in his long life with three dukes of Athole, whose seat was in Niel's native region of Dunkeld. All became involved with Niel and his art, and it is easy to understand his attachment to their house. As time passed, he moved farther and farther afield to balls and assemblies, until no function of consequence could afford to be without him. His son Nathaniel enjoyed a similar celebrity in the early years of the next century.

Once, the ball of the Caledonian Hunt at Cupar had to proceed without Niel on account of his illness. Excellent substitutes were obtained, but the dedication of 'a bumper to the better health of Niel Gow, a true Scottish character, whose absence from the meeting no one could sufficiently regret', brought, we are told, loud acclaim, and tears to the eyes of some of the ladies.[15]

One observer noted at a county ball that there was always a marked stiffness and distance among the nobility and humbler gentry until Niel Gow appeared. Once he set his bow to the strings, however, this reserve disappeared. It was said, too, that no one brought more out of Niel than the Duchess of Gordon. Her presence made him more than ordinarily enthusiastic, and this too is easy to understand, for the duchess, like Abercairney and several others, was of that great breed of unsophisticated Scottish worth which recognized the same in others.

It is strange that Sir Walter Scott never mentions Niel Gow. Certainly his Wandering Willie, the canty chiel in *Redgauntlet* who was 'the best fiddler that ever kittled thairm with horse hair', was a character from a similar mould, but Niel was not an itinerant fiddler of this sort, although he was a professional. Wandering Willie bears a close resemblance to Patie Birnie; but neither Niel nor Patie entirely fits the model.

The meeting of Burns with Niel Gow in 1787 was a remarkable historical event, although it was treated at the time as a casual occurrence. Burns described Niel as 'a short, stout-built honest Highland figure, with his greyish hair shed on his honest social brow', and wrote verses in honour of the famous fiddler. Other versifiers followed suit and probably the best known of these efforts is 'Niel Gow's Farewell to Whisky' set to

Niel's tune of that name; it first appears in the *First Collection*, 2nd ed. and reappears in the *Fifth Collection* with the explanation—'This tune alludes to prohibiting the making of Whisky in 1799. It is expressive of a Highlander's sorrow on being deprived of his favourite beverage.' The verses of the song reveal a different story:

> *You've surely heard o' the famous Niel, The man that played the fiddle weel;*
> *I wat he was a canty chiel, And dearly loved the whisky, O.*
> *And aye sin' he wore tartan hose, He dearly lo'ed the Athole brose;*
> *And wae was he, you may suppose, To bid 'farewell' to whisky, O.*[16]

This is attributed to Agnes Lyon of Glammis (*cf.* Charles Rogers, *The Modern Scottish Minstrel*) but the above quotation is from one of the better versions which were current.

Elizabeth Grant, a daughter of Grant of Rothiemurchus, describes the joy with which she reached Inver, on her journeys to Rothiemurchus each summer, at the prospect of hearing Niel play at the Inn.[17] Of course, in those days most people had little knowledge of music other than that in their own native idioms, and here, active in their midst, was the greatest exponent of the native dance music who had ever lived!

Indeed Niel was what we would now describe as one of the tourist attractions of Inver and Dunkeld. The distinguished scholar, Thomas Garnett, on his tour of the Highlands in 1799 tells us how he and his companion 'took a late dinner at Dunkeld' after which they were favoured with a visit from Niel Gow, 'a singular and well known character, and a celebrated performer on the violin'. Dr Garnett feels it necessary to qualify this by explaining:

> When I call him a celebrated performer, I do not mean that he can execute the sweet Italian airs with the touch of a Cramer. His only music is that of his native country, which he has acquired chiefly by ear, being entirely self-taught, but he plays the Scotch airs with a spirit and enthusiasm peculiar to himself. He is now in his seventy-second year, and has played publicly at assemblies, &c. on this instrument for more than half a century. He is a native of the village of Inver, where he resides, and has acquired, by tuning his lyre, what he considers as an independence, and which is therefore such. He favoured us with several pieces of Scotch music. He excels most in the Strathspeys, which are jigs played with a peculiar spirit and life; but he executes the laments or funeral music, with a great deal of pathos.[18]

Niel was married twice. His first wife, Margaret Wiseman, had family of five sons and three daughters. The sons were William, John, Andrew, Nathaniel and Daniel. The last named died in infancy, the others lived to follow their father's footsteps. William died in 1791 aged 40; Andrew and John settled in London (*c.* 1788) as music publishers in

King Street, Golden Square. Andrew died in 1794, and John continued his lucrative business until 1827.

Niel Gow had no children of his second marriage with Margaret Urquhart of Perth whose death after thirty happy years as Mrs Gow inspired the beautiful 'Lament for the death of his Second wife'.

When son John moved to London he was armed with a letter from his father addressed to the Earl of Breadalbane, Park Lane, London, couched as follows: 'My dear Lord—This letter will be handed you by my son Jock. He is tired of the kail and brose of Inver, and deil kens what he would be at; but doubtless your Lordship will guess—I have the honour to remain your lordships loving friend and countryman, Niel Gow.'[19]

John delivered this note to his lordship while the latter was presiding at the annual dinner of the Caledonian Society. His lordship took an opportunity to read the letter to the company, amidst much laughter and applause, and John Gow was thereupon introduced and appointed leader to the Society's band.

The most famous of Niel's sons, however, was Nathaniel (plate 23), born at Inver, 28th May 1763. He started his career with lessons on the same kit (a small fiddle, plate 8) as had been used by his father as a child, was then sent to Edinburgh for tuition under 'Red Bob' Mackintosh for a time, and also Alexander McGlashan. It is said that his first professional appearance was as cellist in McGlashan's band; he studied cello with Joseph Reinagle. In his twentieth year he received the commission of Herald Trumpeter which he held to the end of his life, 19th January 1831. He was not only a versatile instrumentalist but a well-educated musician, active in the vigorous musical life of the Edinburgh of his day, and in great demand as a teacher.

Nathaniel entered business as a music-seller, in partnership with William Shepherd—Gow and Shepherd, 41, North Bridge, Edinburgh—in 1796. This was a very successful enterprise until Shepherd died in 1812, when, because of poor management, it began to decline and was liquidated in 1814. Nathaniel resumed business with his first son Neil,* at 60 Princess Street, where they remained for five years, then in Hanover Street, then in 60 Princess Street again, changing to Gow and Galbraith in 1826, his son having died in 1823.

Nathaniel was a favourite with the Prince Regent (afterwards George IV), and had the honour of playing for him in London at private parties in Carlton House and apparently also at such august assemblies as Almack's. As testimony to the esteem which his artistry and doubtless also his personable qualities earned for him, he received valuable gifts from distinguished patrons. In 1811 the Earl of Dalhousie gave him a massive silver goblet, Sir Peter Murray of Ochtertyre presented him with a

* Nathaniel's son spelt his name thus.

fine cello and Sir Alexander Don, an enthusiastic amateur, gave him a valuable violin. Then when he was reduced to bankruptcy in 1827 and in failing health, his former patrons were not unmindful of his services to his art. They supported an annual benefit ball which realized about £300. The noblemen and gentlemen of the Caledonian Hunt voted him an annuity of £50 and George IV granted him a pension; every year he received a handsome present from the Hon. William Maule, subsequently Lord Panmure, successor to a name distinguished in the annals of eighteenth-century fashionable life.

What a great period of Scottish music was spanned by his life, and there he was, at the very centre, son of the most celebrated exponent of Scottish fiddle music, and leader of the most requested dance band of his time. As with his father, no really fashionable dance could be arranged without him and large sums were paid to attract him to country parties.

Also, like his father, Nathaniel was married twice; he had five daughters and one son by the first, and three sons and two daughters by the second. His son Neil was a doctor of medicine by profession and a good musician. but he died at the early age of twenty-eight with such tunes as 'Bonnie Prince Charlie' and 'Flora Macdonald's Lament' (the title from the words set by his fellow fiddler, the poet James Hogg), and 'Miss Hay of Hayston's Reel' to his credit. With Nathaniel's death at the age of sixty-eight, a famous era of great fiddlers came to an end, but some of its glory was revived about fifty years later by J. Scott Skinner.

Niel Gow died on 1st March 1807 at Inver, his home during most of his eighty years. Unlike his talented son Nathaniel, he ended his days in comparative affluence, but was unspoiled and couthy to the end.

The laments in music, verse and prose were sincere. My favourite because of its evocative lines (one can hear and see the great fiddler in them) is that of the Rev. James Grahame, writing in English in the style of which his great countryman Thomson was the master:

> The blythe strathspey springs up, reminding some
> Of nights when Gow's old arm (nor old the tale),
> Unceasing, save when reeking cans went round
> Made heart and heel leap light as bounding roe.
> Alas! No more shall we behold that look
> So venerable, yet so blent with mirth,
> And festive joy sedate; that ancient garb,
> Unvaried; tartan hose and bonnet blue!
> No more shall beauty's partial eye draw forth
> The full intoxication of his strain
> Mellifluous, strong, exuberantly rich!
> No more amid the pauses of the dance
> Shall he repeat those measures, that, in days

> *Of other years, could sooth a falling prince,**
> *And light his visage with a transient smile*
> *Of melancholy joy, like autumn sun*
> *Gilding a sere tree with a passing beam!*
> *Or play to sportive children on the green,*
> *Dancing at gloamin' hours, or willing cheer,*
> *With strains unbought, the shepherd's bridal day.*[20]

There is some question of the stature of the Gows as composers. Niel's compositions amount to about eighty-seven tunes of which, however, Glen asserts, at least a quarter are plagiarisms to some extent, or are appropriated without acknowledgment from the publications of others and presented under new titles. His most celebrated compositions are: 'The Duchess of Athol's Slipper' and 'Niel Gow's Lament for his Second Wife'. Nathaniel was perhaps a more polished composer than his father, although Niel's earthier grasp of the idiom has much to be said for it, but neither, in total achievement as composers, for all their fidelity to the old modes, excel the quality of Marshall, Mackintosh and Dow.

Nathaniel Gow claimed 197 tunes, divided approximately into 33 reels, 58 strathspeys, 7 jigs, 10 quicksteps, 6 laments and 83 waltzes and slow airs and others. Of these, the most celebrated reel is 'Largo's Fairy Dance' [51] commonly called 'The Fairy Dance', which like his lyric 'Caller Herrin' is well known today. 'Bothwell Castle', 'Lady Charlotte Durham', 'Loch Earn', 'Lady Elizabeth Lindsay's Strathspey' and 'Lady Charlotte Campbell's Strathspey' are not so well known, but show Nathaniel at his best.

The other sons, William, John and Andrew, to whom Glen attributes seven, sixteen and three tunes respectively, were capable of flights of inspiration. William is still represented by 'Lady Loudon's Strathspey' and 'Mrs Dundas of Arniston', a reel; John by 'Tullymet Hall' and 'Ayr Races'. Andrew's strathspey, 'Major Molle' and William's reel 'Mrs Muir Mackenzie', are possibly superior to any written by other members of their family.

It is intriguing to notice that a Gow and a Dow appear among the instrumentalists at the Court of Mary, Queen of Scots, an interesting and appropriate coincidence.

The Gow music collections are extensive and are in the bibliographical Appendix B, page 249.

The appropriation of tune titles: priority and authorship

We have mentioned occasionally the misappropriation of tunes by the compilers of printed collections, such as Isaac Cooper's complaint that

---

This is an allusion to Niel's playing in the presence of Prince Charlie during his brief period with the rebel army.

people had published what they called 'new' reels, but which were merely old reels with new names; John Glen's censure of Nathaniel Gow for publishing the tunes of others without indicating their source, very often also changing their titles; and William Marshall's complaint on this score.* More serious, however, is the accusation that Nathaniel has claimed some of these tunes as the compositions of his father, and even of himself. This appears the more heinous when we notice that a borrowed tune which is attributed to no composer in the first edition of a collection is claimed for Niel in the second edition some years later. The table on the following pages is an analysis of the specific instances of these various infringements cited by John Glen.

In a number of instances we are dealing with plagiarism of a musical theme rather than with direct copying of the original. For instance, the strathspey 'Cheap Mutton' by Niel Gow in the *Fourth Collection* is a simple variation on the traditional tune 'Ewie wi' the Crooked Horn' which is included in the *First Collection*. 'Major Graham', in the second edition of the *First Collection*, is similar to the second part of Marshall's 'Miss Admiral Gordon's Strathspey' which Gow published in the first edition of the same collection although not in the second; and also in the *First Repository* where he properly attributes it to Marshall. Glen regards 'Major Graham of Inchbrakie' as a plagiarism of 'Miss Admiral Gordon', but Burns distinguished between the two tunes, and used both.

Likewise the second strain of 'Mrs Donaldson's Strathspey' in Gow's *First Collection* appears to be derived from the second strain of Dow's 'Miss McLean of Duart', published some ten years previously. This may or may not be a case of plagiarism, but suspicions are aroused when we notice that although 'Mrs Donaldson' is given no composer in the *First Collection*, it is claimed for Niel Gow in *The Beauties*, 1819. A less excusable plagiarism is represented by 'The Marquis of Huntly's Snuff Mill' attributed to Niel Gow in the *Fourth Collection*, 1800, which is Marshall's 'Miss Dallas' altered in key and in a few notes. In other instances, we have a strathspey converted into a reel, and vice versa, and there is nothing new in that. Where does one draw the dividing line between plagiarisn and originality in traditional music? A certain attitude to this is revealed by Nathaniel Gow in his response to the following remarks of Robert Burns contained in a letter reproduced in Cromek's *Reliques* in 1808:

Speaking of 'McPherson's Farewell' [47], it is said Gow has published a variation of this fine tune as his own composition, which he calls the

* It must be remembered that copyright protection at that time was, by modern standards inadequate. Piracy was common, in spite of the Act of 1709, the first attempt at a comprehensive protective code. There were frequent complaints by London booksellers of the activity of Irish and Scottish printers. The Scottish printers were apparently as willing to print each other's copyright works as they were to copy printed works published in London

'Princess Augusta'. Again, in the same book, 'My Tocher's the Jewel', it is said, this tune is claimed by Nathaniel Gow. It is notoriously taken from the 'Muckin' of Geordie's Byre'! It is also found, long prior to Nathaniel Gow's era, in *Aird's Selection of Airs and Marches*, the first edition under the name of 'The Highway to Edinburgh'.

Nathaniel Gow's response appears in the introduction to the *Fifth Collection* published in the next year. He pointed out that no composer's name was attached to either tune in the Gow collections, and that 'My Tocher's the Jewel' had been taken from Oswald's *Caledonian Pocket Companion*, where it was a quick jig. 'It struck him,' he says, 'that it would be pretty if slow, and, being without a name, called it "Lord Elcho's favourite".'

As it happened, Nathaniel Gow did not claim the new slow version of the jig as his own composition, although he appears to have done this kind of thing, at least on his father's behalf, in other instances. The position is an ambiguous one condoned by traditional practice.

As far as the Gow collections are concerned, Niel is described as the 'author' of the first four, although clearly Nathaniel was their editor. Many of the tunes comprising these collections are ascribed to their respective composers—Niel's sons, and such distinguished amateurs as Sir Alexander Don, Mr Sharpe of Hoddam, Lord Macdonald, Mr Nisbet of Dirleton and others. Those whom we may call the professionals are represented by Malcolm McDonald, John Bowie, William Marshall and James Macdonald. The remaining tunes are unclaimed. Of these, a number, such as 'Tullochgorum' [59], 'This is no my ain Hoose' [32], 'Stumpie', 'The Bob of Fettercairn', 'Jenny Nettles', 'Roy's Wife', 'O'er the Water to Charlie', and several 'Gallic' and Irish airs and incidentals like 'Boolanzie', are traditional or in common currency. The remainder are presumably of unknown authorship, or are we being asked to believe that they are the work of Niel Gow? Niel's name is not prefixed to any of the tunes in these collections, except in the cases of 'Niel Gow's Lamentation for Abercarnay', 'Niel Gow's Lament for his Brother' and 'Niel Gow's Compliments returned to Mr Marshall'.

Glen seems to take the view that the terminology of the title pages— 'Collection of Reels, &c. . . . by Niel Gow'—and the allusion thereon to Niel as 'author', implies that the tunes not otherwise ascribed are the compositions of Niel. But many of these, as we have noted, could not be assumed to be Niel's by any of his subscribers, for they were well known as traditional tunes. Nevertheless in the circumstances, the title-page wording is ambiguous.

At the end of the *Third Collection*, the following note appears: 'Nathaniel Gow hopes it will not appear ostentatious for prefixing his name to the tunes composed by himself, having seen severall of them published lately under fictitious names, and in a very incorrect manner.'

Title of tune in Gow publications	Title of Gow publication	Gow attribution of authorship
Sir John Shaw Stewart	First Collection, 1784	
Lady Madelina Sinclair	Third Collection, 1792	
The Earl of Dalkeith's Reel	Third Collection, 1792	
Mrs Macdonald Grant	Third Collection, 1792	Nathaniel Gow
Mrs Hamilton of Wishaw	Third Collection, 1792	
The Marquis of Huntly's Snuff Mill	Fourth Collection, 1800	Niel Gow
Lord Balgonie's Favourite	Fourth Collection, 1800	'A very Old High Tune'
Cheap Mutton	Fourth Collection, 1800	Niel Gow
The Countess of Dalkeith	Fourth Collection, 1800	
Lady Hamilton Dalrymple's Strathspey	Fourth Collection, 1800	
Miss Margaret Graham of Inchbrakie	First Collection, second edition, 1801	Niel Gow
Hon. George Baillie's Strathspey	First Collection, second edition, 1801	Niel Gow
Hon. Miss Drummond of Perth's Reel	First Collection, second edition, 1801	Niel Gow
Major Graham of Inchbrakie	First Collection, second edition, 1801	Niel Gow
Miss Menzies of Culdare's Reel	First Collection, second edition, 1801	Niel Gow
Miss Drummond of Perth's Strathspey	Third Collection, second edition, 1807	Niel Gow
The Marquis of Huntly's Farewell	Repository, Part First, 1799	
Lord Alexander Gordon's Strathspey	Repository, Part First, 1799	
The Duke of Gordon's Birthday	Repository, Part First, 1799	
The North Bridge of Edinburgh	Repository, Part First, 1799	
Honest Duncan	Repository, Part Second, 1802	
Lady Charlotte Campbell (Medley)	Repository, Part Second, 1802	Published by the Au of Mr John Hamil Proprietor Nathaniel Gow
The Miller of Drone	Repository, Part Second, 1802	
Lady Wallace	Repository, Part Second, 1802	
Look Before You	Repository, Part Second, 1802	
Look Behind You	Repository, Part Second, 1802	

Possible prototype or original	Authorship claimed	Date. Title of publication
Crawford of Donside's Reel	John Riddell	1766
Braes of Aberarder	Charles Duff	1790
onel Crafurd's Reel	Robert Bremner	1759
Hunter of Burnside	Charles Duff	c. 1790
Hamilton of Wishaw	William Marshall	First Collection, 1781
Dallas	William Marshall	First Collection, 1781
Mr Patrick McDonald of Kil- re	Alexander Campbell	Albyn's Anthology, 1815
on's Reel alias wi' the Crooked Horn		{ First Publication Cumming Collection, 1700 Ross Collection, 1780
ara Strathspey	William Marshall	First Collection, 1781
Hamilton Dalrymple's Strath- y	Robert Mackintosh	1793
Marquis of Huntly's Strathspey	William Marshall	First Collection, 1781
and Skip	Daniel Dow	1776 Attributed to Dow by Gow in Repository, Part Third, 1806
Grace Gordon's Strathspey	William Marshall	First Collection, 1781
Admiral Gordon's Strathspey	William Marshall	First Collection, 1781
of Glendochert	Alexander McGlashan	Third Collection, 1786
Sarah Drummond of Perth's thspey	Malcolm McDonald	
Marquis of Huntly's Farewell	William Marshall	First Collection, 1781
Alexander Gordon's Strathspey	William Marshall	First Collection, 1781
Duke of Gordon's Birthday	William Marshall	First Collection, 1781
vie House	William Marshall	First Collection, 1781
Downie's Strathspey	Duncan MacIntyre	[1795]
n Shiel	Robert Petrie	Third Collection [1802]
Charlotte Campbell	Robert Mackintosh	1793
liller of Drone	John Pringle	1801
Wallace's Reel	Robert Mackintosh	Airs, Minuets, Gavotts and Reels, c. 1783
Ross's Strathspey	William Marshall	First Collection, 1781
louse of Letterfourie	William Marshall	First Collection, 1781

Title of tune in Gow publications	Title of Gow publication	Gow attribution of authorship
Loch Erroch Side	Second Collection, second edition, 1803	Niel Gow and Wife
Jonny Pringle	Repository, Part Third, 1806	
The Doctor	Repository, Part Third, 1806	Attributed to Marsha Third Edition. No att tion in earlier edition
The Duchess of Manchester's Strath-spey	Repository, Part Third, 1806	
Lady Grace Douglas	Third Collection, second edition, 1807	Niel Gow
Honest Men and Bonnie Lasses	Fifth Collection, 1809	
Colonel David Stewart of Garth's Reel	Sixth Collection, 1822	

Is Nathaniel suggesting that he did not always attach his name to his own compositions in these collections? If so, why some tunes and not others? For he did attach his name to some. It is a curious remark in the circumstances and no less curious in that it is never repeated in any subsequent edition or collection. He was a bold man to raise the issue at all, being himself so great an offender. Nevertheless, was it this fear of appearing 'ostentatious' which prevented Niel Gow from attaching his name to his own tunes in the first three collections?

This situation was clarified in their second editions. Niel's name was now attached to twenty-eight tunes in the first collection, thirteen in the second and five in the third. A few of these, as we have seen, are disputed; it being asserted that they were composed by others or are plagiarisms, to some degree. But most of them were indeed Niel's.

At best, there was a great deal of carelessness, as, for instance, in the *Repositories* in particular, where tunes by Marshall and Mackintosh and Petrie are included under their composers' titles, but only a few have the composers' names attached to them.

One final curiosity demands notice. This is the strange case of Malcolm McDonald's second collection. He produced this collection in 1797, and a year or so after (according to Glen, for it carries no date) another edition of this appeared, bearing on its title-page, 'Corrected by Niel Gow'. The 'corrections' to the actual notation are very slight, but now four tunes ar

Possible prototype or original	Authorship claimed	Date. Title of publication
Erroch Side	Alexander McGlashan	Third Collection, 1786
urnet's Reel	William Marshall	First Collection, 1781
ine Campbell's Strathspey	John Pringle	1801
ine Stewart's Pittyvaich	William Marshall	1822
ie Castle	William Marshall	First Collection, 1781
Georgina Gordon's Strathspey	William Marshall	First Collection, 1781
ray of Carse	Charles Duff	1790
Duchess of Manchester's Fare- to Scotland	William Marshall	First Collection, 1781
no my ain Hoose	Traditional	Published in Gow, First Collection, 1784

ascribed to Niel Gow (although one, says Glen, is a composition of William Gow) and five to Nathaniel. Some of these reappear in later Gow collections. The 'Hon. Captain Maitland's Strathspey' reappears in Part Second of the *Repository*, but this time unclaimed.

The following provides a simple breakdown of this matter:

Title of tune in McDonald's Second Collection reprinted in 1797	Gow attribution of authorship	Gow publication (First subsequent)
Wha can help it	Niel Gow	Sixth Collection, 1822
Miss Ferguson of Raith Strathspey	Niel Gow	
Lawers House	Niel Gow	Fifth Collection [1809]
Callam's Frollock	Nathaniel Gow	
Mrs Landle's Delight	Nathaniel Gow	
Greenend Park	Nathaniel Gow	As 'Lady Shaftesbury's Strathspey in the Third Collection [1791]
Mrs Duncan's Reel	Nathaniel Gow	Fourth Collection [1800]
Hon. Capt. Maitland's Strathspey	Nathaniel Gow	Repository, Part Second [1802]

Malcolm became Niel Gow's bass player about the time this occurred, and some of his tunes had appeared—and had been acknowledged—in the Gow first and second collections. He also subsequently published two further collections. As it stands, in the absence of rebuttal from McDonald, it looks as though he had heard these tunes of the Gows and used them for his collection, perhaps not realizing that they were claimed by the Gows. Surely the bare-faced appropriation of McDonald's tunes would have stimulated some response from him. One doubts, too, that Niel Gow, particularly, would condone anything quite so outrageous.

In passing judgment on alleged plagiarisms, one must recognize that the melodic and rhythmical clichés inevitable in traditional music produce blood relations among tunes. Some thematic ideas are sufficiently fertile to produce several progeny—'Deil Stick the Minister' spawns 'This is no mine ain Hoose' [32, 33], and 'This is no my ain Lassie'; and the poignant 'Kind Robin' is transmuted into the 'Bonny Banks o' Loch Lomond'. Thus it is a very common thing in Scottish traditional music circles to hear of this or that tune being a 'set' of another.

In chapter 1, Bertrand H. Bronson was cited to the effect that the musical germs of traditional ballads would prove to be less numerous than their narrative or literary germs. It may be suggested that Scottish dance tunes likewise are developed from a mere handful of musical ideas. There is some substance in this, but I think the melodic range of Scottish instrumental dance music is much greater than in the case of folk song, particularly that class of folk song categorized as balladry by Francis Child. Nevertheless, there are undoubtedly a great many rhythmical-cum-melodic clichés in the traditional dance music of any people. This, of course, is an important source of its distinguishing character.

It is possible that some at least of the apparent plagiarisms among alleged original compositions of the late eighteenth-century fiddlers are due to the peculiarities described above. Nor can it be overlooked that two or more composers may have drawn inspiration occasionally from a common source. This source may have been a tune of a different rhythm, or a tune played by this or that folk musician in this or that locality, heard independently. This is not to whitewash the deliberate misappropriation of original compositions which did take place; but it cautions us not to be too presumptuous in accusing this or that composer of the plagiarism of another's work.

Perhaps, too, there is such a thing as acceptable plagiarism in music. It is of the nature of human development that the new derives from the old. Even the most original of composers have elements in their work which are derivative, as well as characteristics which are inevitably shared—use of certain melodic sequences and the like—which can largely be anticipated by the average musician, and which have often become so commonplace that one readily attaches such adjectives as 'vulgar' and 'banal' to them.

A great influence on the transformation of traditional tunes has been their use for the lyrics of various poets, of Robert Burns in particular. It is curious that Burns's schoolmaster, John Murdoch, reported that Burns had no ear for music. Yet it is clear that in manhood he had a great memory for traditional tunes and could scrape them out on his own fiddle.

'Many of our Strathspeys ancient and modern,' he wrote to Thomson, 'give me exquisite enjoyment . . . For instance, I am just now making verses * to Rothiemurche's Rant, an air which puts me into raptures; and in fact, unless I be pleased with the tune, I never can make verses to it . . .' 'Rothiemurchie's Rant' [48] appeared in Bremner's *Collection of Scots Reels or County Dances*, 1759, a tune which, like so many of the older airs, is anonymous. Not all of the tunes which Burns admired were anonymous, the composers of those which he would have described as 'modern' were known; but once Burns set words to them, he gave them new identity. Marshall's beautiful 'Miss Admiral Gordon's Strathspey' [6] has become 'Of a' the airts the win' can blaw' (Johnson's *Scots Musical Museum*, no. 235): 'Lady Mackintosh's Reel', a fine strathspey from Bremner has become 'a man's a man for a' that'; and another from the same source, 'Grant's Rant' is 'Green Grow the Rashes' [30], and so on. The titles of some of the tunes in Bremner certainly suggest songs, and verses to some were current in the countryside as in the case of 'My ain kind dearie O' or 'Lea Rig', which Burns revised.

Since Burns a number of editors of Scottish songs have replaced some of the tunes he used with others which seemed (to them) preferable. Thus, for instance, in such cases as 'Afton Water' and 'My Love is like a Red Red Rose', the airs which are commonly known today are not the ones used by Burns. 'A Red Red Rose' (*Museum*, no. 402) was originally set to that strathspey which appeared under the title of 'Major Graham' in Niel Gow's *First Collection* (second edition), but G. F. Graham replaced this by the beautiful old Scottish tune 'Low Down in the Broom', some fifty years afterwards, and this is the tune associated with the song today.

'Major Graham', as already pointed out, is apparently derived from Marshall's 'Miss Admiral Gordon'. Stenhouse stated that Marshall formed this tune by adding a second part to an air 'Lowlands of Holland' which was published in the *Museum*. This is the air to which Robert Gilfillan (*c.* 1800) set his popular song 'O Why left I my Hame?' Glen points out that there is no evidence that this was an old tune and that a very different tune appears years earlier under the same name in Oswald's *Pocket Companion*. Glen had little doubt that the original version of the tune was Marshall's and that the *Museum*'s 'Lowlands' was a derivative produced by Urbani. Among Burns's MS. notes on the *Museum*, there is the following note—'I have been told by somebody who had it of Marshall himself, that he took the idea of his three most celebrated pieces,

* 'Lassie wi the lint-white locks'.

'The Marquis of Huntley's Reel', 'His Farewell' and 'Miss Admiral Gordon's Reel' from the old air, 'The German Lairdie'.[21]

These disputes of priority and authorship have had their day. They have a certain antiquarian interest for all lovers of Scottish traditional music, but at this point in time we can treat the subject with greater equanimity. The Gow collections, repositories and the others (Appendix B, pages 249–52) for all their occasional plagiarisms, intentional or otherwise, are invaluable to us today. We would have been much the poorer without them.

Dilettantes and distinguished amateurs

The subscribers to the printed collections of Scottish dance music and the personalities honoured by the titles to the new compositions contained in these were, for the most part, members of the landed gentry, or friends of the composer. The dedicatees of the collections were invariably distinguished patrons of the author.*

From the list we see that Niel Gow was the first of the dance music compilers to dedicate his work in this way, and, most appropriately at that, to the wife of his laird and benefactor the Duke of Athole. The personages honoured by tunes embrace a wide range from dukes to the 'Landlady at Inver' or a fellow gut-scraper. One can also determine some of the beauties of the day from these titles—Lady Charlotte Campbell, Miss Drummond of Perth, Miss Lucy Johnston of Hilton and others.

* Niel Gow (First Collection) to the *Duchess of Athole*; Niel Gow (Second) to the *Noblemen & Gentlemen of the Caledonian Hunt*; John Bowie (1789) to the *Countess of Kinnoul*; John Anderson (*c.* 1789) to the *Gentlemen of the Musical Society of Greenock*; Malcolm McDonald (1789) to the *Earl of Breadalbane*; Charles Duff (*c.* 1790) to the *Duke of Athole*; Robert Petrie (1790) to *Mrs Farquharson of Monaltrie*; Niel Gow (Third) (*c.* 1792), to the *Marchioness of Tweeddale*; Malcolm McDonald (*c.* 1792) to *Miss Drummond of Perth*; Robert Mackintosh (1793) to the *Hon. Mrs Campbell of Lochnell*; William Shepherd (1793) to *Miss Abercromby of Tullibody*; Alexander Leburn (1793) to *Mrs Moncrieff of Reedie*; George Jenkins (1793) to *H.R.H. The Prince of Wales*; Daniel McLaren (1794) *Miss Dr. Grant*; Archibald Duff (1794) to *Lady Carnegie of Southesk*; Duncan MacIntyre (1795) to *Lady Charlotte Campbell*; John Clark (1795) to the *Musical Society of Perth*; Robert Mackintosh (1796) to *Mrs Oswald of Auchencruive*; Robert Petrie (1796) to *Mrs Garden of Troup*; Malcolm McDonald (1797) to the *Countess of Breadalbane*; James Walker (1797) to *Sir James Erskine St Clair of Sinclair Bart.* and the *Worthy Brethren of the Free Mason Lodge in Dysart*; John McGlashan (1798) to the *Hon. Mrs Charteris*; A. Gibb (1798) to *Miss C. Dalrymple*; Niel Gow (1799) to the *Duchess of Gordon*; Charles Stewart (1799) *Lady Mary Hay*; Niel Gow (1800) to the *Earl of Eglinton*; James Walker (1800) to *Lady St Clair Erskine of Sinclair*; John Morison (1800) to *Mrs Duff of Fetteresso*; Niel Gow and Sons (1802) to the *Duchess of Buccleugh*, (1806) to the *Countess of Loudoun and Moira*, (1809) to the *Countess of Dalhousie* and (1871) to the *Nobility and Gentry of Scotland*; Nathaniel Gow (1819) to the *Caledonian Hunt* and (1819) to the *Earl of Dalhousie*; Niel Gow and Sons (1822) to the *Marchioness of Huntly*.

The assembly fiddlers or dancing masters were not insensible of the inspirational power of female beauty allied to dancing or musical talent.

The violin, spinet, harpsichord, guitar and flute were the favourite instruments among the aristocracy at this time, and as we have remarked in an earlier chapter, they saw no incongruity in mixing 'Corelli's soft Italian song with "Cowdenknowes" and "Winter Nights are Long"'. They danced avidly, and mostly to their own native reels, strathspeys and jigs. It is not surprising that the more creative among them composed a tune or two. Not all the genteel composers of reels cared to be identified in print, however—there was a kind of stigma about being represented as a common musician and, in the case of a woman, in being creative (except in child-bearing). It showed genteel refinement and modesty, if creative one had to be, to remain anonymous or, at most, have one's name discreetly disguised as 'Selected and Composed by Mr. S. F****r'. Thus we encounter such acknowledgments as 'communicated by a lady in the North', or 'by an amateur'.

Nevertheless, a number of the Scottish gentry saw no shame in acknowledging their compositions, although it is obvious that the most prolific of these, 'Sodger Hugh' Montgomerie of Coylfield and Skelmorlie (1739–1819), was not at all sure of the propriety of this. The collection of 'New Strathspey Reels for the Pianoforte, Violin and Violincello, Composed by a Gentleman and given permission to be published by Nathaniel Gow' (1796), attributed to him, is circumspectly anonymous.

Colonel Hugh Montgomerie (plate 20) became twelfth earl of Eglintoun in the year in which this work appeared. He had served in American campaigns and been elected Member of Parliament for Ayrshire. In the latter capacity, he was honoured by a poetic address from Robert Burns himself ('Earnest Cry and Prayer'). He took over the Eglinton policies with a grand conception of his role as laird, instituted many improvements, maintained a splendid stable and fine equipages, and appointed a family piper. A talented Irish piper, John Murphy, served the Earl in this capacity, *c.* 1820 (*cf.* Francis O'Neill, *Irish Minstrels and Musicians*, Chicago, 1913). A man of action rather than words—he was singularly tongue-tied—Hugh had not much place in his life for the fine arts, but he was passionately fond of the national music and no mean exponent of it on the fiddle, if we may judge from his compositions. His best-known tunes are: 'Lady Montgomerie's Reel', which is familiar to those who have danced 'The Montgomerie's Rant' as published by the Royal Scottish Country Dance Society, and 'Ayrshire Lasses'. In addition to the work mentioned above, Hugh had some tunes in the Gow collections, and indeed he is the dedicatee of the *Fourth Collection* (plate 19); Turnbull of Glasgow later published a further selection of his tunes. Scotland's national instrumental music never had a more enthusiastic patron, and Matthew Hall, a noted fiddler and cellist of Ayr, told the editor of *The*

Ballads and Songs of Ayrshire (Ayr 1846) that he frequented Coilsfield and Eglinton Castle in his capacity of musician over a period of forty-five years, and that the Earl generally took part at the concerts there on the violoncello and the harp.

Sir Alexander Don of Newton-Don is another aristocratic name conspicuous among composers of reels and strathspeys. The fifth and sixth baronets bore the same name and together spanned the period we are considering. The sixth was doubtless the composer of the reels attributed to Sir Alexander Don in the Gow Collections. The family bears a name associated in all ways with the music and dance of Scotland. There was Lady Don who, with Mrs Rochead of Inverleith, was a celebrated directress of the Buccleugh Place Assembly and who, in Cockburn's words, shone first as a hooped beauty in the minuet, then as a lady of ceremonies 'at our stately assemblies'. Each, he writes, 'carried her peculiar qualities and air to the very edge of the grave—Lady Don's dignity softened by gentle sweetness, Mrs Rochead's made more formidable by cold and rather severe solemnity'. She was about the last person in Edinburgh to keep a private sedan chair, adds Cockburn, 'as comfortable as silk, velvet, and gilding could make it', with 'two well-known respectable chairmen, enveloped in her livery cloaks'.[22]

Other distinguished amateurs whose names come to our attention from time to time as the composers of tunes are Sir Alexander Boswell of Auchinleck (James Boswell's son), who had much in him of his mother; Mr and Mrs Sharpe of Hoddam, Mrs Robertson of Ladykirk, Lord Macdonald (of Sleat), Mr MacLeod of Raasay, Miss Murray of Ochtertyre, Miss Baird of Sauchtonhall, and, most romantic of all, Miss Lucy Johnston of Hilton (plate 21).

Many of Miss Lucy's compositions are in the Gow collections. Her skill as a dancer and musician no less than her beauty is attested by the number of tunes addressed to her, as well as the dedication of Mackintosh's second collection. She was one of six girls in a family of eleven. Her sister Suphy became one of the intelligent eccentrics of Edinburgh society—the girl who, as an experiment, was left to educate herself, who dressed in an oddly masculine manner, who practised blacksmithing as a hobby, and played the fiddle! Lady Anne Barnard wrote the words of 'Auld Robin Gray' to Suphy's favourite tune.

Lucy with her delicate beauty formed a marked contrast to this; but she obviously possessed musical gifts of a high order. It is probable that she performed on the spinet or harpsichord (one can scarcely imagine her as a violinist), but no one has thought fit to tell us of it. She was a frequenter of the concerts and the dance assembly until she married Richard Oswald of Auchencruive in 1793. Burns wrote some new verses for 'I'll gang na mair tae yon toun' in honour of her arrival at her husband's family seat not far from Burns's birthplace:

> O' wat ye wha's is yon toun,
>   Ye see the e'ening sun upon?
> The fairest maid's in yon toun,
>   That e'ening sun is shining on.
>   . . . etc.

Charles Kirkpatrick Sharpe wrote that 'None who ever had the delight of seeing her in the ballroom, giving double charms to a minuet, or dignifying a country dance, can question the truth of this feeble encomium:

> " *Whate'er* she *did was done with so much ease,*
> *In* her *alone 'twas natural to please:*
> *Her motions all accompanied with grace;*
> *And Paradise was open'd in her face."* [23]

Alas, the gods had marked her for their own, and doubtless the birth of two daughters hastened her decline. Oswald took her to Portugal in an attempt to check the tuberculosis which now consumed her, but she died in Lisbon in 1797.

After ten years as a widower, Richard Oswald married one of 'Sodger Hugh's' daughters, Lady Lilias Montgomerie, widow of that crude terror of the bench, Lord Braxfield. She it was who was the subject of the only story of Braxfield which Henry Cockburn 'ever heard that had some fun in it without immodesty'. The butler, the story goes, told his Lordship that he was giving up his place because his lordship's wife was always scolding him. 'Lord!' Braxfield exclaimed, 'ye've little to complain o'; ye may be thankfu' ye're no married tae'r.'

The River Ayr flows through the hazels, birks, beeches and elms and by the buttressed overhangs of the property of Auchencruive, and agricultural research thrives where the 'e'ening sun' shone, one happy day in the life of Burns, and in the hall redolent of gentle Lucy Johnston of the dance.

CHAPTER 5

The Nineteenth and Twentieth Centuries

The impression left by the period we have just been discussing is one of great artistic fertility, and awakening of the personality and proud spirit of Scotland. It was a productive, intimate period, which was to expand into something less comfortable as the new century progressed. The division between centuries is never as sharp and decisive as appears on the calendar; but, strangely enough, each century seen in the perspective of time seems to reveal a character or spirit of its own.

The nineteenth century carries us from the last vestiges of feudal society into the fiery torrent of the age of steel and the machine, at once submerging humanity and sweeping a path to its material if not its spiritual good. The new dances—the French Quadrille, the German Waltz and Polka and their many derivatives—dominated the English dance floor, shouldered out the Minuet, Country Dance and even the Scotch Reel which had become very popular. In Scotland the Country Dance and Reel, especially in the combined form of 'Strathspey and Reel' for two couples, held their place, particularly in rural society, throughout the century, although Quadrilles and Waltzes, especially, made increasing inroads in the cities.

So rapid, indeed, was this change, that after all we have seen, Dean Ramsay could write in the eighteen-fifties:

> . . . a taste for that most interesting style of music, the pure Scottish, is in some quarters becoming a matter of reminiscence . . . I refer more particularly to the reels and strathspeys which with many Scotch persons have become nearly quite obsolete . . . It has a peculiar character of its own, and requires to be performed with a particular and *spicy* dexterity of hand, whether for the bow or the keys. Accordingly, young ladies used to take lessons in it as a finish to their musical education. Such teaching would now, I fear, be treated with contempt by many of our modern fair ones. I recollect at the beginning of the present century, my eldest sister, who was a good musician of the school of Pleyel, Kozeluch, Clementi, etc., having such lessons from Nathaniel Gow, a celebrated reel and strathspey performer.'

Dalyell, in his *Musical Memoirs of Scotland*, alludes to the decline in the Scottish repertoire of the orchestra used at the Highland Society's dance competition in Edinburgh by the year 1839. This, however, is rather a reflection on the changes in city dance habits than on the relish for the music in many of the less sophisticated regions of the country, a relish which was still very considerable among the common people well into the next century.

Clearly it was not so vital as before; taking the taste of the nation as a whole, it was in decline; but there were still a number of reel and strathspey collections published in the second half of the nineteenth century, and numerous Scottish song collections. There were also some excellent fiddlers whose celebrity is handed down to us, including at least one in the heroic mould who lived into the twentieth century. It seems to have been worth the effort, too, for William Crawford Honeyman (1845–1919) to publish a *Strathspey, Reel and Hornpipe Tutor for the Violin*, as recently as 1898.

Meantime, romantic Scotland had caught the artistic imagination of Europe through the works of Sir Walter Scott and translations of Macpherson's *Ossian*. Byron, too, whose mother was a Huntly-Gordon and the dedicatee of Isaac Cooper's reel 'Miss Gordon of Gight', shared something of this fashionable fervour. The great Hector Berlioz exercised his original orchestral genius on themes inspired by Scott—*The Pirate (Corsair), Waverley* and *Rob Roy*—and Donizetti wrote *Lucia di Lammermoor*, at the first performance of which, it is said, the actors wore their sporrans round their necks! And many other composers, infected by the contemporary romantic movement in the arts, sought inspiration in Scottish themes. The most celebrated of these, since they have stood the test of time, are Mendelssohn's *Hebrides* or *Fingal's Cave* overture, *Scotch Symphony* (no. 3), and the *Scottish Sonata* (op. 28); and Max Bruch's *Scottish Fantasia* for violin and orchestra.* Bruch's *Schottlands Tränen* and *Schottische Lieder* are not so well known. Bizet wrote an opera, *The Fair Maid of Perth*, and even Tchaikovsky, at the end of the century, set the Scots ballad *Edward* to music. George Thomson had earlier solicited arrangements and tunes from Haydn, Beethoven and Pleyel for his *Select Collection of Original Airs for the Voice*, 1793–1818, and William Whyte (1771–1858) had done likewise for his *Collection of Scotch Airs*, 1806.

The use of folk themes in music was now attracting composers whose native lands provided music which lent itself to symphonic use: Smetana, Dvořák, Greig, Glinka, Borodin, were among the most notable. It was natural for the Scots, possessors of a rich heritage of national music, to expect to produce a composer in this mould.

Their nearest approach to this was Sir Alexander Mackenzie, whose

---

* Bruch's treatment of 'I'm wae for lack o Johnnie' in this work is most felicitous.

father was a well-known musician and compiler of a collection of Scottish music (his 'Linton Lowrie' has come into vogue among folk-singers in the nineteen-sixties). Mackenzie had a distinguished musical career, and although he was never consciously 'nationalist' in his compositions there is a flavour of Scottish idioms where the subject warrants it, as in his *Cottar's Saturday Night* (1888) for chorus and orchestra, *Pibroch* (1889), *From the North* (1895), *Scottish Piano Concerto* (1897) and the *Tam o' Shanter* Scottish Rhapsody.

This takes us into the era of the celebrated Glasgow School of painters, the 'Scottish Colourists', and the avant-garde architectural genius James Rennie MacIntosh. There was something in the air in Scotland and it is not surprising that, in music, Mackenzie's example was followed by Hamish MacCunn (1868–1916), Learmont Drysdale (1866–1909) and J. B. McEwan (1868–1939) to form at least an incipient Scottish 'nationalist' school.

Survival of Scottish song

The Scot's love of his native song remains with him to this day, even if his repertoire is adulterated by the inclusion of numerous music-hall derivatives of the Scottish sentimental strain. Certain singers with excellent voices find a ready market for their gramophone recordings of this repertoire which may occasionally include a song with some claim to be classed with the true folk idiom, such as 'My Love is like a Red Red Rose' or 'Ye Banks and Braes' or 'Whistle and I'll come tae ye my Lad'. 'Annie Laurie', 'Caller Herrin'' and 'The Auld Hoose' have lost the favour of their pre-war days; but 'Loch Lomond' reigns supreme as the most widely recognized Scottish song, apart from 'Auld Lang Syne'. Folk singers of the calibre of Ewan MacColl and Jeannie Robertson now enjoy an immense public at home and abroad.

The celebrated folk-song collectors of the past century or so could never have suspected that their material would be resuscitated in the middle of the twentieth century and find its most ardent devotees among the young. This phenomenon, of course, is not peculiar to Scotland, it is a contemporary vogue in the English-speaking world, a startling restoration of the old love for the ballad lyric of the British Isles, and its descendants.

If there is still life in Scottish traditional song in the middle of the twentieth century, what was its vitality one hundred years earlier? Still considerable, even if a mere shadow of its former substance, which speaks volumes for the place of the native music in Scottish life in earlier centuries

As regards the favourite songs of the early nineteenth century, at least in the Lowland centres, Peter Mackenzie the genial reminiscer of Glasgow mentions 'Rule Britannia', 'John Anderson my Jo', 'Of a' the airts' 'The Rock and the wee pickle tow', 'Roy's Wife of Aldivalloch' and

'Jenny dang the Weaver'.[3] Of these, only the first and third would be widely recognized today, although all the other tunes are probably also familiar to the wide public for Scottish dance music.

It is interesting to note the songs selected by Queen Victoria for John Wilson's recital during her visit to Taymouth Castle in 1842. 'Lochaber no more' and 'The Flowers of the Forest' were old tunes, the first set to words by Allan Ramsay, the second by Jane Elliot and others. 'Cam ye by Athol' had words by James Hogg, music by Nathaniel Gow's son Neil, and 'The Laird of Cockpen' words by Lady Nairne (Caroline Oliphant, early nineteenth century) to the air 'When she cam' ben she bobbit'. The other songs included were 'The Lass o' Gowrie' and 'John Anderson my Jo', and, by special request, 'Waes me for Prince Charlie', which had words by William Glen (d. 1824) to the tune 'Johnnie Faa'.

John Wilson, incidentally, was the most widely acclaimed singer of Scottish songs in his day. He was perhaps the first of the modern generation of professional specialists in Scottish songs.

The poetic tastes of the Lowland Scottish people tended to sentimentality as the nineteenth century progressed, and what passed for poetry was mostly couthy versifying in feeble imitation of the lyrical example of Robert Burns. Worse still, maudlin replacements of the great master's words were often preferred, as, too, were inferior tunes with familiar clichés. The state of Scottish poetry at the end of the nineteenth century, despite Robert Louis Stevenson, was epitomized by a collection of songs 'for the social circle', called *Whistle Binkie*. Nevertheless, George Douglas Brown was writing his *House with the Green Shutters*, 1901, and Hugh MacDiarmid (C. M. Grieve) was born.

One could not claim 'The Star o' Rabbie Burns' or 'Scotland Yet' or 'The March of the Cameron Men' or 'Angus Macdonald,' which now found a ready ear, as lyrics in the tradition of Scottish song. Rather were they in the tradition of its imitators. Nevertheless, there was an impressive public for collections of Scottish song at home and abroad, and an insatiable appetite for Scottish antiquities and anecdote.

A spate of Scottish song collections began with the success of Robert Smith's *Scottish Minstrel* published in Edinburgh in 1821-4. This encouraged Finlay Dun and John Thomson to publish *Vocal Melodies of Scotland* (Edinburgh, 1836 *et seq.*). Many other collections appeared, of which the most important was the *Songs of Scotland* (Edinburgh, 1848-9) by George Farquhar Graham, reissued with additional notes by John M. Wood in 1884.

The work of harvesting the music of the countryside continued and its results appeared in such works as *Traditional Ballad Airs*, Edinburgh, 1876 and 1881, from the counties of Aberdeen, Banff and Moray, by Dean William Christie; the *Killin Collection of Gaelic Songs*, Edinburgh, 1884, by Charles Stewart; *Ancient Orkeney Melodies*, London, 1885, by David

Balfour; *Vagabond Songs and Ballads of Scotland*, Paisley, 1899–1901, by Robert Ford and the celebrated *Songs of the Hebrides*, 1909, 1917, 1919, by Marjory Kennedy Fraser. In addition, there are important contributions in the publications of the English Folk Dance and Song Society by Lucy Broadwood (*d.* 1939) and Anne Geddes Gilchrist (1863–1948). This work is being continued with the help of the tape recorder by the School of Scottish Studies, Edinburgh University.

So much for the survival of Scottish song tunes into our time; tunes which for the most part are dance tunes, whether they be rendered in their natural dance rhythms or transmuted into slow airs. In addition, we are still left with a considerable corpus of instrumental dance music which, as far as the Scoto-Saxon tongue is concerned, has not been associated with words. Many of the strathspeys, reels, jigs, etc., current in the repertoire of the exponents of traditional dance music in the nineteenth century were original compositions of no great age. Often the composer of a tune was widely known, but perhaps even more often, he was not known and the tune did not reach the printed page. Numerous fiddlers, and pipers, composed dance tunes which, if they were committed to paper at all were only handed round in manuscript. Others printed their tunes for private circulation.

A list of the publications of Scottish dance music during this period will be found in Appendix B, and it will be seen from this that some of the collections which we have already discussed were published, or had editions published, in the early decades of the nineteenth century. One of the most valuable, on account of the number of old tunes it presents in print for the first time, is Captain Simon Fraser of Knockie's *Airs and Melodies peculiar to the Highlands*, Edinburgh, 1816. This work contains a large number of airs which Fraser associates with the period 1715–45.

Towards the end of the century appears the Glen collection gleaned from eighteenth-century sources; it is a most valuable work in that the composers of the tunes are identified where possible and the selection is that of a man of impeccable taste in this music. Then the 'Atholl' collection (1884) by James Stewart Robertson,* which is the largest single compendium of Scottish dance tunes yet printed. Unfortunately, only the composers of a few tunes are identified in it. After these, the *Gesto Collection of Highland Music*, 1895, and the *Skye Collection of the best Reels and Strathspeys*, 1897, both compiled by Keith Norman MacDonald, which contain many tunes appearing for the first time in print.

The Kerr collection (James Spiers Kerr, 1841–83) has no great claim to originality, but has enjoyed wide currency in many editions right into

---

* Robertson, a lawyer, founded the Edinburgh Highland Reel and Strathspey Society in 1881 and was its first president. He hailed from Edradynat, Perthshire, where he was born (1823) and was instructed in Scottish fiddle music by Duncan McKercher.

the present time on account of its diversity and its suitability for the dance repertoire of the late nineteenth and early twentieth centuries.

Numerous manuscripts or fiddlers' tune books are in private collections here and there, many undoubtedly have been lost forever. Of the earlier nineteenth-century unpublished collections, mention must be made of John Hall's Music Book, in Glasgow University Library, Simon Fraser's second collection in Edinburgh University Library and Christie's collection at Aberdeen University. These, however, are only the more distinguishable examples.

The new dancing fashions, quadrilles, polkas, waltzes and galops, spreading to Scotland from continental Europe and England, are first noticed in the high society functions and public dances of the towns and villages. These were patronized predominantly by the young. The traditional occasions associated with the kirn, hiring fairs or weddings in which members of the older generation participated, retained the Reels and Country Dances. While the Quadrille began its conquest of the Lowland assemblies, the Country Dance became more familiar in the Hebrides. Hitherto, the favourite dances in the West Highlands and Isles had been the native reels, including the common Highland Reel for three or four. Towards the end of the century we find the following Country Dances being enjoyed there: Haymakers, Flowers of Edinburgh, Petro-nella, Triumph, Rory O'More, Cumberland Reel, The Queen's Wel-come, Young Prince of Wales—supplemented by Strip the Willow, Glasgow Highlanders and the Eightsome Reel and even the Schottische and Polka, and very often to the music of the bagpipe.[4] Dancing was still enjoyed upon the slightest excuse as of old, at weddings, fireside ceilidhs, Beltane, New Year, or simply on dry moonlight nights at some favourite part of the road or green.

The Reel and Strathspey, otherwise known as the Foursome Reel; the Reel of Tulloch and the Eightsome Reel, held a dominant place on the programmes of the typical Scottish ball despite the intrusion of the Quadrille (particularly in its form of the Lancers) and of the Waltz and Polka in their several forms. Thus even in the nineteenth century, when lovers of the native dance music were reflecting nostalgically on the golden days of the recent past, there was still a large public and social place for the traditional music in the dance.

Nineteenth-century fiddlers

But it was also good music to listen to. A good fiddler could command a considerable audience at concert or ceilidh. Bands of fiddlers joined together to form what were called Reel and Strathspey societies, that in Edinburgh being founded in 1881 by J. S. Robertson, the compiler of the Atholl Collection. These societies were very active in many larger towns

and held annual concerts right up to the Second World War, which
unfortunately seems to have marked the end of this active phase in most
regions.

Some fiddlers joined concert parties which toured the halls and pur-
veyed Scottish music old and new to enthusiastic audiences from Aberdeen to Liverpool and London. This was a new phase and one which has
not yet disappeared, although fiddlers have become scarce and have had a
lean time on the concert platform in the face of competition from the reedy
sonorities of the accordion and the coarsening of popular taste in this
music.

There were still many sensitive and discerning ears for the traditional
fiddle music in the nineteenth century, and still a certain amount of
patronage of good fiddlers among the Scottish gentry, and indeed no
insignificant number of good fiddlers both amateur and professional. The
great names of the previous century, however, seem to transcend those
which follow in their train and doubtless, with the obvious exception of
Niel Gow, these names owe much of their fame to the quality of their
published compositions. One suspects that a number of the nineteenth-
century fiddlers, such as Archie Allan (1794–1837) and James Allan
(1800–77) of Forfar (plate 26), and Charles Grant (1810–92) of Aberlour, were comparable with the best of the previous generation, and if not
in all respects, at least in some. A pupil of Niel Gow's told a Mr J. S
Marshall of Dundee that the nearest approach to Niel Gow's style was
Jamie Allan's performance of Dow's reel 'Bonnie Annie', and James
Scott Skinner (plate 27) who was to surpass all his contemporaries
records that Charles Grant was in his time probably the best exponent of
what he called the 'good auld style'.[5] Another writer in the nineteen
twenties whose father was an enthusiastic fiddler confirms this by saying
that 'the old style of playing Strathspeys never had a better exponent'.[6]

Thus we come to some vague conclusions about the relative merits of
musicians who, before the days of recorded sound, could leave only
reputation. Others, again, like Patie Birnie of old (plate 15), earn their
fame as much by their colourful personalities as by their musical skill
However that may be, certain names come to our attention, in addition
the Allans and Charles Grant just mentioned, and Simon Fraser (plate
24), of whom a president of the Gaelic Society of London once said, '
never heard anyone make the fiddle speak Gaelic so beautifully!' Notice
must be taken of Pate Baillie, James Paterson, Alex Walker, Peter Milne
William Martin, James McIntosh and family, Duncan McKerracher
Archie Menzies, John Strachan, Geordie Donald, James Young, Alex
Skinner, and Charlie Hardie. Some of these are mentioned by Scott
Skinner, who thought that a more tutored technique could have enabled
them to 'soar higher', while they could still, he thought, have rendered
'their country's music by the light of nature'. Certainly it is precisely the

ich Skinner himself contrived to do, and with great success, for his
ne now almost ranks with that of Gow and Marshall in Scottish fiddle-
sic circles.

n considering certain names one is conscious of the possibility that
ne equally worthy musicians are being overlooked because no one
ficiently literate has been available to sing their praises, some 'mute
lorious' Gow indeed! However, starting with the Allans of Forfar, it
uld be noted that Baptie describes Archie and James as brothers, but
s is wrong; they were cousins. Archie was a violin pupil with Barclay
nn (according to Lowson, but more probably Finlay Dun) and Sandy
rray of Edinburgh, and is said to have played in Nathaniel Gow's
d for a time, which is probable. His playing was described by
exander Lowson as clean and neat, and characterized by immense
wer, especially in strathspeys.[7] His best-known composition is the
thspey 'Miss Gray of Carse', familiarly known today as 'Dean
dge'.
Archie died in his prime and was survived by his cousin and pupil,
nes, by many years. James was the son of George Allan, a barber in
rfar, who also played the violin and enjoyed local celebrity for his
ying of jigs. While playing at a 'maiden-feast' or kirn, James ex-
anged fiddles with the farmer and thus acquired his rather beaten
trument which he called the 'shoe'.* This had a superior tone to that
his former instrument and with it he gained most of his laurels as an
tstanding player of reels. In 1856 he was engaged by Julian Adams for
 touring Scottish concert party, as leader of a thirty-piece string band
ich included Duncan McKerracher, one of the many products of the
tive territory of the Gows, and Willie Stewart, another Forfar fiddler.
was Stewart, Lowson tells us, who recalled in later years that he 'never
t onybody that cud tak a grip o' a tune in the way Jamie did'.
The tour, of three months' duration, embraced the principal towns of
gland and Scotland, and set up James Allan as a concert performer, in
ich role he was billed in later years as 'Reel-player to the Earl of
rlie'. He included the Glasgow City Hall concerts in his itinerary and
s succeeded by his two fiddler sons, R. B. Allan who settled in
asgow, and J. S. Allan who was a pupil of Sir A. C. Mackenzie.
testifies to Jamie's local celebrity that in 1894, seventeen years after his
ath, there remained sufficient enthusiasm to honour his memory by the
ction of an inscribed granite obelisk over his grave in Forfar cemetery.
 left a number of compositions in MS. of which the best-known is *The
r of Strathmore*. Some of these MSS. came into the possession of Robert

lastair Steven writes in his publication *Speir* (1969), that he examined this smallish fiddle
d to have been the product of Tom Perry of Dublin) while it was in the possession of a
s MacFarlane, a daughter of the kenspeckle Strathmore dancing master, 'Dancie' Neill,
 whose hands it had fallen after Allan's death.

Scott, a member of the 'Angus Occasionals', a reel and straths)
orchestra which enjoyed a vigorous heyday around the turn of the cent'
and included in its number the vaunted Cameron brothers of the Ki
district. Angus Cameron who is a well-known contemporary fiddler
the Scottish tradition, is a son of one of these brothers. Scott compile
scrapbook of Strathmore fiddlers which is of considerable interest
students of the subject. Also in his possession is his father's fiddle, said
be an Amati, which, in the tradition of the region, was given a name,
this case 'Mysie' (or Maisie).

Turning now to Charles Grant, a farmer's son, born and raised
Strondhu, Knockando, Morayshire, in the Craigellachie district
Strathspey to which William Marshall retired. Being of a scholar
disposition, Charles proceeded to Aberdeen University, from which
graduated in 1827 to become a schoolmaster, first in Elchies then, fr
1841, in Aberlour in the same Craigellachie region he regarded as hor
He was only twenty-six when Marshall died and it is said that he wa
pupil of the great fiddler-composer, and this is very likely, whet]
formally or informally. Marshall's family held Charles in sufficient reg;
to present him with the master's fiddle, in 1851.

Aberlour was a town in Scott Skinner's circuit as a dancing master a
indeed he lived there for a short time, so Charles doubtless had ma
opportunities to meet and share a fiddling session with him, thus bridg}
the eighteenth and nineteenth century generations of Scottish fidd]
through their greatest composers—Marshall and Skinner.

Grant's name suggests other fiddlers of his clan who left an imprint
the memory of Strathspey—Donald Grant, of Grantown, whom c
informant described as the 'best Strathspey and Reel player of his tim
who had two sons 'nearly equal to him', and two brothers, William a
John, distinguished as the 'two Glennies', having been born in Gl
arder, parish of Knockando.[8]

It is often remarked how the skilled musician is not necessarily endow
with commensurate musicianship. Charles Grant had a good word to }
of John Hay of Delldonald on the opposite ground that although he v
not a skilled musician, he played 'so lively that even cripples wh
listening to his playing, were induced to throw away their crutches a
dance'.[2] This, of course, is the highest testimonial possible for a dar
musician.

Charles Grant retired from schoolmastering in 1871 and devoted]
later years to his fiddle and angling rod. He composed about fifty-
strathspeys and reels which were published for private circulation, (
best known of which is 'Belrinnes Strathspey'.

Remaining in the same area and period, James Paterson (1819–(
should be mentioned as the composer of a collection of forty-eight stra
speys, reels, etc., published in Glasgow in 1867. He spent his days a

tailor and teacher of dancing in the region of Gamrie, Banffshire, and is said to have collected upwards of seven hundred tunes from the Northern counties; one wonders what happened to this valuable property.

Born in the same year in Rhynie, Strathbogie, Aberdeenshire, was Alexander Walker, who acquired a knowledge of mensuration and surveying but who devoted himself to gardening and fiddling. He invented instruments for levelling and land-surveying which he intended for the Great Exhibition of 1851, through which he came to the attention of Sir Charles Forbes of Castle Newe who had a residence in Kensington. Thus it happened that Alexander Walker came to lead the music for the Scotch Reels at the great ball given at the Guildhall in London on the occasion of the Exhibition, and attended by the Royal Family and 1,700 guests. Sir Charles thereafter employed him as gardener at Castle Newe from which Alex sallied forth on occasion to join the orchestra at the Queen's Balmoral parties. He published in 1866 a collection of two hundred of his own tunes, dedicated to Sir Charles.

With so much to hold him among his native hills, it comes as a surprise to notice his uprooting himself, at the age of fifty-one, to join his brother in far-off Vermont, and then moving, first near Albany, then to a market garden of his own called Forrestdale in Williamston, Massachusetts. He was still going strong in 1898 as farmer and land surveyor and writing home occasionally to the local newspapers, through which source we learn that he had composed about one hundred and eighty 'melodies in the Scottish style' since going to America. The best known of his earlier compositions is 'The Braes o' Letterfourie'.

Before leaving the North-East, we should notice William Martin (1836–1908) who, though born in East Lothian, served as a schoolmaster at Inverkeithny in Banffshire until he retired to Edinburgh in 1901. His strathspey, 'Mr Martin's Compliments to Dr Keith Macdonald', and reel, 'Mr Joseph Bank', are reproduced in the Skye Collection, and his strathspey 'Mr Murray of Pittendreich' has been a considerable favourite.

Moving now to the 'source of Tay' and the parish of Dunkeld immortalized by Niel Gow, we find James McIntosh (1791–1877) who is said to have been the last pupil of Niel Gow,[10] and his brothers Charles (1797–1867) and Donald (1808–90), and his nephew Charles (*b.* 1836) who played the cello. These McIntoshes were not related to their more illustrious namesake 'Red Bob', nor, likewise, to Red Bob's grand-nephew, James MacIntosh, son of a lint-miller, born at Carsie, 1801, whose claim to fame is as a fiddle-maker. He has been credited with 204 violins, 10 violas and 35 cellos (*cf.* Alastair Steven, *Fiddling around Blair*, Speir, vol. i, 1969), James McIntosh of Dunkeld played in Nathaniel Gow's band; Charles, a hand-loom weaver, enjoyed a widespread teaching practice and led the orchestra on Queen Victoria's memorable visit to Taymouth Castle in 1842; Donald settled in Dundee. Charles junr. resorted to the cello and double bass after he lost the fingers of his left hand and laid some claim to fame as a distinguished field botanist, an avocation he exercised while employed as a post runner over a period of thirty-two years. He published a collection of reels and strathspeys including some original compositions, and his brother, James, led a band in Dunkeld well into the present century.

Another famous Athol fiddler was Duncan McKerracher (1796–1873), the so-called 'Dunkeld Paganini'. His grandson, Mr A. McKercher, who lives in Blairgowrie, told Alastair Steven, to whose researches I am much indebted, that it had been handed down in the family that, as a child, Duncan had danced on a table to Niel Gow's playing. In his later years Duncan procured Niel's cottage in Inver as his home. He made a reputation on the concert platform, where he was wont to appear in a long black coat and tartan sash or plaid. There is a picture of him extant in this garb, wearing in addition his masonic apron. It is said that he wore the apron for the playing of his favourite encore 'The Mason's Apron'.

At the conclusion of a selection he would dramatically throw his arms in the air, fiddle in one hand and bow in the other. Henry Dryerre tells us in his *Blairmore and Strathmore Worthies* (Edinburgh, 1903), that McKerracher was a very poor performer of slow airs, which may have resulted from his peculiar bowing technique, what James Allan called 'that damn'd diddrie-fa style o' McKercher's!' But, surprisingly enough, this did not preclude his developing a good connection as a teacher. He gave lessons to some of the best families in Perthshire and neighbouring counties, and published two collections of dance music, one in 1830 in which the bulk of the tunes were composed by Captain Daniel Menzies. He was very much a Highlander, and very much of a personality. It is believed that his last public appearance was at a concert in Edinburgh, 15th November, 1873.

One fiddler from the Lothians to whom we have referred, and who enjoyed great repute among his contemporaries was Pate Bailie (1774–1841). He is believed to have been raised in Liberton, but lived most of his life in Loanhead, Midlothian, where he followed the trade of stonemason. He also carved spoons and articles in horn and sold them, which led to his being called the 'Fiddling Tinker'. His appetite for the 'barley bree' was in every way commensurate with that expected of one of his avocation in those days, but he had the advantage over most fiddlers (if this is true) in that he could fiddle a reel while flat on his back! We are told that his fingering was remarkably rapid and distinct and that double-stopping was something of a speciality with him. He had the honour of succeeding Nathaniel Gow in playing for functions at Dalkeith Palace, and there his celebrity seems to end. We know nothing of any compositions from his hand, although he is reputed to have published some of his work in 1825. He was succeeded by his fiddling sons, William and Robert, and grandson, Robert Bailie of Pennecuik.

From Dalkeith into the Border valleys seems a natural progression. There we encounter Johnny Pringle who was selected by Lord Minto to lead his lordship's band when he was governor-general of India, and John Howieson of Hawick, son of another celebrated Border fiddler, Adam Howieson, of whom we read in the Hawick records for the years around 1800. Thomas and Robert Rutherford and James Moffat, along with the foregoing, were still remembered in Hawick in the early years of the present century as skilful performers. John Howieson and John Pringle both composed several airs which were favourites in Teviotdale in their time.

Moving to Dumfries, Murdoch tells us that a correspondent to the *Courier* newspaper in 1837 described James Porteous of Meinfoot, Ecclefechan, and Andrew Jamieson of Lockerbie, as celebrated violinists who were then 'far advanced in the vale of years'.[11] This would make them contemporaries of Burns, whom Jamieson apparently claimed to have known. Of wider celebrity in the first half of the nineteenth century, however, was 'Johnstone of Turnmuir' as he was called, a ploughman on his father's farm. It was not unusual for him to be seen leaving his task in the fields to try out some new tune which had taken shape in his head. He joined concert parties in his later years as yet another of the so-called 'Scottish Paganinis', and Murdoch tells us that contemporary journals described Johnstone as the 'chiefest and most noble master of the violin that at any time appeared in these parts', and that a writer who knew the fiddler well claimed that he had no living equal in Scotland, not even in such familiar names as Ralf Gleeson, McLauchlan of Ayrshire or the erratic Pate Bailie. The last named, we have noticed, and there is little we know of the first; James McLauchlan, however, is mentioned by Burns in his *Brigs of Ayr* (1786):

> *O had McLauchlan, thairm-inspiring sage,*
> *Been there to hear this heavenly band engage,*
> *When thro' his dear strathspeys they bore with Highland rage,*
> · · · · ·
> *How would his Highland lug been nobler fired,*
> *And ev'n his matchless hand with finer touch inspired!*

Accompanied by Matthew Hall on the cello, he performed at balls and other occasions throughout the South-West of the country. Hall told the editor of *The Ballads and Songs of Ayrshire*, 1846, that they had in one week 'passed twenty-six parish kirks, and returned to Ayr on Friday to a ball, never getting to bed till Saturday night', and Strang in his *Glasgow and its Clubs* tells us that 'McLachlan and his Bass' were the 'best and only orchestra for the social functions of the Glasgow Gaelic Club in its early days'. Of course, as Burns's lines suggest, McLauchlan (or McLachlan:

both spellings are used) was a Highlander, a fact which would not detract from his favour with the Gaelic Club.

Matthew Hall was a native of Ayr and had been one of John Riddell's pupils (page 58). Originally a fiddler, he later concentrated on the cello, and was associated with McLauchlan in the patronage of 'Sodger Hugh' (page 85). It is evident from Hall's recollections and other circumstances that McLauchlan came to Hugh's attention when he joined the Argyle and Western Fencibles, raised jointly by the Argyll and Eglinton families in 1778, in which Hugh was a Major. It is difficult to see how McLauchlan could earlier have served as a footman to Lord John Campbell at Inverary, as Hall appears to have believed, when Lord John was only about a year old at the time the fencible regiment was formed. It is likely that Lord John is being mistaken for his uncle, Lord Frederick Campbell, who was colonel in that regiment.

In any case, McLauchlan and Hall and 'blind Gilmour from Stevenston' were frequenters of Coilston and Eglinton Castle, and we may be sure Hugh Montgomery was very particular about his musical company. It seems likely, although by no means certain, that John Hall (d. 1862) of Ayr whose *Selection of Strathspeys, Reels* was published in Ayr in 1818 and whose autograph *John Hall, his Music Book* is in Glasgow University Library, was one of Matt Hall's family. Certainly there was a family of Halls in Ayr who maintained high repute as fiddlers in the first half of the nineteenth century.

Other Ayrshire fiddlers of distinction were the Andrews of Lave-mill, near Dundonald, and another celebrated by Burns was the droll and witty Major William Logan, 'thairm-inspirin, rattlin Willie! . . . Hale be your heart! hale be your fiddle! Lang may your elbuck jink and diddle' (Epistle to Major Logan, 1786). He is said to have composed a variety of airs, some of which were so difficult apparently that few would attempt them, and like Sodger Hugh's fiddles and cellos appear to have disappeared through the indifference of the subsequent generation.

By the middle of the nineteenth century, the greatest concentration of strathspey and reel fiddlers of merit was still to be found in the heart of the countryside traditionally associated with the art—the North-East counties and Perthshire—but voices were raised here and there deploring the passing of a great age of fiddlers and fiddler-composers.

The Skinners of Deeside

We turn our attention to the banks of Dee in the county of Kincardine. Here in the first half of the nineteenth century William Skinner is moving up and down Deeside following the profession of itinerant dancing master and fiddler. A correspondent to the *Aberdeen Weekly Free Press* (3rd September 1881) tells us that whenever 'Dancie Skinner' opened a class, in a hall or barn, the young generation and Skinner's older friends mustered to attend. He was, the correspondent adds, 'a first class performer when dancing *was dancing*!' Highland Flings, hornpipes, and the country dances, he says, 'were really exercises'.

William Skinner held his bow in the left hand, having lost most of the fingers of that hand in his youth through an accident with a gun. This accident happened during the old ceremony of shooting off firearms at bridals, causing William to abandon his work as a gardener and seek a livelihood as a 'left-handed' fiddler and dancing master. He was assisted after a time by his son 'Sandy', the 'Alex Skinner' of our list above, and at Banchory, on 5th August 1843, another son, James (plate 26) was born. Little did he suspect that this son was destined to carry the family profession to considerable heights and add lustre to his name, or that he would leave the infant fatherless before eighteen months were out.

Sandy continued to provide for his mother and infant brother, and when the child was about six years of age, gave him his first lessons on the fiddle. We soon find the boy accompanying Sandy on the cello at the local dances and dancing-school balls which were part of their livelihood. And when Sandy did not require his help, James partnered Peter Milne, a kind and genial fiddler, who played at dances in the same territory. All this by the time James was nine years of age. Peter Milne (1824–1908), it should be noted, published a collection of strathspeys containing many of his own compositions.

James's mother now re-married and sent him to complete his meagre education at Connell's School, Aberdeen. It was during this period that he attended a concert in the County Rooms, given by a boy's band known as 'Dr Mark's Little Men', from Manchester. The impression this made on James was to lead him to apply to Dr Mark to become a member of the band. He was accepted, and, with Sandy's support, he left Aberdeen in 1855 at the age of twelve to realize his new-found ambition, to be indentured for six years to Dr Mark and his 'Little Men'.

During his period with the band, James studied with Charles Rougier, an accomplished French violinist and member of the Hallé Orchestra. Engagements with the band carried him all over the British Isles and, in 1858, to a command performance before Queen Victoria and Prince Albert at Buckingham Palace.

But James Skinner's heart was Highland and in dreams he saw the salmon pools of Dee and felt a longing for the kindly faces and tongues of his own people. That he persevered so long in exile in the face of such attachments is the measure of his determination to master his instrument. We might never have suspected the presence of these tensions had he not absconded from the band when but three months were left to complete his tenure. He returned to his mother in Aberdeen with no prospect but to apply himself, in the tradition of his family, to the calling of dancing master and fiddler in his native country. His old mentor, Peter Milne, conducted him to a 'Professor' Scott—dancing masters were commonly called 'Professor' or 'Dancie'—with whom agreement was reached to prepare him for the profession of dancing master, and within a year we find him competing at Highland games as far afield as Belfast and Bray near Dublin. Skinner must have felt a deep obligation to Scott for, on the completion of his studies, he styled himself henceforth, James Scott Skinner. His most memorable success as a competitive Highland dancer, it should be added, was to gain a decision in the Highland Fling over the famous contemporary dancer, John McNeill of Edinburgh.

Fiddle competitions had been fairly common for over a century and in 1863, the year following his venture into dancing, Skinner was awarded first prize in an open fiddling competition at Inverness against some of the acknowledged masters of the time. Despite this impressive performance, it was as a teacher of dancing that Skinner was best known for many years, including in his circuit the Ballater district and numbering some of the children of tenants of the Balmoral estate among his pupils. His work at Balmoral merited the approbation of the great Queen herself, in consequence of which Skinner was honoured with an invitation to dance at a ball in the castle. An 'assembly' usually terminated the course of instruction and so we read in the *Aberdeen Free Press* of Skinner's Balmoral class of children on such an occasion dancing a Country Dance, 'Long Live the Queen', the pupils also singing as they danced 'God Bless the Prince of Wales' and 'The Bonnie Wood of Craigielea'. Then four boys in kilts danced the 'Lonach Highland Fling' and 'Gillie Callum', in a 'masterly style, such as has not been witnessed in this locality before'. The music was provided by James Skinner and his brother Sandy, along with Willie Blair and son, reel players to the Queen and the Prince of Wales, supported by Mr Thomson, Balmoral, on the cello and relieved at intervals by Mr Ross, piper to the late Duchess of Sutherland, and W. McHardy, piper to Ballater Rifle Volunteers.

Willie Blair (1794–1884) was the son of a Crathie fiddler and was known locally as 'The Queen's Fiddler'. He was born in Abergeldie and lived until he was ninety years of age, was tall, stout and 'plain of speech and manner'. He was apparently much addicted to snuff and often set those near him to sneezing when in the thick of a tune he would snort and puff. He was a carpenter by trade and turned his hand to making violins but resorted to the method of accelerating the seasoning of the wood by baking it, which gave good immediate results but led to a decline in quality as the instrument aged. His sons, James and John, were both fiddlers, and John in particular became very accomplished. He lived in Aberdeen, while James succeeded to his father's house in Crathie. We can see that many of the notable fiddlers mentioned here had opportunities to meet and be influenced by each other.

The usual practice of the itinerant dancing master was to remain for a few weeks in any given region on his circuit, teaching every night of the week. In addition, there were private classes for the nobility and special classes for the well-to-do. The evening classes were largely devoted to social dancing, and the well-to-do and labouring classes alternated evening about, each covering the same material but the one costing a guinea and the other 7s. 6d. for a four week series.[12] White gloves were requisite for the guinea classes but not for the others. At Elgin we find Skinner's 'advanced lady pupils' dancing 'La Gorlitza par Delferir', 'Ghillie Callum' and 'Cane Hornpipe', and at Invergordon 'one or two smart boys' dancing the 'Sailor's Hornpipe' and 'Highland Fling'.

Skinner met his first wife, Jean Stuart, while on a brief tour with a concert party and after a short sojourn in Aberlour, took up residence at 95 High Street, Elgin, from which centre he moved out on a circuit embracing Dingwall, Invergordon, Tain, Nairn, Peterhead, Banff, Balmoral, Rothes, Fochabers, Carron, Keith, Forres and Aberlour. He appears to have been assisted by his wife, for in several instances we read of 'Mr and Mrs Skinner's pupils' closing assemblies. He also began to organize his own concert parties with which he toured numerous towns and villages of the North East, and also appears to have found time to provide the orchestra for various balls. Skinner's young son Manson performed as a dancer with the concert parties and we notice that 'Miss Skinner' danced 'the Scotch Jig' at Fochabers Dancing Assembly.

This busy fruitful period was brought to a tragic end by Jean's sudden death after almost twelve years of marriage. James seems to have been very upset by his loss and, returning to Aberdeen in 1883, he abandoned his profession for a time. By now he had published the first of those collections of his works which were to perpetuate his name—twelve new *Strathspeys and Reels* in 1865, thirty more in 1868 and the celebrated *Miller O'Hirn Collection*, 1881, followed by the *Elgin Collection*, 1884, the *Logie Collection*, 1888, *The Harp and Claymore*, 1904, and several others of less importance. He composed many light classical virtuoso pieces in the taste of his time as well as reels, strathspeys and marches.

An introduction to the famous piper and dancer Willie McLennan of Edinburgh led to their forming a concert party for a three-month tour of North America. They set sail for New York with their party of nine, in 1893, inspired by high expectations which seemed fully realized by the resounding success of their first concert. But great must have been their consternation when Willie McLennan, the great Highland dancer, was stricken with meningitis, and died. The tour was first curtailed, then abandoned with great sorrow.

On his return to Scotland, Skinner was married again to Dr Gertrude Park, and took up residence in Monikie, near Dundee. William McHardy, the Laird of Drumblair, near Huntly, placed a rent-free

[9] THE LAIRD O' DRUMBLAIR
J. Scott Skinner

cottage at his disposal, and it was appropriate that it was in this cottage that Skinner composed the best known of his many strathspeys—'The Laird o' Drumblair' [9].

By the turn of the century we find Skinner on tour and making a great success of performing Scottish violin music on the stage. Perhaps his artistic and nomadic life was too big a strain on his new wife, for she left him to emigrate to Rhodesia in 1909. In 1911 he was in London as one of 'The Caledonian Four' at the opening of the London Palladium. The idea for this venture came from Harry Lauder although he was not one of the party. After this and many other successful engagements the manager fell ill and the party broke up.

Scott Skinner was now a household word in the realms of Scottish fiddle music. Through his numerous concert appearances he became known the length and breadth of the land. He projected himself and his music with masterly flourish and aplomb and many recall his cavalier manner of bowing the final chord, flicking the bow from the strings as though to rid it of a surfeit of moisture.

In 1917, at a ceremony in Edinburgh, J. Scott Skinner was presented with his portrait in oils commissioned by his admirers from the eminent artist J. Young Hunter. (It is now in Dundee Art Gallery.) He was proud to number among his friends and admirers Sir Granville Bantock, Professor Blackie of Edinburgh, Sir W. S. Gilbert, Harry Lauder, Si

James Cantlie (a noted Harley Street specialist) and Dr K. N. Macdonald, editor of the *Gesto Collection* of Highland music and the Skye Collection of strathspeys and reels, etc. So, full of honours, he returned to Aberdeen in 1922, after thirteen years of steady concert work. He was a 'weel-kent' and well-loved figure on the Northern concert platforms until about 1925, when, at eighty-two, he felt no longer equal to the task. His last years were clouded by the financial difficulties which had dogged his career. These were relieved somewhat by his being granted a civil pension and by the generosity of his friends. He died on 17th March 1927 and was interred in the presence of a great crowd at Allenvale Cemetery, Aberdeen. Four years later, Sir Harry Lauder there unveiled a handsome granite memorial stone surmounted by a bronze bust of the great fiddler, now affectionately remembered as the 'Strathspey King'.

Shortly before his death, Skinner rashly allowed himself to be 'ower persuadit' and accepted an invitation to compete in a grand fiddling competition in America. There he was mortified to find the accompanist unable to keep up with him and with no knowledge of how to accompany reels and strathspeys. Skinner stopped playing and walked off the plat-form, absolutely refusing to participate further. This long and ill-advised journey doubtless took heavy toll of the aged fiddler's strength.

Skinner's was a long and full life, and fortunately he lived into an age in which his great art could be recorded, however imperfectly, but until his recordings are re-issued in some form, they will be classed as very rare.

Into the twentieth century

J. Scott Skinner takes us into the present century, and the decline in the numbers of fiddlers interested in the 'traditional music', which was evident when that century dawned, has continued. The place of the fiddler in the dancing life of Scotland has disappeared. The Royal Scottish Country Dance Society has done much to restore and re-create the Country Dance; but the dance assembly habits are such that a band is required. The tradi-tional arts exist in an alien environment; they must be protected and nourished by organized action in the way that rare species of animals or birds are preserved. In the case of dancing, however, a way of survival has been found, and with it the music has survived.

Ignorance of this music, however, is as yet too widespread for the dying art of the fiddler to be resurrected. His place in dancing has been largely usurped by the accordion. But this should not and indeed does not apply to listening. Skinner played mainly for a 'listening' as opposed to a 'dancing' audience, so too could the fiddlers of today and tomorrow. Radio has widened this audience, but the B.B.C., despite its great work for British music, has not yet done enough for the great tradition of

Scottish fiddle music.* Despite the neglect, it certainly survives, however tenuously, and leading into the present times, one notes Dr Grant of Banff writing in 1920 that James Henry (*b.* 1877), shoemaker at Macduff and Portsoy, was 'perhaps the finest living player of Scottish reels'.[13] Entering his heyday at this time was James F. Dickie, of New Deer, Aberdeenshire, who was highly esteemed. John W. R. Junner, now of Banchory, whose authority and judgment I respect in these matters, found it thrilling to hear Jamie's renderings of his 'specials' even in more recent times, when he was past his best.

'He was in a class by himself', Mr Junner tells me, 'in such grand tunes as "The Dean Brig o' Edinburgh", "Madam Frederick", "Millhills", "The Braes o' Auchtertyre", "Macpherson's Rant", "The Smith's a Gallant Fireman", etc . . .' He did not turn his hand to composition, but he had his own variations to tunes, which Mr Junner describes as 'absolutely fascinating'.

Likewise Mr Alastair Steven of Blairgowrie draws my attention to some noted Athol fiddlers of this period, such as Joseph Johnston of Rattray who won many of the fiddling competitions which were a feature in Perthshire well into the 1920's, and 'Dancie' Reid, who died still clutching his violin while leading his Kirriemuir dance class in the Sean Triubhas in 1942. Also from the same airt was fiddler Ian Powrie, son of a ploughman at Bendochy Farm, whose Scottish Country Dance band achieved much fame in the 1960's before he emigrated to Australia.

Of outstanding fiddlers still to the fore we must mention the following:

William J. (Bill) Hardie of Aberdeen, believed by certain authorities to be the finest living exponent of the Scott Skinner style. Fortunately he has been recorded by Beltona. Hector MacAndrew, of Cults, Aberdeen, was born at Fyvie early is the century (plate 28). He is an authoritative and very distinguished musician in his native idioms. Having composed over fifty tunes, we must rank him among the hallowed band of fiddler-composers. He has been recorded on Waverley records.

Tom Anderson (plate 29), a native of Shetland and residing in Lerwick, has been very active in preserving his art not only as an exponent in the Shetland style and as a prolific composer, but as a collector and as founder and leader of the Shetland Fiddlers' Association—often referred to as 'The Forty Fiddlers'. He also has been recorded on Waverley Records. Ron Aim (plate 30), has acted in a similar capacity in the neighbouring island of Orkney's Strathspey and Reel Society. Unfortunately he has not been commercially recorded.

Ron Gonnella (plate 31), born at Dundee, brings to bear something of

* A fiddling competition has recently been sponsored by the B.B.C. in Aberdeen with the intention of making it an annual event. It is to be hoped that the adjudicators shall be drawn from those who really understand the Scottish idiom and the traditional art of the fiddler.

the talent of his ancestors on the reels and strathspeys of the adopted land of Stabilini, Urbani and Rizzio. His rendering of Strathspeys is broad and warm and his musicianship sensitive and intelligent. He also has been recorded by Beltona.

The increasing use of the accordion for accompaniment to Scottish Country Dancing and for entertainment purposes has already led to the composing of tunes in the traditional style by performers on that instrument. Just what characteristics will emanate from this is difficult to say at this time, other than to observe that the harmonic character of the accordion and its technical peculiarities must constrain the music in a different way from the violin or bagpipe; similar remarks are appropriate to the piano. Accordionists, admittedly, have not been very prolific as composers and not unexpectedly show marked favour towards jig and reel when the muse inspires them. Pianists appear to be making a greater contribution to the composition of new tunes.

Some recent compositions, however, are disturbing, exhibiting a loss of the old tonality and characteristics of melody essential to the Scottish tune. The giving of a Scottish name to a tune and calling it a 'reel' or 'strathspey' is no justification for classing it with the traditional airs. A simple illustration of what I mean may be provided by treating the well-known Australian tune 'Waltzing Matilda' as a strathspey. The rhythm may be strathspey but the essential characteristic of melody and tonality are absent.

The traditional structure of four- or eight-bar measures and repeats is also intimately wedded to the dance and should be respected. Is it too much to ask that aspiring composers of music in the traditional style should make certain that they know what that style is, absorb its essence, and try to understand it before setting the creative wheels in operation?

CHAPTER 6

Accompaniment to the Dance

We have noted the supreme place of the bagpiper as the purveyor of dance music at all social functions of the ordinary people from medieval times. Most of these functions had to be conducted outdoors or in a large farm building, such as a barn, and that only when it was empty. The fiddle held sway indoors but it is not until the eighteenth century that one sees it really offer serious competition to the bagpipe in popular social dance, and then particularly in the Central Highlands, Breadalbane and Strathspey.

In an old Gaelic song printed by Simon Fraser, 'Feadan glan a' Phiobair' (The Pipe Slang), the noisy rattling piper at a country wedding makes a comparison between the bagpipe and the fiddle. While the fiddle so frequently interrupted the progress of the dancing through the breaking of strings and tuning, his bagpipe chanter could be depended upon. Was it ever known to fail, he asks the 'bonny lasses', while they continued dancing? [1]

But in another Gaelic song in the same collection, 'Mari nighean Dheorsa', this time by a fiddler, Grant of Sheugly, it is claimed that the 'sprightly youth and bonny lasses . . . all declare that at wedding, dance or ball' the fiddle with its bass in attendance had no competitor—'thy music', he claims, 'having the effect of electricity on those who listen to it'. J. Scott Skinner tells us that the cello played 'only *one* drone note at a time' and usually vamped 'giving much character to some tunes'.

This was the most highly favoured combination in the golden age of Scottish dancing. Niel Gow with his brother Donald on the cello formed the most illustrious combination of their time. We read, too, of the Glasgow Gaelic Society balls being served by 'McLachlan and his Bass', [2] and we have seen how Scott Skinner started his career playing bass to Peter Milne and his brother. This, too, as we have also seen, was the combination for which the printed collections were arranged, with, or without, harpsichord.

The harpsichord or spinet were luxury furnishings to be found only in the homes of the more wealthy (plate 16). There, however, dancing reels to the harpsichord was not unknown. In the Farington Diary (23rd September 1801) we read of Mr Bell, a wine merchant in Leith, 'dancing ɔtch reels' with three others, 'with great spirit, one of the ladies playing a Harpsichord'.[3]

t is apparent, too, from some of David Allan's pictures, that the piper ɪnetimes alternated with the fiddler at weddings and the like (plate 17). ɪmetimes the piper was also a fiddler, as was the case with Joseph and ɪrick MacDonald, whom we discussed earlier, and with such burgh ɪsicians as Johnny McGill of Girvan, and John Hastie of Jedburgh:

When bagpipes new fangl'd lugs had tir'd	*A fiddle spring he'd let us hear,*
They'd sneer; then he, like ane in-spired,	*I think they ca'd it ' nidge-nodge-near;'*
Wi's fiddle their flaggin' spirits fir'd,	*He'd gi' a punk, and look sae queer, Without a joke,*
Or e'er they wist;	*You'd sware he spoke words plain and clear,*
Gi' every taste that they desir'd, He never mist.	*At ilka stroke.[4]*

ɪn the absence of the more sophisticated instruments, the Jew's-harp or ɪmp was very popular in the West Highlands, where it was commonly ɪwn as the 'Lochaber Trump'. It is mentioned in the *Complaynt of ɔtland* in the sixteenth century, and its use for dancing in remote St ɪda was remarked by Martin Martin in his book *A Late Voyage to St 'da*, 1698. Even more rudimentary was the paper and comb, resorted to ɪmany a ceilidh in the nineteenth century, a practice doubtless as old as ɪbs and paper.

ɪhe melodeon and concertina were inventions of the nineteenth century, ɪich found ready acceptance in Scotland and Ireland, as did their ɪcendants, the accordions. The dancing in Highland regions today, ɪwever, has become very cosmopolitan, and the music likewise.

The dance orchestra

ɪe development of orchestras to play Scottish reels, strathspeys and jigs, ɔongs to the eighteenth century dance assemblies. In the countryside it ɪs uncommon to find even two fiddlers playing together at social dances. ɪthere were two fiddlers, they preferred to alternate. So we notice in ɪvid Allan's 'Penny Wedding', one fiddler reaching for his stoppan of ɪ while the other plays. The homes of the nobility were not without their ɪlroom with what was commonly known in country parlance as the ɪddler's bike' (the musicians' gallery) but the orchestra was used for the ɪrt dances, the 'pavins', 'gaillyerts', 'currants' and, later, 'minuets'. ɪe music for dancing at the Scottish Court in the sixteenth century was ɔvided by assorted consorts of viols, hautboys, lutes and virginals; but ɪ dances at Court, except for the occasional country round, were not the ɪces of the countryside.

At the formal dancing assemblies which developed in the towns Scotland in the eighteenth century, a fiddle alone was never adequate. 1 constitution of the band was arbitrary but, of course, it had to be able play minuets and gavottes as well as reels, jigs and hornpipes for the R(and Country Dances.

The band at the Edinburgh Assembly in 1747 consisted of four fidd two oboes and one bassoon. The fiddles were John Reoch, Jar Cameron, John Wilson and Robert Hutton; oboes, Thomas Roberts and Charles Calder; and bassoon, John Thompson. There were m; woodwind players in Scotland at this time and the regimental bar employed them. It is very likely that one of the 'fiddles' was a cello.

In the seventeen-seventies and perhaps a little before, the favourite ba at the fashionable assemblies was that of Alexander McGlashan who account of his stately and dressy appearance, as we have seen, was co monly called 'King' McGlashan. William Gow was a member of band and so at one time, apparently, was Nathaniel Gow. WI McGlashan retired from the leadership of the band, William Gow to over and continued with the ensemble until he died in 1791.

It may be of interest to quote the payments awarded musicians for th services at balls in the late eighteenth century as shown by the followir 'St. Michael's Lodge of Freemasons, Crieff, 1783, 27th Dec. to N Gow, 15s., and John McNeell 2s. 6d., and pipers, 5s. each.' This does 1 compare well with that given at the Edinburgh Assembly in 1747, wh the band was paid according to the number of dancers—not exceedi 100 persons, 6s. per player; between 100 and 150, 7s. 6d., over 150, 1 A maximum of 1s. 9d. was allowed the band for 'ale-money'.

As a yardstick we can take the normal earnings of the artisan mas(weaver, or carpenter—6d. per day in 1750 and 1s. by 1790. Ale was . per pint and whisky 5d. per pint. It was therefore possible to beco1 inebriated at small cost and this was borne in mind by the assem| directors.

In 1820 the English dancing master, Thomas Wilson, describes t musician's lot in London:

Their being considered as *obliged* to play for hire for their Employe Amusement, they are frequently treated worse than their servants, a1 never, or seldom spoken too, but in an imperious haughty mann generally addressing them, and speaking of them, by the names fiddlers, endeavouring thereby to shew a superior consequence in the1 selves, and the dependance of the Musicians: or otherwise, adopt t other extreme, and become very familiar, and ply them with Liquor, order to make them drunk, being with those persons a common opini(and saying, that nothing is so amusing as a drunken fiddler, the wh(of the Musicians coming under this title whatever instrument they pl;

This is a base and pitiful advantage, and reflects no credit on those who practice it. That these persons should occasionally drink is no wonder, from the Dust arising from the Room, and great Exertions in playing long Dances; but more should not be forced on them than is needful. Another thing that requires remark, is, that Musicians are seldom payed for their playing, without their Employers complaining of the high price of their Labour; yet these employers never think, that the Musicians cannot find employment for more than five or six months in the year, and that generally in the winter Season, when the weather is bad . . .[5]

I do not think the prestige of the musician ever sank so low in Scotland. For one thing, the people for whom he played had a different attitude to his function. For instance, Niel Gow and his patron the Duke of Athole enjoyed a chief-clansman relationship in character with Scottish society.* Other fiddlers of distinction enjoyed like patronage.

The nineteenth-century band and the pipes

On the famous visit of George IV to Edinburgh in 1822 Nathaniel Gow's band did the honours at the Dalkeith Palace reception and His Majesty is said to have expressed much pleasure in the music. Captain Gronow is mistaking Niel for Nathaniel when in his celebrated *Recollections* (1866) he writes of Niel Gow's orchestra playing at Almack's in 1817.

Not content with his many engagements, Nathaniel held from 1797 until 1830 (excepting 1826) an annual ball of his own, usually in March. This was a lucrative venture and a notice of that of 1810 reveals its popularity: 'Mr Gow's rout (we cannot call it a ball, there being no dancing) on Tuesday, was as usual crowded, with all the beauty and fashion in and about the metropolis'.[6] No band, we can safely say, established such preeminence in the performance of Scottish dance music until recent times.

Of course, by the early nineteenth century, the city dance band had to be able to play waltzes, polkas and quadrilles as well as Country Dances and Highland reels. There were still balls exclusively devoted to Reels or Country Dances such as the Gaelic or Caledonian Society functions held at wide intervals. Dalyell,[7] writing in 1849 of the Edinburgh Highland dance competitions, for which the music was provided by a dance band (!) tells us that many of the tunes 'most effectually enlivening the dance thirty or forty years ago, and then in highest vogue, have been gradually

An interesting letter from a village piper in Ireland to his patron is reproduced by T. Crofton Croker in his *Researches in the South of Ireland*, London, 1824: *Madam, The bearer hereof is the piper that played for your Lordable family at the Terrace on the 12th inst. and I am referred to your Honour for my hire, Your Ladyship's pardon for my boldness would be almost sufficient compensation for my labour. Patrick Walsh.*

falling into oblivion. The sterility of the orchestra being remarkably conspicuous in 1839, a list of twelve former favourites sent to the leader proved almost totally unknown'.

Press notices of balls held by Scott Skinner in the eighteen-seventies in the north-east show his band to vary according to his instrumental resources. At Nairn he had violin, flute, piccolo, piano and cornet; and at Keith Volunteer Ball three violins, cornet and double bass. On another occasion at Keith he had violin, bass, cornet, flute, clarinet, piano. The programme at his dance school ball in Forres 1880 comprised German Schottische and Hungarian Polka; Country Dance, 'Long Live the Queen'; Reel, 'Marquis of Huntly's Farewell'; 'French Quadrille'; Scotch steps, Sword Dance, The Graces, Highland Fling, Cane Horn-pipe, Scotch Medley, Jack Tar, Mazurka, Vals Country Dance, Galop and Reel of Tulloch. This was not of course a typical ball, but it gives us some indication of the curriculum of the typical dancing school in the north-east of Scotland.

Queen Victoria remarked that the band from Glasgow which per-formed at her reception at Inverary Castle in 1874 could not play reels, and that the Reels which interspersed the Country Dances and Schot-tisches had to be danced to a piper. It was customary, however, for the Highland Strathspey and Reel, and Reel of Tulloch to be danced to the bagpipe in Argyll at this period.[8] Indeed, at the annual ball at Kilberry, Argyll, about the turn of the present century, Reels, Schottisches and even Polkas were performed to the pipes, several pipers taking turns to play The pipers, as J. F. and T. M. Flett have reported, determined what was to be danced as the inclination moved them.

It was customary also from the later years of the nineteenth century to very recent times, for a piper to provide the music for the Reels at such balls as the Northern Meeting and certain Caledonian Society balls in various towns.

The modern dance band and the accordion

For the origin of the modern Scottish dance band, as we will call the band specializing in Scottish traditional dance music, we must look to the so-called bothy bands and Irish ceilidh bands of the early years of the century. The bothies were the Scottish bunk-houses for farm labourers at potato lifting ('howkan') or harvest ('hairst'). Ensembles of this kind included marches, 'Valeta', 'Military Two-Step' and similar popular dance tunes in their repertoire. But as the nineteen-twenties progressed, the development of broadcasting and the work of the Royal Scottish Country Dance Society (founded in 1923), proved that there were thousands of Scots who were deeply attached to the Reels and Strathspeys of the native land, and not averse to numerous Irish interpolations.

The Piper to the Laird of Grant, 1730, the oldest known picture of a three-drone Highland bagpipe. Original painting in the Earl of Seafield's collection.

A reel in a kitchen at a social occasion in the eighteenth century. When the women took their rocks or distaffs it became a spinning party or 'a rocking', the title of A. Maclure's painting (c. 1840). Engraving by H. Robinson for Whitelaw's *Scots Songs*, 1884.

3 James Livingstone, piper of Haddington, and Andrew Simpson, town drummer, uniformed in 'ane doublet of Lyonis cameis, ane pair of blue breeks, and schone'; Harry Barrie, the town simpleton, follows. The single-drone bagpipe and swesch was still well known in Scottish burghs in the eighteenth century. Drawn by Rob Mabon, a local artist, about 1770.

4 A Scottish shepherd with stock-and-horn, piobcorn or hornpipe, illustrating a scene in Allan Ramsay's ballad opera, *The Gentle Shepherd*, engraved after a painting by Sir David Wilkie, 1823.

5 The 'Queen Mary' clarsach, presented by Mary Queen of Scots to Beatrice Gardyn. 31 in.

6 Rebec, rybab or rybid, a popular medieval member of the fiddle family. 22 in.
7 Crwth, bowed cruit or crowd, mentioned by Giraldus, twelfth century. 22 in. 8 Kit, a narrowed-down fiddle, eighteenth century. 15¾ in.

9 An eighteenth-century stock-and-horn. 25 in.

10 Old bagpipe with two drones. The common stock is engraved with the letters 'RMcD', a galley (borne or quartered in Arms of the Macdonalds) and date 1409.

11 Three-drone Piob Mór or Great Highland Pipe (nineteenth century) from a diagram in C. N. M. North's *Leabhar Comunn nam Fior Ghael*, 1881–2. Upper drone, 32 in.; the blow-pipe is vertical, chanter *right*.

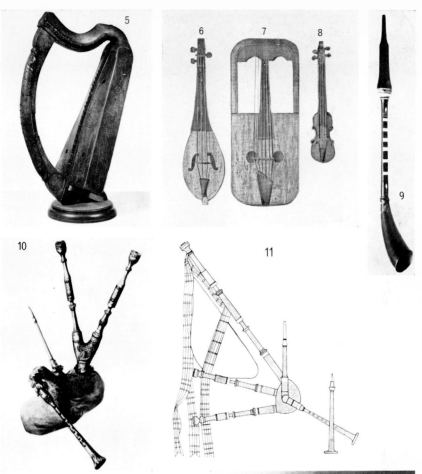

12 Irish piper from Derrick's
Image of Ireland, 1581.

13 English piper from Hogarth's
engraving 'Southwark Fair', 1737.

14 Scottish piper with Border or Lowland
bagpipe, with bellows under the right arm.
Engraving after Sir David Wilkie, 1813.

15 Patie Birnie, born about 1635, a fiddler of Kinghorn, Fife, has 'a face mingling cleverness, drollery, roguery and impudence' (Robert Chambers). Engraving after William Aikman.

16 The spinet, a square-shaped harpsichord, w 'bass' (violoncello) accompaniment, a favourite co bination for Scottish dance music among nobil and gentry in the eighteenth century. An illustration Ramsay's *Musick for Scots Songs in the Tea-T Miscellany*.

17 'The Highland Dance'. Niel Gow accompanied by his brother Donald on the 'cello at a occasion on the Athol Estate in the summer of 1780. The older man filling his pipe may be Mu Abercairney. The piper is refreshing himself in the background, ready to relieve the fiddlers. Dona the old violer's way of holding the bow. Painting by David Allan, 1780.

18 Niel Gow (1727-1807), born at Inver, near Dunkeld, the most celebrated fiddler in the golden age of Scottish fiddling, father of a distinguished family of fiddlers-composers. He wears his customary habit. Portrait by Sir Henry Raeburn, 1787.

19 Frontispiece of Niel Gow's *Fourth Collection* in his series of Strathspey reels, 1800, dedicated to the Earl of Eglinton and obtainable from 'the Author at Dunkeld and John Gow, No. 31 Carnaby Street Golden Sqr. London'.

20 Hugh Montgomerie, twelfth Earl of Eglinton (1749-1819), an enthusiast in Scottish dance music, whom Burns called 'Sodger Hugh'. Painting probably by J. S. Copley, *c.* 1780.

21 Lucy Johnston of Hilton (1765-97), a composer of reels, a belle of the Edinburgh Dance Assembly, much admired by the Gows, Mackintosh and Burns—'Her motions all accompanied with grace; And Paradise was open'd in her face'.

22

23

24

22 William Marshall (1748–1833), 'first composer of strathspeys of the age'. 23 Nathaniel Gow (1766–1831), 'Royal Trumpeter', composer and publisher. 24 Capt. Simon Fraser of Knockie (1773–1852) made famous collections.

25 James Allan (1800–77), most distinguished member of a family of fiddlers. 26 James Scott Skinner (1845–1927), dancing-master, fiddler and composer. 27 William J. Hardie (b. 1898), leading exponent of the Scott Skinner style.

31

32

33

28 Hector MacAndrew, born at Fyvie, distinguished member of a fiddling family. 29 Tom Anderson of Lerwick, fiddler-composer, exponent of the Shetland style. 30 Ron Aim of Kirkwall, leader of the Orkney Reel and Strathspey Society.

31 Ron Gonnella of Dundee, fiddler, sensitive performer of reels and strathspeys. 32 Jimmy Shand of Auchtermuchty, most celebrated pioneer of the accordion-based band. 33 Stan Hamilton of Ayr and Toronto, band-leader pianist.

34 The Montgomerie's Rant at a Royal Scottish Country Dance Society ball in Edinburgh, 1956, with Tim Wright's band in the 'fiddler's bike'.

35 The Deuks dang ower my Daddie, a Scottish Country Dance at a semi-formal ball at the University of Western Ontario, 1966, with Stan Hamilton's band (R. Brown and R. Frew, accordions).

Since that time thousands of enthusiasts have studied the Scottish Country Dances and now not only perform them regularly at classes promoted or inspired by the Society but organize and attend balls exclusively devoted to them, throughout Britain and the Commonwealth. This is particularly true of Canada which, in so many respects, can be regarded as an extension of Scotland in North America. Something of the same can be said of New Zealand.

The accordion, in virtue of its greater volume of sound, the variety of its chording and its relative simplicity, has now largely supplanted the violin in Scottish dance bands. It cannot be said that it can supplant the violin in execution, but one accordion will suffice in a busy ballroom where three violins would be required. Much of the Scottish dance music, nevertheless, is violin music, and the wide leaps, slurs, and sharp contrasts of this are impossible on the accordion. Neither violin nor accordion, however, has the percussive power of the piano, but compensation for this can be made in a band. The piano may not be thought a suitable instrument for reels and strathspeys; but it is just as suitable as its more portable keyboard relative, the accordion. Much, however, depends upon the skill of the performer. One celebrated exponent of Scottish dance music on the piano, known to me, can make one forget that the violin has a tone quality, a flavour, that centuries of music-making have recognized, and which make it, in talented hands and in intimate surroundings, the most moving and eloquent vehicle of the slow air or strathspey.

It can probably be said that there is a growing tradition of playing Scottish—and Irish—dance music on the accordion. Although an accordion performance can be exciting, I find it difficult to imagine one being moved by it. There are two specific classes of the instrument, commonly distinguished by their fingerboard, 'button' or 'piano', and many different makes, German, Austrian or Italian. The tone-colour of the instrument varies according to its construction and, in addition, each instrument has 'couplers' analogous to the 'stops' in the organ or harmonium, which alter range and tone colour within certain limits.

The most successful of the pioneers of the accordion-based Scottish dance band was Jimmy Shand (plate 32) of Auchtermuchty in Fife who dominated the field from the nineteen-thirties into the nineteen-sixties. He and his many successors have been recorded on gramophone records which have brought their performances before a vastly wider public than that enjoyed by any band or performer in the past. There are now numerous bands of this type, usually identified by their leaders. Ian Powrie, Bobby Macleod, Alastair Downie, Andrew Rankine and Tim Wright are notable names of recent years, while Stan Hamilton's band is reaching new heights of a highly musical order in performing for dancers as well as entertainment.

Only a few of the modern Scottish dance band leaders have any deep awareness of their material or indeed any musicianship of the quality associated with the great fiddler-composers. Some are very limited not only in repertoire of tunes but in ability to arrange sequences of contrasting but related tunes, and to use a wide range of keys. Much depends upon whether the band is performing for listening or dancing. For Country Dances, for instance, the selection of tunes and tempo of performance are very important, the one to maintain interest and the other to facilitate comfortable dancing. The nature of each dance has a bearing on both and demands some very special knowledge on the part of the arranger of the music; knowledge of the character of the dance and a large repertoire of tunes.

A typical combination for the modern Scottish dance band would be two accordions, piano, and double bass and drums, with a violin (or violins perhaps) or a trumpet, or both. The advent of electronics has solved the problems of inadequate volume of sound, and most bands now use amplifiers in public. More than a little musical vulgarity is creeping, nay striding in, and there is some loss of grasp of the idiom and modal structure of the traditional Scottish tune, but at least there is a public for the music such as would astonish any Scot living at the turn of the century.

CHAPTER 7

The Elements of Scottish Traditional Dance Music

The rhythms involved in Scottish traditional dancing are popularly classed as reel, strathspey, hornpipe, and jig. The subject is surprisingly difficult to discuss because the terms 'reel' and 'hornpipe' can mean many different things.

Evidence indicates that the term reel was originally used in Scotland to refer to any communal dance. This generic use of the term remains with us, but it is confused by its familiar use with reference to a specific dance, or class of dance, more properly called the 'Highland Reel' or 'Scotch Reel', and with reference to the music for that dance. In medieval times, the most distinctive figure in the communal social dances of the country-side was the interweaving figure which we call reel today, and which was called reel or 'haye' in medieval Scotland. Thus reel can be used of any communal social dance, of a specific dance, of a specific figure and of dance music.

Reel and hornpipe

With respect to music, the term reel, today and at least for the past three hundred years, is reserved for the quadruple-time music associated with the 'Highland' or 'Scotch' Reel; but it should not surprise us to encounter folk dances called Reels, as in the Hebrides, which are performed to 6/8 and 9/8 jigs. The major part of Scottish dance music, however is in 4/4 or 2/4 and is commonly catalogued in two principal categories—reel and strathspey. Most so-called reels, however, are more precisely 'rants', as we shall see. The Scottish measure is another category of the same but is not suitable for the 'Highland Reel' as a dance and therefore is usually distinguished from reels in the dance music collections. All, however, were used for Country Dances, and many of the early publications of Scottish dance music are described as collections of reels *or* country dances, i.e. music for Reels or Country Dances.

Similarly, with the word 'hornpipe'. This is the name of a particular reed-pipe called the stock-'n-horn in Lowland Scotland. It is also the name for a step-dance, or, in modern parlance, a 'tap' dance. The music to which this was commonly executed in those parts of England where it was most popular was of a peculiar jaunty limping-gait of a rhythm under the time signature of 3/2, or sometimes 6/4 or 3/4. Nor was the word hornpipe used of any other class of tune until later in the eighteenth century. Any step-dance, however, tended to be called a hornpipe even if it were performed to a jig. The 'hornpipe' which Nancy Dawson danced in the *Beggar's Opera* in the seventeen-sixties, and for which she earned so much fame, was performed to a jig tune, called 'Nancy Dawson's Hornpipe' in contemporary music publications, although later the title was usually shortened to 'Nancy Dawson' [10].

[10] NANCY DAWSON

The hornpipe as a dance was originally associated with shepherds (as was the instrument) and this seems to suggest that the link between the instrument and the dance lies in the possible habit of shepherds stepping out the jaunty rhythm to their own playing. Country dances to hornpipe tunes were certainly familiar in Elizabethan times. The steps in the country hornpipe-round were doubtless of the 'treepling' variety familiar in Scottish rural country dancing within living memory [1] and to be encountered among English sword dancers and in North American square dancing.

The class of tune familiarly thought of when the word 'hornpipe' is used today, is that to which the solo step-dance 'Sailor's Hornpipe' is performed and of which 'College Hornpipe' [88] is the most familiar example; the Irish probably think first of their own hornpipes. This style of hornpipe tune is in common time and bears only slight resemblance to the original triple-time hornpipe tune which enjoys no practical dance use today. It is considered further on page 122.

The hornpipe as an instrument was referred to by its Gaelic name in the Gaelic regions of Britain, but not so the dance form or the music. The Irish have a step dance they call 'hornpipe', not *piobcorn*. It is curious, too, that whereas the hornpipe as an instrument was familiar in Anglesey in the eighteenth century, the style of music called 'hornpipe' has no evident association with that island nor with the mainland of Wales, yet it does have associations with Lancashire not far away.

To move from the 3/2 hornpipe to the 9/8 jig seems natural; both are in triple time, i.e. beating three to the bar. The 6/8 jig, although constructed of triplet rhythm, beats two to the bar, not three. The jig is related in turn to the slow Gaelic airs, Irish and Scottish, in triple time, which, in recent years, in Scotland have been vulgarly called 'Scottish Waltzes'. These tunes are of the character of the ancient 'ports' of the harp. The tune of Burns's 'Ae Fond Kiss' is a good example, as also is the well-known and beautiful air 'Mairi ban Og'.

[11] LESLIE'S LILT
Skene MS. Dauney's *Ancient Scotish Melodies*, 1838

[12] LADY ROTHEMAY'S LILT
Skene MS. Dauney's *Ancient Scotish Melodies*, 1838

The mention of slow triple-time tunes brings to mind the 'lilts' in the Skene MS. *c.* 1620. 'Leslie's Lilt' [11] is one, but strangely 'Lady Rothemay's Lilt' [12] in the same MS. is in common time. Henry Farmer refers to the lilt as a dance, but this is pure conjecture. Certainly the tune 'Leslie's Lilt' has something of the grace of the minuet, although that dance was not introduced until at least thirty years after. There is nothing 'traditional' in the character of the lilts in the Skene MS.; they are simply pleasant lute tunes of the nature of songs without words, and, of course, this is the sense in which the word 'lilting' is used in Scottish poetry. In Ireland the term is particularly used of a form of mouth-music, although a dance called 'Irish Lilt' was performed on the early eighteenth-century London stage.

The relationships between the various categories of dance tune lead to the easy conversion of tunes from one rhythm into another, and many Scots and Irish tunes can be discovered in different guises because of this. Nor should this particularly surprise us when we recall that even in the days of stately risings and fallings and sprightly caprioles, it was not uncommon to find pavanes played as galliards or saltarellos, the pavane being simply an andante treatment of the same rhythm.

British traditional dance idioms

The traditional dance music of the British Isles, as one would expect, comprises a common body of rhythms, with certain individualities super-imposed by the constituent regions. Thus we have Irish and English, and perhaps Scottish, jigs; triple-time hornpipes peculiar to England; reels peculiar to Scotland and others peculiar to Ireland and including what could be called common-time hornpipes. The varieties of individual utterance in music are not dissimilar to those of speech. It is certain that in earlier times, several regions of Scotland retained something of their own diction in music as well as speech. This was true of the Highlands and Lowlands in broad division, of course, but also within the Highlands in Strathspey, Breadalbane, Athol, Skye, the Hebrides (even between islands), and Sutherland; and also within the Lowlands in Moray, Kin-cardine, the Lothians, Galloway, Roxburgh, and the particularly Norse islands of Orkney and Shetland.

These regions expressed something of their own individuality in styles of performance and taste.* Tunes were widely shared and crossed the natural and national frontiers with ease. The familiar jig 'Cock o' the North', became the Irish 'Auntie Mary' or the English 'Joan's Placket' [83]; and the reel called 'Bob o' Fettercairn' or 'Had I the Wight' in Scotland, is embroidered with *arpeggi* when it moves into the repertoire of

* Even in the nineteenth century, as Henry Dryerre tells us, there were 'pervervid advocates of Perthshire, Aberdeenshire, Fifeshire and Forfarshire styles of playing (*Blairgowrie an Strathmore Worthies,* Edinburgh 1903), and we are told by Jamie Allan's most distinguishe pupil, J. S. Marshall of Carnoustie, that Jamie's playing of strathspeys and reels was ' happy medium between the Edinburgh style and that of the Highlands' (Alexande Lowson, *Portrait Gallery of Forfar Notables,* Forfar [1880]).

the Northumbrian pipes, and takes the name 'Newburn Lasses'. Like-wise 'John Paterson's Mare' becomes the 'Black and the Grey', and 'Struan Robertson' becomes 'Cuckold come out of the Amrey'. It all represents a great heritage of music, which has spilled over its original boundaries and is now to be found in the common currency of folk musicians in all the settlements with which the British have been asso-ciated the world over. In tracing the origins of the traditional streams to which these countless airs belong, one can still discern the distinction drawn by Giraldus in the twelfth century between the Irish and Scots on the one hand and the English and Welsh on the other. The same division is valid in the art of dance.

The instruments which have exerted most influence on Scottish dance music are the fiddle and the bagpipe in its several forms. Remembering that the chanter of the Highland pipes was only of nine degrees compass we can certainly identify tunes which are likely to have been composed for that instrument, or identify tunes which could not have been. We must always remember, however, that the human voice also has exerted an influence.

Despite the common influences on the various styles of Scottish dance music, which obscure the categories, we must distinguish between them, as far as we can. It will be best, therefore, if we consider the basic cate-gories in turn, beginning with the hornpipe since that is the term most frequently applied to the indigenous dances of the British Isles.

Triple-time hornpipe

When we consult those collections of Country Dances and country tunes which were published so generously in England during the seventeenth century, we notice the use of such terms as jig-hornpipe, hornpipe-jig and bagpipe-hornpipe as well as, simply, *hornpipe*. These, as we have remarked, are in a distinctive rhythm under the time signature 3/2, 6/4 or 3/4. One in *Apollo's Banquet*, 1663, called a hornpipe-jig is in 9/4. Such, then, were the hornpipes of England, thriving with particular virility in the counties of Derby, Nottingham and Lancaster.

Handel and Purcell both regarded the triple-time hornpipe as a charac-teristically English rhythm and employed it in certain of their works. Stenhouse, the industrious annotator of *The Scots Musical Museum*, wrote (*c.* 1824) that tunes of the category of 3/2 hornpipes had been played in Scotland 'time out of mind', and that James Allan, piper to the Duke of Northumberland, had assured him that this 'particular measure originated in the borders of England and Scotland'. This we can well believe as it is in these districts that the rhythm has survived longest. It obviously enjoyed a wider currency in former days; but it is not to be found in the music of the Gael.

The earliest *printed* hornpipe is a remarkable keyboard composition by Hugh Aston (*c.* 1525).[2] Then came the 'traditional' examples in Playford's publications, and a valuable collection of 'Original Lancashire Hornpipes' by John Ravenscroft, dated 1705, of which John Hawkins reproduced some examples. Hawkins tells us that Ravenscroft (*d.* 1745) was a very corpulent man and one of the waits of the 'Tower Hamlets' in London, and that he was much sought after to play at balls and dancing parties and 'was singularly excellent in the playing of hornpipes in which he had a manner none could imitate'.[3]

A compilation of hornpipes bearing the same title as Ravenscroft's was published by one Thomas Marsden about 1697, but this appears to have been lost.[4]

The best known surviving lyrics in this metre are 'The Dusty Miller' [13], 'Robin Shure in Hairst', 'Go to Berwick Johnnie', 'Jockey said to Jenny' and 'Dance to your daddie':

> *Dance tae y'r daddie*   *And ye'll get a fishie,*
>   *My bonnie laddie,*   *In a wee wee dishie,*
> *Dance tae y'r daddie*   *And ye'll get a fishie,*
>   *My bonnie lamb!*   *When the boat comes hame.*

This, of course, is a 'nursery' setting of the tune, and there are others; but even the more adult lines tend to be humorous. The rhythm, it seems, wears a perpetual smile.

> *Hey, the dusty millar and his dusty coat,*
> *He will win a shilling or he spend a groat,*
> *Dusty was the coat,*
> *Dusty was the colour,*
> *Dusty was the coat that I gat frae the millar.*

Hawkins writes (1776) that '. . . the measure of the Hornpipe is triple time of six crotchets in a bar, four whereof are to be beat with a down, and two with an uphand'. It lends itself to syncopation, perhaps its most noticeable—and attractive—characteristic. Certainly, this does not find expression when the tune is constrained to a framework of words, but when treated instrumentally, the propensity for syncopation becomes evident.

The hornpipe's propensity thereto is illustrated in an early version of 'The Dusty Miller' [14] and an un-named example [15] from the Patrick Cumming MS. of 1723, in the Scottish National Library, both of which we reproduce here. Dauney states that 'The Dusty Miller' appears as 'Binny's Jig' in the Blaikie MS., usually dated 1692 [5], but the similarity is apparent only in the first strain.

An example taken from the second Gow collection, 'The Marchioness of Tweed-dale's Delight' [16], which is to be found in the Bodleian

[13] THE DUSTY MILLER
Kershaw MS, Lancashire. *c.* 1820

(Early copies show crotchet in place of two quavers at position of stars)

[14] As a jig
Elizabeth Maclachlan's *First Border Dance Book*, 1931

[15] UN-NAMED HORNPIPE
Patrick Cumming MS, Edinburgh, 1723

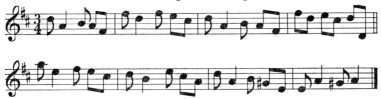

[16] THE MARCHIONESS OF TWEED-DALE'S DELIGHT
or 'The Keys of the Cellar'
Niel Gow's *Second Collection*, Second Ed., 1803

Country Dance MS. as 'The Keys of the Cellar' is especially interesting in this respect and is also reproduced here. If each minim in this tune can be replaced by two crotchets, the rhythmic motif stands out, ♩ ♩̂ ♩̂ which obviously provides a link between the 3/2 hornpipe and its namesake in 4/4. An attempt to convert a triple-time hornpipe into jig rhythm is illustrated [14].

Country Dances to triple-time hornpipe were still performed well into the eighteenth century, but it enjoyed no hold in Scotland and has been unknown there since that time as the music for any form of dance.

The Scottish double hornpipe

Scottish step dances to the native common-time dance tunes were sometimes distinguished as 'Double' Hornpipes in the late eighteenth and early nineteenth centuries.[6] Thus *Sean Triubhas* was classed as a 'double hornpipe', so also *King of Sweden*, in the dancing schools. (Alan Cunningham in his Scottish Songs, 1825, refers to 'Shaun truish Willighan' as a 'popular hornpipe air'.) The term double was used, presumably, to distinguish step dances to quadruple-time tunes from those to the triple-time hornpipe, sometimes called the 'single' hornpipe.[7]

The Irish use the terms single and double with respect to reels and hornpipes, but here the distinction is not one of rhythm, as in the Scottish instance, but of tempo.

The Scottish dance tunes in quadruple time, although used for the native step-dances sometimes classed as 'hornpipes', are better not referred to as hornpipes at all. The principal classes have names which adequately distinguish them—'Scottish measure', rant and strathspey. Most so-called reels are a class of rant, conforming to the general structure of the rant. The local characteristics which may have distinguished a Skye reel from a Sutherland reel are too obscure for us now to identify. Only the Strathspey reel is clearly distinguishable to most musicians and dancers today.

The Scottish measure

The earliest identifiable Scottish common-time dance tune (or double hornpipe) in the published and manuscript sources, conforms to the class later identified as 'Scottish measure'. This name is not found in print prior to Playford's *Collection of Original Scotch Tunes (Full of the Highland Humours)*, 1700, which we considered earlier. The earliest recorded use of the term, as far as I have been able to discover (and I have searched diligently) is 'Maclean's Scots Measure' in the Blaikie MS. In the eighteenth century it appears in several collections both as part of the title of a tune, e.g. 'Watson's Scotch Measure' or in description of a tune as 'Dumbarton's Drums—a Scottish Measure'. There are inconsistencies in this practice, in that a tune which is obviously a Scottish measure sometimes appears undesignated as such in the same collection as takes pains to designate others of the same class. Then, McGlashan designates 'Wap at the Window' as a Scottish measure, although it is a jig! However, we must always be on our guard for printer's errors.

The basic characteristic of the Scottish measure is the emphasis on the first three beats of the bar, the phrase beginning on the 'up' beat viz.:

$$ \text{♫} \mid \text{♩ ♩ ♩} \quad \text{or} \quad \text{♫.} \mid \text{♩ ♩ ♩} $$

The second and third beats are frequently stressed in certain bars in the phrase by being on the same note; the phrase usually ending on the triple repetition of the final note—*pom-pom-pom*. The rhythmic motifs

$$ \text{♫} \mid \text{♩ ♫♩ ♫} \quad \text{and} \quad \text{♫} \mid \text{♩ ♩ ♩} $$

constantly recurring and underlying the tune even where they are not overtly expressed.

Good familiar examples of this are: 'The White Cockade' [17], 'Petronella' [18] and 'Dumbarton's Drums' [19]. Further examples, though perhaps not so familiar, which are worthy of study are 'Corn Rigs' [22], 'The Blue Ribbon Scottish Measure' [24] and 'Watson's Scotch Measure' [26]. The prototypes of these are to be found in *Apollo's Banquet* and, in the case of 'Dumbarton's Drums' and the 'Blue Ribbon Scottish Measure', also in the Skene MS., *c*. 1620. Compare 'Sawney' [23] (i.e. 'Sandy') in *Apollo's Banquet* with 'Corn Rigs' [22] from the *Scots Musical Museum* over a century later. Also a 'Scotch Tune' [21], reproduced here from *Apollo's Banquet*, should be compared to 'Dumbarton's Drums' [19] from Gow and 'I Serve a Worthie Ladie' [20] from the Skene MS.

'Watson's Scotch Measure' can be traced to the *Gude and Godlie Ballates*, 1567, through the title of a song with which it was associated, 'O, an ye were dead gudeman'. Of course there is no written record of the music associated with the song at that early date. In more recent times it is the tune associated with Burns's 'There was a Lad', although Burns used it for 'A Highland Lad my Love was born' (which now is commonly set to 'The White Cockade'). Through this, our attention is drawn to the close affinity between 'Watson's Scotch Measure' and the 'White Cockade'. However, the 'Duke of Buccleugh's Tune' [27] in *Apollo's Banquet* (sixth ed.), is obviously an early version of 'Watson's Scotch Measure'.

Another interesting tune of the category of Scottish measure in the Skene MS. is 'Pitt on your shirt on Monday' [28] which, with its long closing run of quavers, hints at the 'Jacky Tar' class of hornpipe of over a century later.

Two imitation Scottish tunes, from *Apollo's Banquet,* one by Purcell, [92], and the other entitled 'Scotchman's Dance' [56], are presented here for comparison with the above. It will be seen that they are of the same genre.

As regards the name Scottish Measure, it seems unlikely that the Scots would themselves create the term. Nor can we claim the Scottish measure as a Lowland class of tune without being brought up sharply by the recollection of such tunes as 'Highland Laddie' [29], 'The Peat Fire Flame' and 'Mairi's Wedding' from the Hebrides.*

Was the Scottish Measure the name of a dance? There are suggestions that it was a Scottish 'twosome'. Although there is much to suggest that the term Scottish Measure was the name of a social dance, no one has left any mention of it as such. A study of London playbills shows that a dance of this name was performed on the London stage in the years 1750–1757, and on an isolated occasion by Fishar the ballet master in 1775.

If the Scottish Measure was indeed a twosome social dance it may well have acquired its name by analogy with the 'English Measure' or what were called 'the Measures' at the Courts of Elizabeth and James—the basse dance and the pavan—although these had given way to the 'Coranto' and minuet by the time the term Scottish Measure first appeared in written record. On the other hand, the word measure may relate to the rhythm of the music; the drum accompaniment to the pavan,[8] strikingly enough, is suggestive of that of the Scottish measure:

Did either or both of these analogies lead to the adoption of the name Scottish Measure?

* Robert Burns refers to the Scottish measure, 'Dumbarton's Drums' as a 'West Highland' air in his MS notes (appended to James C. Dick, *The Songs of Robert Burns.* Hatboro, Pa., 1962).

[17] THE WHITE COCKADE
Atholl Collection

[18] PETRONELLA
Gow's *Repository*, Part Fourth, 1817

[19] DUMBARTON'S DRUMS
Gow's *Repository*, Part Second, 1802

[20] I SERVE A WORTHIE LADIE
Prototype of 'Dumbarton's Drums'
Skene MS. Dauney's *Ancient Scotish Melodies*, 1838

[21] 'SCOTCH TUNE' [DUMBARTON'S DRUMS]
John Playford's *Apollo's Banquet*, Sixth Ed., 1690

* Bar missing on original

[22] CORN RIGS
Fiddle set from Atholl Collection, 1884

[23] SAWNEY
Prototype of 'Corn Rigs'
John Playford's *Apollo's Banquet*, Fifth Ed., 1687

[24] THE BLUE RIBBON SCOTTISH MEASURE
Gows' *Repository*, Part First, 1799

[25] BLUE RIBBENN AT THE BOUND ROD
Skene MS. Dauney's *Ancient Scotish Melodies*, 1838

[26] WATSON'S SCOTCH MEASURE
Gow's *Repository*, Part First, 1799

[27] THE DUKE OF BUCCLEUGH'S TUNE
Prototype of 'Watson's Scottish Measure'
John Playford's *Apollo's Banquet*, Sixth Ed., 1690

[28] PITT ON YOUR SHIRT ON MONDAY
Skene MS. Dauney's *Ancient Scotish Melodies*, 1838

[29] HIGHLAND LADDIE
Gow's *Repository*, Part Second, 1802

It is a peculiarity of instrumental dance tunes that they are often named after people, e.g. 'The Earl of March's Pavane' and 'Mrs MacLeod's Reel'. This is notably true of the 'Scottish Measure'. We have noted the titles included in Henry Playford's *Collection*, 1700 (page 53). In the McGlashan Collection of Scots Measures, of the late eighteenth century, we find the name of 'Watson's', 'Miss Andy Campbell's', 'MacLach-lan's', 'Invercauld's' and, of particular note, 'Pique's Scottish Measure'. Pique was the name of a well-known dancing family of whom one was a teacher of dancing in Edinburgh in the seventeen-sixties. It seems probable, too, that Watson and MacLachlan may have been dancers or musicians, otherwise the 'Mr' would have been inserted. The 'Maclean Scots Measure' in the Blaikie MS. could be another of this kind, for at that time there was a notable Edinburgh dancing master called Maclean.

Clearly it was tunes of the character of Scottish measures which were to English ears 'full of the Highland humours', as Henry Playford expressed it in the sub-title of his *Collection* in 1700. The strathspey was not in the picture at all as far as the seventeenth century publications were concerned.

Rants and reels

There is no dance, nor any hint of a dance called the 'Rant'; it is a name used solely of a style of dance tune. It is a Germanic, not a Gaelic, word, and it means to frolic or to romp. The spirit of a tune described as a 'rant' we must expect to be gleeful, even roistering. Compared to the more leisurely Scottish measure, the rant is, in fact, very spirited. It is of the same structure as the measure, but compresses the measure's eight-bar phrase into four bars. The interjection of the figure ♪♪♩ is frequent, and usually on the first beat of the bar. A considerable number of Scottish songs are set to tunes of this kind. Consider 'Green Grow the Rashes', which tune was originally called 'The Grant's Rant' [30, 31] and 'This is no my ain Hoose' [32, 33] which is a set of 'De'il Stick the Minister', a very old tune, and relative of 'This is no my ain Lassie' [33], as is 'Sean Triubhas'. Two versions of the old 'Sean Triubhas' are presented here [34–35] as a matter of interest. This is not the tune to which the dance is performed today. Now the tune associated with 'Sean Triubhas' is 'Whistle o'er the lave o't' [36], also a rant in structure, and sometimes rendered as a strathspey [37].*

A number of instrumental rants are particularly lively and show considerable partiality for runs of the following shape:

and

* Whether a tune of this character emerges as a Scottish measure or a rant is essentially only a matter of emphasis and tempo. In other words, whether the phrase is spaced out such that the heavy stresses fall with deliberation on the first three beats of the bar or furtively between the third and fourth beats.

[30] GREEN GROW THE RASHES originally 'THE GRANT'S RANT'
Johnson's *Scots Musical Museum*, no. 77, 1787

[31] Fiddler's version
Atholl Collection, 1884

[32] THIS IS NO MINE AIN HOOSE
A set of 'De'il Stick the Minister'
Dick no. 96. W. Thomson's *Orpheus Caledonius* no. 32, 1733

[33] Another set of the same

[34] SEAN TRIUBHAS UILLACHAN
Simon Fraser, *Airs and Melodies*, 1816

[35] SEAN TRIUBHAS UILLACHAN
A second version
Wilson's *Companion to the Ballroom*, 1817

[36] WHISTLE O'ER THE LAVE O'T
Commonly used for the dance 'Sean Triubhas'
Dick no. 250. *Bremner's Scots Reels*, p. 56, 1759

[37] As a strathspey
Atholl Collection, 1884

[38] STEWART'S RANT
Commonly used for the Country Dance 'General Stewart's Reel'
Atholl Collection, 1884

[39] MISS MAY HAY
Atholl Collection, 1884

[40] DRUMMOND'S RANT
Atholl Collection, 1884

'Stewart's Rant' [38], which is the tune associated with the Country Dance 'General Stuart's Reel', and 'Drummond's Rant' [40], are two examples of the livelier instrumental rant. As is to be expected, there are many tunes which, though structurally of this class, do not carry the word rant in their titles, such as 'Miss May Hay' [39] used as an example here, and some indeed, which are called 'reels' such as the familiar 'Duke of Perth's Reel' [41, 42].

Accepting our identification of the rant, it soon becomes apparent that a very large proportion of Scottish reel tunes are of this structure. Even the 'Reel o' Tulloch' which seems at first glance to be of a category of tune very different from the typical rant, reveals itself on close examination to be simply an elaborately disguised one.

In Strathspey style, the rant retains the same characteristics as its allegro form with the addition of the dotted rhythm and snap of the strathspey. Thus some typical rants which we have mentioned—'Green Grow the Rashes', 'Sean Triubhas' and 'Whistle o'er the lave o't' are often rendered in strathspey style, as also is the celebrated 'MacPherson's Rant' [47].

Two fascinating examples of the Strathspey rant are 'Rothiemurchus Rant' [48], a great favourite of Robert Burns, and 'Struan Robertson's Rant'.

Returning to the 'Reel o' Tulloch', we must note that it is the name of a specific dance as well as the name of the tune to which the dance is performed. It has every appearance of having been composed for the bagpipe, being within the compass of that instrument and replete with intervals of thirds and fifths to which the chanter lends itself. The first appearance of this fascinating tune in written record is as a violin set [43] in the Drummond Castle MS., 1734, where it runs to 160 bars of variations, not including repeats.

James Logan presents a pipe set of the tune in his *Scottish Gael*, 1831, which is reproduced here [44] for comparison and study. It will be noticed that in this two bars are added to the second variation to provide a coda. These would be omitted in playing for the dance.

Of a similar style, but less elaborate, are those reels which Captain Fraser published as 'pipe' reels (though they are set by him for the violin) in his celebrated collection of tunes from the Highlands. He gives a number of examples of this class of tune and remarks that 'ordinary performers on the violin are not ready to take them up, as they require a distinct bow to each note' (which, of course, was how the untrained fiddler performed). One which we have reproduced here—'Druimuachdair' or 'Highland Road to Inverness' [45], has peurt-a-beul words which 'describe two foot passengers [travellers], overtaken by a frosty wind of such extreme cold, that they could scarcely preserve life by trotting to the measure of this air'. The word 'trotting' describes the character of this reel and others classed by Fraser as 'pipe' reels. We can

[41] DUKE OF PERTH'S REEL
Drummond Castle MS, 1734

[42] A second version

[43] REEL O' TULLOCH
First two measures, Drummond Castle MS, 1734

and continue for twenty measures of variations

[44] RIGHIL THULAICHEAN

A bagpipe set

James Logan. *The Scottish Gael*, 1831

[45] DRUIMUACHDAIR or HIGHLAND ROAD TO INVERNESS

Described as a 'pipe reel'

Simon Fraser, *Airs and Melodies*, 1884

[46] A' CHRIODHAILEACHD—THE MERRY-MAKING
Described as a 'pipe reel'
Simon Fraser, *Airs and Melodies*, 1884

feel the two pulses to a bar and can hear the handclapping reinforcing them. Another example, 'A Chriodhaileachd'—The Merry-making [46] showing a little more variety, is presented for comparison. Can it be that these tunes belong to an extinct bellows-pipe? They have the staccato characteristics of the 'closed' chanter, and of course we know that bellows-pipes were familiar in the Isles and Highlands some time before the eighteenth century.

Another style of reel which perhaps we can identify as a class is exemplified by the familiar 'De'il amang the Tailors' [49] and 'Largo's Fairy Dance' [51] with their ♩ ♫♩ ♫ phrases reminiscent of Scottish measures. Other well-known tunes of this category which come to mind are 'Rachel Rae', and 'The Wind that Shakes the Barley' (which is substantially a set of the 'Fairy Dance'). These form a link between the rant and reels of the style of 'Timour the Tartar' [50].

[47] MacPHERSON'S RANT

Directed to be played 'slow with much expression', but the spirit of Burns's words to this tune—'sae rantingly, sae wantonly, sae dauntingly gaed he'—suggests a more vigorous treatment.

Gow's *Repository*, Part First, 1799

[48] ROTHIEMURCHUS RANT

A strathspey rant
Atholl Collection, 1884

[49] THE DE'IL AMONG THE TAILORS
Atholl Collection, 1884

Another popular reel of a decorative cast, 'Mrs McLeod of Raasay's Reel' [52], was 'communicated' to Nathaniel Gow by Mr McLeod of Raasay as 'an original Isle of Skye Reel'. This tune appears basically to be a Scottish measure, of the same category as such tunes as 'Kate Dalrymple'. Thus are the characteristics of specific types of reel tune permuted and elaborated, and we have yet to consider the most distinctive variant of all, the strathspey.

It is not unexpected that one encounters musical borrowings, between Irish and Scottish dance tunes, but the Irish reel is of a smoother rhythmical structure than the Scottish, as is revealed by a study of the Irish reels presented here—a 4/4 'Sutra Seana Cnocaine' [53], a 2/4 'O'Flaherty's Gamble' [54] and an Irish 'fling' in common time, 'The Flax in Bloom' [55].

These tunes are very lively, but are not syncopated and have no terminal 'pom-poms'. The accent is on the first beat of the bar, although the intuitive performer, especially on the violin, places stress on other parts of the bar occasionally to give 'pith and birr' to the phrasing.

[50] TIMOUR THE TARTAR
Atholl Collection, 1884

[51] LARGO'S FAIRY DANCE
Nathaniel Gow. Niel Gow's *Fifth Collection*, 1809

[52] MRS McLEOD OF RAASAY'S REEL
Niel Gow's *Fifth Collection*, 1809

[53] SUTRA SEANA CNOCAINE
or 'The Humours of Old Knockane'
Roche Collection

[54] O'FLAHERTY'S GAMBLE
Roche Collection

[55] THE FLAX IN BLOOM
Roche Collection

The strathspey

Early in the nineteenth century, Captain Simon Fraser of Knockie (plate 24) wrote in one of the notes to his published collection of Gaelic tunes, *The Airs and Melodies peculiar to the Highlands of Scotland and the Isles*, 1816: 'In passing through the district of Strathspey, the traveller may be apt to forget, that among the long ranges of fir-wood and heath on each side, originated that sprightly stile of performing and dancing the music which bears its name, now in universal request from the Spey to the Ganges.' Perhaps it is too much to claim the origin of the strathspey for the district which bears it name, for we must still explain how numerous dance tunes, sung *puirt-a-beul* in the Western Isles, are strathspeys, and perhaps we are closer to the truth when we quote Angus Cumming, the last of a long line of family fiddlers in Strathspey, who said in the eighteenth century that he belonged to that country in which 'that species of music [the strathspey] was *preserved in the greatest purity*'! He also calls strathspeys 'Old Highland Reels'. Thomas Newte Esq., in his *Tour in England and Scotland in 1785*, 1788, wrote:

According to the tradition of the country [Strathspey], the first who played them [strathspeys] were the Browns of Kincardine, to whom are ascribed a few of the most ancient tunes. After these men the Cummings of Freuchie, now Castle Grant, were in the highest estimation for their knowledge and execution in Strathspey music, and most of the tunes handed down to us are certainly of their composing ... The last of that name, made famous for his skill in music, was John Roy Cumming. He died about forty years ago, and there are many persons still alive who speak of his performance with the greatest delight.'

Angus Cumming was doubtless a member of the same family, for he tells us in the preface that he 'follows the profession of his forefathers, who have been for many generations musicians in Strathspey'. He makes no claim for his family being creators of the idiom, nor does he mention John Roy Cumming who, according to Newte, died around 1750, about thirty years before Angus published his collection.

It can be said that the strathspey is a way of playing reels *andante*, and indeed James Logan appears to be implying this when he writes in 1831:

'There are certain differences very perceptible to a musical ear in the style and character of the music of certain districts. The Caithness and Sutherland people are noted for playing in quick time, and the people of Strathspey, or rather the part of Scotland in which that valley is situated, are celebrated for their partiality to slow time.'[3]

Certainly, all reels and rants can be performed as strathspeys.

The peculiarity of the strathspey lies in its dotted rhythm, the shorter note coming first: ♪♩ and ♩♪.

It is obvious to look for the origin of this in some characteristic of the bagpipe or fiddle. Certainly, both instruments cope with it very well. The peculiar flick or jerk of the wrist in the up-bow of the Scottish fiddler and the florid fingering of the bagpiper, especially on the 'open' chanter bagpipe, suggest themselves as sources of the style. Some have surmised, however, that the 'snap'—as this rhythmic peculiarity is called—is a product of Gaelic vocal inflection. One need only hear a strathspey rendered in puirt-a-beul 'mouth music', to see the force of this. It may be significant, too, that both puirt-a-beul and the strathspey are peculiar to Scotland.

Francis Peacock alludes to this in his book on dancing[10] where he treats of the Highland Reel, suggesting that the rhythm of the strathspey was a fundamental rhythm of Ossianic verse (trochaic tetrameter) but this does not account for the snap.

Arnold Schering,[11] a German musicologist, in a series of papers (1912–1914) tried to establish criteria for the identification of instrumental as opposed to vocal music, with particular reference to European music of the twelfth to sixteenth centuries. Among these criteria he lists certain rhythmic characteristics—frequent syncopations, tying of short notes to long ones, alternating very long and very short notes, and the use of dotted rhythms! The more obvious criteria, such as range and melodic sequences, we need not consider here.

Accepting these rhythmic criteria, it follows that the strathspey, which embraces them all to a marked degree, is an instrumental rather than a vocal style. Lloyd Hibbert,[12] however, has questioned the validity of Schering's hypotheses and points out that the ability to execute complicated rhythms depends more upon the performer's rhythmic sense than upon his medium, and that the earliest textbooks on vocal ornamentation —those of Sovicelli (1594), Conforto (1607), and Rognone (1620) among others—decidedly favoured the employment of dotted rhythms, including those in which (as in the strathspey), the shorter note comes first.

The evidence is that the earliest melodic accompaniment to dance was vocal, the melodic instrumental accompaniment coming quite late, with instrumental dance melody developing, not from instrumental rhythmic music, but from the 'instrumentalizing' of dance songs, for which the words have been abandoned.[13]

The Scottish snap then, may conceivably have been taken by the instrument from the voice; but the term puirt-a-beul, suggests that the voice is assuming the role of the instrument. Here we have a vocalized instrumental music. It is still conceivable that the voice in turn contributed the snap through this.

The snap is an essential peculiarity of the strathspey, but Scottish exponents of the traditional dance music habitually introduce it to jigs and Scottish measures and the like. The *motifs* ♩♩ ♩ and ♩. ♪♩ (the inverse of the 'snap') are characteristic of the Scottish measure, and a phrase of the shape ♩ | ♩. ♪♩ ♩ | ♩. ♪♩ ♩ | seems to exhibit the snap in performance, although it does not do so in print. In a run of dotted notes the order of precedence—short before the long—is obscured. It is interesting to note that in 'The Scotch-man's dance' [56], a tune composed, presumably, in the Scottish manner, and published by Playford in his *Apollo's Banquet*, Sixth Edition, 1690, the ♩. ♪♩ and ♩♩ ♩ of the Scottish measure are conspicuous.

Henry Farmer[14] has suggested that the 'snap' comes from the *port* of the harp, which exhibits the characteristic ♩♩ ♩ which, he suggests, is close to the ♪♩. ♩ of the strathspey. But, of course, as we shall see, both are related to the rhythm of the Single Jig.

These suggestions pale, to my mind, before the strong case for a vocal origin for the snap through puirt-a-beul, or even through the vocal habits of the Gael in performing his own songs. The rhythmic characteristics of strathspeys can, perhaps, best be illustrated by the following examples:

or

or   etc.

Grace notes and flourishes add embellishment and provide a range of what we may call 'styles' of strathspey—from those which are akin to jigs to those which are *legato, andante* airs. A large number can be treated in either way, after the taste of the performer. Indeed, to the uninitiated, many strathspeys appear to be in jig rhythm 6/8 │ ♩ ♪♩ ♪ │ ♩ ♪♩ ♪ │ Hence the remark by Barclay Dun in the year 1816 that the strathspey was 'accented in exact resemblance to a jig'.[15] Thomas Garnett, M.D., who was not a musician, makes a similar remark on being entertained by Niel Gow at the inn at Inver. 'He [Gow] excels most in the Strathspeys, which are jigs played with a peculiar spirit and life; but he executes the laments, or funeral music, with a great deal of pathos.'[16] No doubt the latter were the 'slow airs' as Gow described them.

These somewhat superficial observations by Barclay Dun and Garnett do hint at the fact, however, that strathspeys can easily be rendered as jigs, each bar being convertible into two of 6/8 jig rhythm, although as in the case of converting strathspeys to rants, or Scottish measures, some tunes lend themselves to this more readily than others. Of course, in any event, some modifications to the melodic line are usually requisite, and the results do not often justify the effort. Nor, indeed, are there many instances, at least obvious instances, of strathspey-jig conversion, in the literature. 'Lady Belhaven's Delight' (Gow, *Fourth Collection*) nevertheless, makes a very good jig of Marshall's strathspey 'Mrs Hamilton of Wishaw'.

These comments bring us to Thomas Morley's remarks in his book on music published in 1597: '. . . And I dare boldly affirme that looke which is hee who thinketh himselfe the best descanter of all his neighbors, enjoin him to make but a Scottish Jygge, he will grossly err in the true nature and qualitie of it.'[17]

Morley was trying to illustrate how the art of composition required a somewhat different talent from that necessarily possessed by the good harmonizer ('descanter'). What he meant by a 'Scottish Jygge' is open to some doubt. Its general usage in Morley's time was of a characteristic kind of 'Jockey and Jennie' dialogue in doggerel verse. Whether all of these were set to jig rhythm it is not possible to determine. 'Jenney come tye my Cravat' in *Apollo's Banquet* is an example of such a tune:

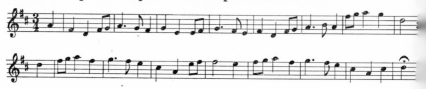

[56] THE SCOTCH-MAN'S DANCE in *The Northern Lass*
John Playford's *Apollo's Banquet*, Sixth Ed. 1690

This tune is not of the category of what was known as 'Scottish Jig' in the eighteenth century. No strathspeys reached the printed page before the eighteenth century, nor is the name even mentioned in connection with music or dance until that century. The temptation is, therefore, to claim that the strathspey was unknown in the seventeenth century. It is less justifiable to claim that the snap which distinguishes it was not a familiar Scottish characteristic before the eighteenth century, for this does occasionally appear in some of the 'Scotch' tunes printed by the Playfords.

There were likewise no written copies of the most characteristic Hebridean Gaelic songs, but no one has suggested that such songs and their mainland relatives did not then exist. No one had yet seen the need to commit a healthy oral tradition to written record. As for the term 'strathspey', it probably came into the vocabulary with the spread in popularity of the Strathspey style of dancing the common Reel in the eighteenth century, first appearing in the Menzies MS. (Appendix A, p. 224) of c. 1749, in which we find 'The Montgomerie's Rant—a strathspey reele'. Its first appearance in print is in James Oswald's *Caledonian Pocket Companion*, vol. iii, 1751, where we find two tunes entitled 'A New Strathspey Reel', then in Robert Bremner's *Collection of Scots Reels or Country Dances, c.* 1760, 'Straglass House—a Strathspey'; and the first title page to include the term 'strathspey' was Daniel Dow's, 1775, after which the term strathspey or strathspey reel was rarely absent from a collection of Scottish dance music. We have also noted Cumming's remarks which allow no suggestion that the strathspey was something new in the eighteenth century, and it would be strange indeed if Burney [18] isolated as a characteristic of Scottish music a rhythmic figure (the 'snap') that had only recently been introduced. If this is not enough, we would have to explain why no one remarks on the sudden appearance of the new style of Scottish music and how Patie Birnie, for instance, already sixty years of age by the turn of the century, set verses to, and sang, 'The Auld Man's Mare's Deid' [57], a song full of 'snap' and, in our parlance, a strathspey.

In the oldest manuscript collection of Highland Reels, the Drummond Castle MS., 1734 (Appendix A, p. 225–6) there are no tunes which one could say are notated in the strathspey style. Nor, on the other hand are there many tunes included which are best known today as strathspeys. One of the latter few, however, is 'Tullochgorum'. It is interesting to compare the Dummond Castle MS. version [58] with the tune as the Rev. John Skinner set words to it, as it is reproduced in Johnston's *Scots Musical Museum* [59], and further with the setting in the Athole Collection [60] which is typical of the later fiddle sets. It will be seen from this that the Atholl version is unquestionably in strathspey style; the *Museum* version with the 'snap' reversed resembles this style and the Drummond version bears no apparent hint of it.

[57] THE AULD MAN'S MARE'S DEID
Robert Chambers's *The Songs of Scotland prior to Burns*, 1862

[58] TULLOCHGORUM
Drummond Castle MS, 1734

[59] A second version
Johnson's *Scots Musical Museum*, no. 289, 1790

[60] Typical of later fiddle setting
Atholl Collection, 1884

[61] MISS ADMIRAL GORDON'S STRATHSPEY
Burns's 'Of a' the airts the win' can blow'
William Marshall, *First Collection*, 1781

[62] THE MARQUIS OF HUNTLY'S FAREWELL
William Marshall, *First Collection*, 1781

Most of the settings in the Drummond MS. are simple and unadorned, but many, such as 'Reel o' Tulloch', 'Merrie Annie', 'Fettercairn Reel', 'Brig o' Turk', 'Caper Fei', and 'Tail Todle', are elaborated with variations, a favourite Scottish taste which is crowned by Pibroch, the supreme variations form of British folk music. There is no justification for assuming that the Drummond MS. is a transcription of versions of the tunes current among the best fiddlers; in any case there is no graphical method of indicating all the subtleties and irregularities of style which constitute the performance of the traditional musician and give character to the music.

We can draw no definite conclusions about the strathspey from the Drummond MS. We can remark its absence therefrom, and in noting the later treatment of 'Tullochgorum' as a strathspey we can note that many other tunes best known to us in strathspey style—such as 'Green Grow the Rashes' (*The Grant's Rant*) [30] and 'Whistle o'er the Lave o't'—first appear in written records as rants.

I think we may conclude from Burns's remark to Thomson about having one of 'our ancienter Scots Fiddlers' play him 'The Moudiewart', a jig, in 'Strathspey time',[19] that it was the habit among untutored fiddlers of the countryside to render tunes in strathspey style at their pleasure. This is really what we would expect. The vogue of the Strathspey dance forms, and particularly of the Highland Reel in its Strathspey form, in the eighteenth century, probably brought the strathspey style of music to wider attention. Most of the great fiddler-composers, as we have seen, produced many grand examples of the genre; but the printed collections testify to a considerable store of strathspey reels in the traditional repertoire.

The Scottish snap became widely recognized as an obvious trait of Scottish music, and had some vogue in late eighteenth-century Europe. Numerous composers, among them, Handel and Haydn, exploited the device and by the time the Waverley novels had swept the Continent, everyone was ready for the Scottish rhapsodies and overtures, and the ballrooms were ready for the introduction of the new polka in imitation of the strathspey both as a dance and music—the *Schottisch*.

A more lyrical form of strathspey which lent itself to the 'largo lento' treatment Burns desired for his songs, became a favourite of fiddlers when they were not playing to dancing. Many of these are designated 'slow' strathspeys in the publications but in many instances these were also suitable for dancing if played faster. A good number reach a high level of melodic inspiration, such as William Marshall's 'Miss Admiral Gordon's Strathspey' ('Of a' the airts') [61] and 'The Marquis of Huntly's Farewell' [62]. With these we are bridging two extremes—the sprightly strathspey and the *andante* air with only a trace of strathspey flavour. A good example of the first is 'Monymusk' [63] or, of course, 'The Marquis of Huntly's Highland Fling' [64], and of the second, the familiar 'Loch Lomond'.* The sprightly strathspey is appropriate for the Highland Fling, Strathspey Reel or indeed any Highland dance to strathspey rhythm. The 'kindlan' bauld' strathspey as Burns called it, has a prominent place in Scottish Country Dancing as well as in song.

The Royal Scottish Country Dance Society has tended to emphasize the lyrical quality of the strathspey, and the nature of the appropriate steps and their style of execution has been based upon that quality, thus filling a gap in the spectrum of Scottish dance. Perhaps there is room for an extension of Country Dance technique to accommodate the more 'sprightly' style of treatment; but that is another matter. As it is, the slow strathspey seems to offer difficulties to many dance orchestras and they often mix the styles of the tunes they select; a legato tune will be treated staccato and so on. It is not a matter of smoothing out the snap! The snap is essential to the Scottish character of the tune.

Certain Country Dances involving the so-called 'Highland Scottisch' steps were popular on the Borders. These, properly speaking, should be performed to Scottisch-type tunes. The 'Scottisch' is distinguished by its two accents to the bar instead of one—on the first and third beats of a two-bar phrase, as for instance:

The 'Haughs of Cromdale' [65] is an example of a strathspey of 'Scottisch' structure, although what we have called the 'jig' type of strathspey above, is also suitable.

In the eighteenth century, there are allusions to the 'Strathspey Minuet' which was clearly a twasome performed to the strathspey, and it is interesting to find in Watlen's collection of *Celebrated Circus Tunes* (1791), 'The celebrated Strathspey Minuet as danced by Mr Lassells and Mrs Parker at the Royal Circus, London and Edinburgh'. This was a tune, a strathspey, entitled 'Mrs Biggs (of Newcastle's) Delight' [66].

Two of what I might call genetic mutations of the strathspey, called *The Strathspey Waltz* [67] and *The Strathspey Quadrille* [68], by one F. W. Grant published on a sheet by Walker and Anderson, Edinburgh,

---

* Anne Geddes Gilchrist has said that 'Loch Lomond' was the only Scottish tune in which she could trace any affinity with Danish folk airs. *Journal of the English Folk Dance and Song Society*, vol. iv, no. 1, 1940. It is really a set of the old air 'Kind Robin'.

[63] MONYMUSK

In G with the ♯ 3rd. Daniel Dow. Gow's *Repository*, Part First, 1799

[64] THE MARQUIS OF HUNTLY'S HIGHLAND FLING

George Jenkins. Gow's *Repository*, Part Second, [1802]

[65] THE HAUGHS OF CROMDALE

Atholl Collection

[66] MRS BIGGS (OF NEWCASTLE'S) DELIGHT
'The Celebrated Strathspey Minuet'
Watlen's *Celebrated Circus Tunes*, 1791

[67] THE STRATHSPEY WALTZ
F. W. Grant, *c*. 1819

[68] THE STRATHSPEY QUADRILLE
F. W. Grant, *c*. 1819

c. 1819, are a subject of curiosity. It is difficult to see any relationship to the strathspey in these except for the figure ♩. ♪♩. ♪ which the strathspey shares with the Irish Hornpipe. The waltz is in 3/8 and the quadrille in 6/8. The tunes are reproduced here for comparison.

The jig

We turn now to the jig. The many fascinating tunes in 9/8 triplet rhythm form the bridge between the triple-time hornpipe and jig. Here the Irish are granted prior claim, although these tunes have been very popular with the bellows pipers of the Border. The Irish pipes, of course, were of similar form. The dance performed to this rhythm is the 'hop jig' [69] These tunes have the same bob-wheel effect as the triple-time hornpipe 'Drops of Brandy' [75] is a rather delightful example.

[69] BARNEY BALLAGHAN
Irish hop jig
I. Blewitt. Set to the words of 'Barney Ballaghan's Courtship' by Hudson, *c.* 1850
Roche Collection, 1911

[70] COCK YOUR PISTOL CHARLEY
Irish single jig
Roche Collection, 1911

The common jig, however, is in 6/8 triplet rhythm. The basic Irish jig rhythms are: | ♩ ♪♩ ♪ | ♩ ♪♩ ♪ | and ♫♫ ♫♫ | ♫♫ ♫♫ |

The characteristic English jig has the rhythm 6/8 | ♩. ♫ ♩. ♫ |, the spirit light and tripping. Many composers gave it the time-signature '2' because of its beating two to the bar, or '3 in 1' and was written in 3/8, 6/8, 3/4, 6/4, or 12/8. Sometimes, it seems, it was the spirit of the music that justified the title 'jig' for we find in the *Fitzwilliam Virginal Book, c.* 1650, two jigs in common time: 'Nobodyes Gigge' and 'Giles Farnaby's Gigge'.

[71] PADDY McFADDEN
Irish double jig
'Accent-strong and medium well marked.' Roche Collection, 1911

[72] RORY DALL'S PORT
Burns's 'Ae Fond Kiss'. Johnson's *Scots Musical Museum*, no. 347, 1792

[73] APPROXIMATE THEME OF 'PIBROCH OF DONUIL DHU'
Piobaireachd Dhomhnuill Duibh

[74] PIBROCH OF DONUIL DHU
Jig or march version
G. Farquhar Graham's *Songs of Scotland*, 1864

[75] DROPS OF BRANDY
Wilson's *Companion to the Ballroom*, 1817

[76] THE BLYTHESOME BRIDAL
Johnson's *Scots Musical Museum*, no. 58, 1787

[77] Dancing set
Wilson's *Companion to the Ballroom*, 1817

[78] O DEAR MOTHER WHAT SHALL I DO?
Giga
Oswald's *Caledonian Pocket Companion*, viii, 1756

The word 'jig' has been widely used with reference to a particular style of ditty and theatrical song and dance interlude, encountered particularly in Elizabethan England, and consequently there has been a temptation to claim the 'jig' for England.

William Chappell, the learned student of English folk music, whose attacks on Scottish music have been so competently dealt with by Glen,[20] attacked the claim of the Irish to the jig. He said that he found no Irish jig bearing that name before the latter part of the seventeenth century. That is, no written record. But Grattan Flood calls attention to a letter from Sir Henry Sidney to Queen Elizabeth in 1569, containing a reference to the dancing of jigs by the Anglo-Irish ladies of Galway.[21] The same author claims that the Irish jig is more than a thousand years old, although his earliest authorities do not use the name 'jig' but 'port', which in Gaelic signifies an air, either vocal or instrumental.

What we know of Irish music, together with Giraldus's remarks on its sportiveness in the twelfth century, support an Irish origin for the jig and possibly also the common-time hornpipe. Certainly, none of the 'ports' I have examined could be called 'sportive'; rather are they slow airs for the harp in common time. Burns set 'Ae Fond Kiss' to 'Rory Dall's Port' [72] which has been mentioned in connection with the strathspey. He took this from Oswald's collection, and here it is 6/8 in the rhythm but Burns directed it to be played 'slow and tender' ♩. ♪♩ ♪| ♩. ♪♩ ♪|

Observe how this rhythm coincides with that of the 'Pibroch of Donuil Dhu' [74], a very old set of variations, and of some other Scottish tunes [75-7], which only shows how variations on any port could well fall into any of the several jig rhythms.

When we recall that the Irish clergy carried their harps to Europe and what Vincenzo Galilei, father of the astronomer, said of the Irish harp,* we should have no hesitation in claiming Irish origin for the Italian *gige*, or *giga*, which is in the rhythm of running triplets:

| ♫♩ ♫♩ ♫♩ ♫♩ |

In his *Caledonian Pocket Companion*, Oswald uses the word *giga* of a style of jig rhythm which is used a great deal for Scottish solo jigs, such as 'O'er the Water to Charlie' and 'Blue Bonnets'. Characteristic of this rhythm is the phrase: 6/8 ♩ ♪♫♩ | ♫♩ ♩ ♪| ♩ ♪♫♩ | ♩ ♪♫♩ | and variations thereof. One of Oswald's own giga variations is presented here [78], along with a familiar example of the style, 'Drummond Castle' [79], described as 'old' in the Gow collection. Another example is 'The Haddington Assembly' [80], composed by William Fraser, the celebrated eighteenth-century oboist. The reader may well identify o

---

* Vincenzo Galilei (1520-91) quotes Dante (1265-1321) as his authority for stating that the harp was brought to Italy from Ireland. *Dialogo di Vincenzo Galilei*, 1589.

[79] DRUMMOND CASTLE
Jig of Oswald's giga form
Niel Gow's *Second Collection*, [1788]

[80] THE HADDINGTON ASSEMBLY
William Fraser. Niel Gow's *Second Collection*, [1788]

recall others, for they are very common in Scottish music and are much favoured as marches by pipe bands. The Scottish musician, today, would habitually dot all or most of the triplets in these tunes, viz.: ♪.♫ although they are not thus dotted in their earliest printed forms.

There is another class of jig, however, which Oswald and others designate as 'Scotch Jig'. These appear to be the Scottish Measure in jig rhythm, and the reader may find it instructive to confirm this by playing in jig rhythm some of the Scottish Measures named here. The phrases of the Scotch Jig are punctuated in the manner of the Scottish Measure: 6/8

[81] THE CAMPBELLS ARE COMING
Johnson's *Scots Musical Museum*, no. 299, 1790

[82] SCOTCH JIG
Set of the air of 'The Moudiewart'
Oswald's *Caledonian Pocket Companion*, iv, 1752

[83] JOHNNIE McGILL
Johnson's *Scots Musical Museum*, no. 207, 1790

[84] JOAN'S PLACKETT
Wilson's *Companion to the Ballroom*, 1817

Two familiar examples of this class of jig which come to mind are 'The
Campbells are Coming' [81] and 'A Hundred Pipers and a' and a'';
they also make excellent march tunes.* Gratton Flood [22] claims the first
for the Irish, who called it 'An seanduine' ('The Old Man') and it
appears in John Walsh's *Caledonian Country Dances* (*c.* 1744) as 'Hob or
Nob'. In the Robert Wodrow *Correspondence* (vol. xi, n. 96) we read that
in 1716, each of three companies of Argyle's Highlanders which entered
Perth and Dundee was led by a piper, and that the pipers respectively
played 'The Campbells are coming, Oho, Oho', 'Wilt thou play me
fair play, Highland Laddie', and 'Stay and take the breiks with thee'.
We can take it from this that 'The Campbells are Coming' has long had
currency as a Scottish pipe march.

A tune designated 'Scotch Jig' [82] by Oswald is a set of the air to an
old Jacobite song called 'The Moudiewart' ('The Mole': William of
Orange met his death through a fall from a horse which tripped on a
mole-hill) and is a good example of the form. Scottish country dancers
may note that this is the style of jig which they appropriate for a favourite
country Dance, 'Fergus McIvor'.

Another Scotch jig from Johnson's *Museum*, is 'Johnnie McGill' [83]
Burns's 'Tibbie Dunbar' (Dick no. 35) and McNeil's 'Come under
my Plaidie'. The English 'Joan's Plackett' [84] is a set of the Scots
'Cock of the North' and the Irish 'Aunty Mary'.

Burns used 'The Moudiewart' for his song 'O for ane-and-twenty
am'. The set of the tune used in the *Museum* is a little different and did
not please Burns, so he recommended Thomson to publish the song in
strathspey rhythm.[23]

The 'Jacky Tar' hornpipe

Towards the end of the eighteenth century a new class of dance tune
became very popular for stage hornpipes performed by the numerous
entr'acte dancers then so much in fashion. Many of them took the name
of the dancer for whom they were composed—'Aldridge's Hornpipe'
Played as Scottish measures, these jigs become 'Mrs Macleod of Raasay' and 'The
White Cockade' respectively!

[85], 'Miss Baker's Hornpipe' [86], 'West's', 'Fishar's', 'Durang' [87], 'Richer's' and others. More obscure titles are borne by a very fe' like 'The Dorsetshire Hornpipe' and 'College Hornpipe' [88]; th latter is the most commonly associated with the 'Sailor's Hornpipe' danc·

Grove attributes the origin of this class of tune to Thomas Arne (1710 1778), and cites as the prototypes the two hornpipes Arne composed f· his edition of Purcell's *King Arthur* in 1767.

But these 'new' hornpipe tunes were not so new, for they had numero' Scottish relatives such as 'East Neuk of Fife' [89] and the tune to th Jacobite song 'The Cuckoo'. The last named, alternatively 'Th Cuckoo's Nest' or 'I do confess thou art sae fair' was published in the la' eighteenth century by the Glasgow publisher, James Aird, as 'Com Ashore Jolly Tar' [90], a tune which was used for a now popul· character dance 'The Sailor's Hornpipe', referred to as 'Jacky Tar' in th Glasgow dancing schools of the period.

Scottish tunes of this class seem the obvious ancestors of the new horr pipes, although one suspects that Arne arrived at his versions through th influence of Purcell. Purcell composed a few dance tunes of a rhyth' which is very suggestive of them, one of which, incidentally, is 'Th Sailor's Dance' [91] in his opera *Dido and Aeneas*. Who knows but th· Purcell came to that rhythm through the influence of the 'Scotch tune' he condescended to imitate on occasion, and one of which is reproduc· here [92].

Whatever their antecedents, the new hornpipes—so called, not fro' their musical structure but from their use—showed a marked preferenc for the *pom-pom-pom* emphasis of the Scottish measure and for the thr· repetitions of the same note at the end of phrases—which is very chara· teristic of Irish music. They have, too, more cascades of half-notes and tl faster pace that this lends them. This, combined with the occasion holding of the note on the second beat of the bar (more common in tl early versions) and the syncopation effected, produce a character which rousing and brilliant.

In considering the relationship of this rhythm to the old triple-tir' hornpipe it is instructive to consider the 'Original Scots Hornpipe' [9· described as 'very old' and published by Gow in 2/4; but which, · closer examination, can be seen to be really in 3/2.

A subtle characteristic distinguishing the new hornpipes from th· Scottish ancestors is their tonality; they are invariably major in mode, ar are rarely the vehicles of song. Their popularity was unquestioned, ar their use for Country Dances maintained it even to the present day. T' old triple-time hornpipe practically disappeared; not displaced by anoth 'hornpipe', but because it belonged to the dancing fashions of a form' age and was already dropping from practical dancing use in the ballroo' before the new hornpipes appeared. Scottish dance tunes in general h·

[85] ALDRIDGE'S HORNPIPE
Atholl Collection

[86] MISS BAKER'S HORNPIPE
Wilson's *Companion to the Ballroom*, 1817

[87] DURANG'S HORNPIPE
Kerr Collection

[88] COLLEGE HORNPIPE
Atholl Collection

[89] EAST NEUK OF FIFE
Atholl Collection

[90] COME ASHORE JOLLY TAR
James Aird's *Airs*, vol. i, no. 190, 1782

[91] THE SAILOR'S DANCE
Henry Purcell, *Dido and Aeneas*, 1689

[92] 'SCOTCH TUNE'
Henry Purcell, *Amphitrion*. John Playford's *Apollo's Banquet*, Fifth Ed. 1687

something to do with this in England. The stage hornpipe did not affect the traditional use of the old triple-time hornpipes by the village step-dancers at the local tavern in many an English village.

What place, it may be asked, has the Irish hornpipe in this? We have taken notice in an earlier chapter, of the fertilizing force of the Irish musical tradition in early medieval times and remarked on the community of the music of the British Isles. The Irish dance tunes classed as 'hornpipes' (though how long has that word been used of them?) are similar to the new hornpipes and to the Scottish tunes of the same class, but have only two accents to the bar. They seem to be an offshoot of those very characteristic and jaunty Irish marches, although in their early written form the Irish hornpipe is not 'jaunty'. The jaunty Irish hornpipe may be of comparatively recent introduction, for a large proportion of those we now hear are nineteenth century compositions. These have the appearance of strathspeys, with their perpetual dotted quavers and 'one-two-three-hop', and the occasional snap.

The earlier Irish hornpipe was not written in this way—whatever the fiddlers and pipers did with it in performance. 'Roger was a Plowboy' [94] is given here as an example of the early lyrical 'variations' style of the Irish hornpipe. This particular hornpipe is apparently derived from the march form of the tune 'Young Roger' [95] published by P. W. Joyce in his *Ancient Irish Music*. The march form of the tune shows the hornpipe rhythm more clearly.

Another example is 'The First of May' [96], which seems to be a double hornpipe variant of a well-known jig 'Let us leave that as it is' [97]. The jaunty treatment of the Irish hornpipe which is now so characteristic is illustrated by a set of this tune [98] taken from Roche's Collection, 1911.

The 'new' common-time hornpipes of the category we have here called 'Jacky Tar', are, within the British context, cosmopolitan derivatives of the native music of the British Isles. Though products of the London theatre of the eighteenth century they are now fully accepted alongside the reels and jigs of more legitimate parentage in the traditional family.

Dance and measure

Traditional Scottish and English and—with certain exceptions—Irish dance music, is compounded of measures of eight bars. The eight bars may be made up of two four-bar phrases, one four-bar phrase repeated twice or an eight-bar phrase. The four-bar phrase usually complies with the formula A-B-A-C or A-B-C-D. In the dance, the eight-bar measure is repeated before the music turns to another measure. Some Irish dances have odd numbers of bars to the measure. In certain instances in Scottish Country Dancing we encounter tunes written as rants which, today at any rate, are commonly played and treated by dancers as Scottish Measures (e.g., 'Duke of Perth's Reel' [39] and 'Maxwell's Rant'). It will be remembered that the phrases of the rant are in four bars of common time; expanding these to eight bars produces Scottish measure. Thus 'Duke of Perth', written as a four bar rant from its earliest appearance in

[93] OLD HORNPIPE
Niel Gow's *First Collection*. Second Ed. 1801

[94] ROGER WAS A PLOWBOY
Early Irish hornpipe

[95] YOUNG ROGER WAS A PLOWBOY
Old Irish March
P. W. Joyce, *Ancient Irish Music*, 1873

[96] THE FIRST OF MAY
Irish double hornpipe

[97] LET US LEAVE THAT AS IT IS
(FAGAMAOID SUD MAR ATA SE)
Early jig set of 'The First of May'
Petrie Collection, 1855

[98] THE FIRST OF MAY
Irish hornpipe, a set of the above
The dotted rhythm is now customary
Roche Collection, 1911

written record, is slowed down and treated by dancers today as though it were in eight bars. This tendency arises, somehow, from the structure and shape of the tune. Other rants, such as 'Stewart's Rant' [36] do not lend themselves to this. It may be said, of course, that the 'Stewart's Rant' has an eight-bar phrase (cf. [36]); but in fact, close inspection shall show this to be a four-bar rant phrase repeated.

Music for Scottish country dances

Scottish Country Dances are performed to reels (including rants, Scottish measures, etc.), strathspeys, jigs and hornpipes of the 'Jacky Tar' variety. In England, the 3/2 hornpipe, 6/8 and 9/8 jigs were the most popular for Country Dances at the beginning of the eighteenth century; but some were set to minuet, rigadon, gavotte and Scottish measure. The Highland Reel, Scottish Measure and Rant, and even the Strathspey were imported from Scotland in the eighteenth century, but the form died out in England when the Quadrille and Waltz were introduced, excepting the 'Waltz Country Dance' and some similar forms in the mid-nineteenth century.

There was no such variety in the Scottish development of the Country Dance. The Drummond Castle MS. (Appendix A, p. 225) contains some Country Dances set to 9/8 jig but of this class only 'Haymakers' (the Scottish name for 'Sir Roger de Coverley') was popular in eighteenth-century Scotland.

It is curious that in the Atholl Collection of Scottish Dance Music 1884, the tunes are arranged under the headings: strathspeys, reels, country dances, jigs and hornpipes. The Country Dances, however, are made up of jigs and tunes of the Scottish measure variety. Possibly James Stewart Robertson, the editor of the collection, was uncertain of how otherwise to classify these tunes. Almost all of them, certainly, are well-known as Country Dances; but many Country Dances still in vogue were set to reels and strathspeys included under 'reel' and 'strathspey' in the collection. Some of the jigs in the collection, not included under Country Dances, have been associated with Country Dances also, such as 'I'll mak ye fain', 'Off she goes' and 'Teviot Brig', but possibly Robertson was unaware of this. His list is as follows (J, jig; SM, Scottish measure):

Blue Bonnets	J	Jenny drinks nae Water	SM
Corn Rigs	SM	Jenny Nettles	
East Neuk of Fife	SM	Jinglin Johnnie	
Edradynate Medley	SM	Kenmore Lads	J
Flowers of Edinburgh	SM	Lady of the Lake	
The Stewart's March		The Triumph	
Haste to the Wedding	J	Waterloo	SM

Willie Davie		Petronella	SM
MacLauchlane's Scotch		Rory O'More	J
Measure	SM	Soldier's Joy	SM
Meg Merrilees		The Bottom of the Punch-	
Miss Forbes's Farewell to		bowl	SM
Banff	SM	The Dashing White Ser-	
Neil Gow's Farewell to		geant	
Whisky	SM	The Deuks Dang o'er my	
O Gin ye were dead Gude-		Daddie	J
man		The White Cockade	SM
Old Dumbarton Drums	SM	What's a' the Steer	

The Royal Scottish Country Dance Society has published its restored dances along with the tunes to be associated with them. The early dances are named after their tunes, but not the more recent ones. The Society publishes two tunes for each dance; but since there are many repetitions of the dance in performance it is incumbent on the musicians to supply some further supporting tunes for the sake of musical interest. A few knowledgeable musicians select and match these very carefully to the dance and to each other and even arrange them for maximum musical interest. Most bands, however, have too limited a range of tunes and too little musical skill to facilitate the performance of these in appropriate and contrasting keys. Even the Society has been known to err in its selection of tunes for a dance, and occasionally in the selection of key and time signature.

Playing and arranging music for dancing poses very different problems from those encountered in presenting dance music for entertainment. The dance imposes severe and obvious restrictions. The tempo is controlled, but there must be as much life, spirit, and variety and compatibility between each dance and its music, as will sweep the dancers into that course of 'free fluent and continuous motion' which characterizes the Scottish Country Dance. How this is achieved is a secret known only to the best ensembles.

It is customary in Scottish Country Dance circles to refer to Country Dances as strathspeys, jigs or reels according to their tunes; all common-time tunes, apart from strathspeys, are classed as reels whether they are hornpipes, Scottish measures or others.

Some dances still enjoyed along with Country Dances and loosely included among their number are not, by definition, Country Dances. 'Strip the Willow', for instance, is a folk dance (9/8), likewise the 'Foula Reel'. The popular 'Glasgow Highlanders' is part Highland Reel, part Country dance. Its 'name' tune is a kind of strathspey in the way that one could say the same of an Irish hornpipe, and is (or should be) usually supported with strathspeys of the 'fling' type. Here, as in all dances of the kind, the musician should understand the dance before he selects tunes for it

The Reel

The 'Highland' Reel, comprising for the dancer eight bars of travel in the figure of a 'reel' and eight bars of setting alternately, poses no special problems for the musician. It has been customary, certainly from the early nineteenth century, to combine the Strathspey and Reel styles, so that a Strathspey Reel is followed by a common Reel, forming the 'Strathspey and Reel'. The tunes selected are entirely at the discretion of the musician.

In music, this combination is called a medley as also is the combination jig and reel, but never jig and strathspey. Some Country Dances are set to medleys and are so called, e.g. the 'Perth Medley'.

The 'Reel of Tulloch' has its own tune and is sometimes combined with the Strathspey and Reel. At some 'Caledonian' balls these have even been combined further with the Eightsome Reel, a round reel devised in the late nineteenth century which remains uniquely popular. In this case again, the selection of tunes is at the discretion of the musician.

These reels demand a degree of technical excellence and physical fitness of the dancers which has militated against their popularity today. Country dancers tend more and more to neglect them because of these demands, but apply the music to less arduous ends. The important thing from the musical point of view is that the restoration of the Scottish Country Dance inevitably stimulates the restoration of a wide range of traditional music, not only of Scotland, but of the British Isles as a whole. The thoughtful Scottish musician will not overlook this.

Tempo

Apart from phrasing, and those characteristics of nuance and stress which give 'lift' to the music, the most crucial matter from the point of view of the dancer is tempo. This must be appropriate to the dance and to the dancer. In general, Scottish dance musicians tend to the fast rather than the slow side of the range of acceptable tempi. Fast tempi, except in certain step dances, are essential to the inferior dancer, and it is striking, in the case of Scottish Country Dancing, that as the general level of proficiency and appreciation ascended during the nineteen-thirties and forties, the desirable tempi became slower. There can be no fixed metronome setting for Scottish dance music, for even the nature of the dances themselves has an influence; but excessive tempo is the enemy of good dancing. The ideal tempo is that which enables the dancer to articulate steps and movements with fluency, shape and continuity.

It is interesting to examine the hints gleaned here and there of the tempi favoured by Scottish dancing masters and musicians in the past and present, for the performance of Scottish dance music. Some of these are presented in the following table:

Authority	Bars per minute			
	Reel	Strathspey	Tulloch	Highland Fling
Surrene (c. 1850)	63	47	60	
J. G. Atkinson (1900)	63	44		
D. R. Mackenzie (1910)	68	38	70	38
John Glen (c. 1900)	64	40		
J. Scott Skinner (c. 1900)	64	48		
Fiddle Competition in Aberdeen (c. 1860)	64	44		
Scottish Official Board of Highland Dancing 1955	66	38		
1961	60	34		
Royal Scottish Country Dance Society (Country Dance) (recommended) 1928	58	42		
(favoured) 1949		38		
„ 1953		36		
„ 1959		32		
Jimmy Shand (c. 1965)		36		
Stan Hamilton (c. 1965)	60	31		

Metronome Number M(Minim) = Bars/min × 2; M(Crotchet) = Bars/min × 4.

A variation of one bar per minute may not seem particularly important. This is true for the faster dance measures, but in the strathspey a bar per minute means a noticeable difference.

The slow Strathspey in Country Dancing is a great test of a dancer; only the very accomplished can make the slow tempo expressive and satisfying. Then indeed is it a thing of largo-lento beauty, 'kindlin bauld' as Burns expressed it, as dance and music. Even the sprightly rhythm desirable for certain tunes and such dances as the 'Strathspey Reel' and the 'Highland Fling' should be taken at an easy pace. Then it is a matter of expression and shape. Without these, however, a slow tempo is a drag, and herein lies the challenge both to dancer and musician.

CHAPTER 8

The Principal Instruments Associated with Scottish Traditional Dance Music

The fiddle

In medieval times, the instruments of the violin family to be found in the British Isles were variously identified as fiddle (*fydel, fithele*), rebec (*rybybe*) and croud (*crwth, cruit*) (plates 6, 7) and *gigue*. Their distinguishing characteristics are described in the many excellent works on ancient instruments now available to us. They were all small-sounding and relatively crude. The croud was the Celtic bowed harp, of which Otto Andersson has written so exhaustively.[1] It was rectangular in shape with a hole suitably located through which the fingers of the left hand could be passed to stop the strings. These ranged from two horsehair strands to the six strings of the Welsh *crwth* in the eighteenth and nineteenth centuries. Of this strain, too, is the Shetland *gue* or *goe*.

The viol family was much favoured in the sixteenth century Scottish and English courts and by the middle classes in the seventeenth century. The tenor viol, however was rapidly superseded by the improved Italian violin in the seventeenth century.

Whatever the motley array of fiddles in the hands of Scottish minstrels and amateurs, it was the violin which dominated the scene in the eighteenth century. There were many connoisseurs of a good violin in Scotland at that time and, it is said, Niel Gow even attained to a Gasparo. Several Scottish fiddle-makers applied themselves to the manufacture of violins after the Italian model. The most important of these were John Dickson (born *c.* 1725) of Stirling, and later London; John Blair of Edinburgh (instruments dated 1790–1805), and Matthew Hardie of Edinburgh (1755–1826) who produced a school of craftsmen. Alexander Kennedy (1695–1785) settled in London and founded a family of violin-makers, his model was Jacob Stainer (1621–83), a distinguished Austrian craftsman whom Joseph Ruddiman of Aberdeen (1733–1810) also followed before he turned to Stradivari. These are the most notable names. There grew a considerable body of amateur violin-makers throughout the country, and that bizarre genius, Sir Thomas Urquhart (1611–60), included violin-making among his many interests. For further study of this subject, the reader should turn to the works of William C. Honeyman, William Sandys and Simon Andrew Forster, and Peter Davidson.[2]

The fiddler's technique

What most distinguished the fiddler from the violinist was his technique, his bowing and his intimate association with a music which was inseparable from this technique. The fiddler arrives at his technique by watching and listening to others. The bow is scraped over the strings, with short travel, but with nuance and bite as suits the character of the music. This is true of all fiddlers, whether they be in Norway, France, Cape Breton, Quebec, or Scotland, yet all have music that is their own, although in the case of North America much of the fiddler's music is Scottish and Irish.

Nowadays, the violinist holds his instrument horizontally from the chin, the left elbow being free to adjust slightly to the needs of wrist and fingers to span the strings. The right hand holds the bow and the chin is placed to the left side of the tailpiece. This was not always the case. The eighteenth-century fiddler rested his elbow on his knee, leaning over in a cramped position and, in the case of Niel Gow, according to one of his portraits, held his fiddle with his chin on the right side of the tailpiece. There was the occasional left-handed fiddler too.

The violin bow of the seventeenth century and earlier was much shorter than it was to become later, and of a different shape. The rod was convex and the hair was held taut by the thumb, the 'screwed' bow not being introduced until about 1694; and throughout the eighteenth century the size of violin bows varied greatly. There is no reason to believe that most Scottish fiddlers of the eighteenth century did not adhere to the short bow of previous times. David Boyden, in his excellent and comprehensive book, states that 'owing to the short bow and that violinists commonly played for dancing, the run of violin music was probably played in a somewhat more articulated and non-legato style than would be usual now'.[3]

The precise, well-defined rhythms required by music for dancing favoured this treatment. It is also apparent that 'dance' players commonly held their violins against the breast rather than under the chin. This favoured the short bow, and was quite satisfactory for music in the first position. The art of fingering and shifting was developed by court violinists in the seventeenth century. The traditional fiddler, however, was indifferent to such technique.

One of the devices used by some of the Scottish fiddlers to facilitate the execution of certain recurrent intervals in some tunes was what the Italians called a *scordatura* (lit. mistuning, as against *accordatura*). Normally the violin's strings are tuned G/D/a/e/, but it may be advantageous in some instances to tune them A/E/a/e/, for example. A mistuning of this kind is called a *scordatura*. The advantage of the particular scordatura instanced is its simplification of the repeated use of the interval A — E. Otherwise, with normal tuning, the first finger would have to move awkwardly from the G to the D string to produce A — E. In this way an appropriate scordatura can eliminate the need for cross or double fingering in certain passages and thus reduce the technical skill required of the performer.

In illustration of this, consider the following passage from the reel 'Grieg's Pipes':

By a change in the tuning of the G and D strings to A and E, the fiddler now plays the reel as if it were written thus with the correct tuning (when he plays open *G* string he produces *A*; and likewise the open *D* string produces *E*):

Another example is the following jig in the same key (A)—the favourite key of fiddlers—which would be difficult to play in this key with normal tuning:

Here again, the crucial interval is A — E. This, of course, in the key of A major is the tonic-dominant (i.e. *doh* — *soh*), and tuning the strings to A/E/a/e/ as before, this interval can be executed by the playing of open strings as against the use of the first finger on both in succession:

As Henry Farmer has pointed out, the resonant tone obtained by the use of the open strings serves to give the necessary stress to the accented beats of the bar. For other examples the reader should consult Sir George Grove's *Dictionary of Music and Musicians*, 1954.

Very often a recommended scordatura was marked at the beginning of printed tunes, but one imagines that may of the itinerant fiddlers may have arrived at such devices by experience as they had little use for the printed page. It certainly explains how fiddlers with much less skill than a Heifetz or Menuhin could perform some difficult reels and strathspeys as written. The subject was dealt with in some detail in a manuscript violin tutor written by James Gillespie, published at Perth, 1768, which came into the hands of Henry Farmer and is deposited in the National Library of Scotland.[4]

Niel Gow's most notable characteristic seems to have been his bowing action, particularly a zestful up-bow occasionally accompanied by a shout. The story is told that he first came to attention at a fiddling competition in the year 1745, at which a blind musician, John McCraw, acting as judge, declared in favour of young Gow, saying, 'I would ken his bow hand among a hunder players'. Judging from the notation of strathspeys composed in the 'style of Niel Gow' in Captain Simon Fraser's *Airs and Melodies*, 1816, the Gow style was distinguished by the liberal employment of snap, grace notes, trills, and strong syncopation. Gow's snap was produced, no doubt, by the peculiar jerk of the wrist which characterizes the traditional fiddler's technique in recent times, particularly, as Collinson points out, those fiddlers who trace their lineage to Niel Gow.[5] This undoubtedly must have influenced the performance and conception of the strathspey in the post-Gow period.

A Dr McKnight wrote in the *Scots Magazine* in 1809, on the second anniversary of Niel Gow's death, as follows:

The livelier airs which belong to the class of what are called the Strathspey and Reel, and which have long been peculiar to the northern part of the island, assumed, in his hand, a style of spirit, fire and beauty, which had never been heard before . . . There is perhaps no species whatever of music executed on the violin, in which the characteristic expression depends more on the power of the *bow*, particularly in what is called the *upward* or returning *stroke*, than the Highland reel. Here accordingly was Gow's forte. His bow-hand, as a suitable instrument of his genius, was uncommonly powerful; and where the note produced by the up-bow was often feeble and indistinct in other hands, it was struck, in his playing, with a strength and certainty which never failed to surprise and delight the skilful hearer. To this extraordinary power of the bow, in the hand of this great original genius, must be ascribed the singular felicity of expression which he gave to all his music, and the native Highland goût of certain tunes, such as 'Tulloch Gorum', in which his taste and style of bowing could never be exactly reached by any other performer. We may add the effect of the *sudden shout* with which he frequently accompanied his playing in the quick tunes, and which seemed instantly to *electrify* the dancers, inspiring them with new life and energy, and rousing the spirits of the most inanimate.

[99] CAOIDH NA H 'ALBA' AIRSON NIAL GOBHA
'Caledonia's Wail for Niel Gow Her Favourite Minstrel'
Slow Strathspey Style, 'in his own Strain'. Simon Fraser, 1800

Niel always gave a shout when he changed from strathspey to reel. P. R. Drummond wrote that an 'intelligent old gentleman of the name of Cameron from Stix by Kenmore' thus described Niel Gow's playing to him: '"Some men try to give spirit to dance music by short jerking strokes, with a strong descending bow and a weak ascending, but his was a continuous stream of gorgeous sounds, *like an organ at full gallop*".' [6] The simile may not be the most felicitous, but the meaning is clear and confirms Dr McKnight's observations above.

One further comment is particularly valuable, since it comes from another of Niel's contemporaries who was well skilled in music, Alexander Campbell, the author of *Albyn's Anthology* and other works referred to in these pages. This is to be found in his journal—*A Journey from Edinburgh through parts of North Britain* (vol. i, p. 275), London, 1802, where he refers to Niel Gow as follows: 'His manner of playing his native airs is faithful, correct, and spirited. He slurs none, but plays distinctly, with accuracy, precision, and peculiar accentuation; hence the excellency of his touch and intonation, so essential to true taste and just expression, the very soul of reels and Strathspeys.'

The contemporaries and countrymen of Niel Gow, he incidentally added, were Daniel Dow and Alexander McGlashan, both then deceased.

These observations are consistent with the early comment made of Gow's 'bow hand'. It was unique, zestful and pithy. His tone was relatively rich and his fingering was sure and articulate. Above all, of course, his command of the idioms of Scottish dance music was without peer. No one has ever questioned that.

The traditional fiddler had his own bag of tricks acquired from his predecessors, double stoppings with the open string, 'shakes', 'trebblings' and glides, although the latter are more characteristic of Irish fiddling. The Irish fiddler will stop appropriate notes in the phrase about a quarter of a tone flat or sharp as the case may be, then slide his finger to the true position. In quick passages there is still the suggestion of inflections of this kind which give much character to the music. Such idiosyncrasies are difficult to convey in print. Add to this, too, the traditional conception of tonality, which well-tempered ears destroy.

It has been claimed in recent times that in Shetland there must be more fiddlers relative to size of population than in any other part of the British Isles. Many of the instruments are home-made; some with elaborate decorations inlaid on the back and most handsome in appearance. The piano-accordion has been making inroads, however, and the repertoire has been considerably mixed with importations, the indigenous Shetland tunes being more and more neglected. Efforts to preserve Shetland folklore of all kinds have increased in recent years, which is a hopeful augury.

The Shetland style of fiddling differs from the Scottish, but bears certain affinities with the Irish style. As Patrick Shuldham-Shaw reported:

> The style of playing varies very considerably from place to place ranging from a single flowing melodic line with little ornamentation to a highly elaborate style with so many 'shivers' and so much playing across the strings that it is difficult to distinguish the tune, and the instrument becomes harmonic and rhythmic rather than melodic . . . At its best it is clear, melodious and very vital with a certain amount of ornamentation performed so neatly as never to interfere with the rhythm and flow of melody. The third and seventh degrees of the scale are often neither flat nor sharp but somewhere between the two, though in these cases I usually found that the player had a definite impression of the tune being major or minor in flavour. This I found by playing back the tunes, after noting them, on a keyboard instrument, with both major and minor intervals, and the player invariably decided that one version was right and the other wrong.[7]

One wishes that there had been a similarly skilled observer of Scottish fiddling prior to the eighteenth century and later developments in the art.

It has been suggested that the Scots fiddler-composers of the eighteenth century were influenced by the music of Corelli, the great Italian composer for the violin, but this is unlikely. The music heard at the concerts in Edinburgh, and later at Aberdeen and Glasgow, was mainly by Handel, Pergolesi, Bach, Jommelli and Haydn as well as Corelli, and occasionally Purcell and Arne. The musical fare of the violinist of the time may be indicated by a volume containing Six Solos for the Violin … 'Composed by a Gentleman' (1740), formerly possessed by Henry Farmer, in which there are violin works by Pasquali, Giardini, Borghi, Festing and others. (The 'Gentleman' composer referred to was Dr Foulis of Heriot's Hospital.)

While this music and the teaching of some of the classically trained violinists drawn to Edinburgh by the 'Concerts', had its influence on the repertoire and technique of gentlemen amateurs and some native professionals such as William McGibbon (who studied in Germany) in the early part of the century, and 'Red Bob' Mackintosh, Nathaniel Gow and Alexander McGlashan in the later part, it could not have made any serious impact on the country-bred fiddler. Niel Gow, William Marshall, Robert Petrie and the many other notable fiddler-composers whose work reached the printed page, were largely country-bred, self-taught fiddlers, and there is no hint of Corelli in their compositions. Perhaps they were influenced by the classical bowing technique which, possibly in the case of Marshall, suggested a wider sweep of melody; but that is about all.* To force the self-taught fiddler out of the habits he has assiduously cultivated would be easier said than done.

Stabilini was occasionally invited to Gordon Castle and other seats of the Duke, where, of course, he met William Marshall, at that time the Duke's butler, and it is said that the celebrated violinist was not only 'exceedingly pleased' with Marshall's compositions, but delighted to hear him perform them.[8] Marshall, however, was writing fine strathspeys before he met Stabilini.

Classical music was invading the musical repertoire of the middle and upper classes in direct competition with the native strains, and this occasioned some rallying to the defence of the latter. The Rev. John Skinner (1721–1807) penned the following in his celebrated verses to Tullochgorum:

There needsna be sae great a phrase,   *They're douff and dowie at the best,*
Wi' dringing dull Italian lays,   *Wi' a' their variorum:*
I wadna' gi'e our ain Strathspeys   *They're douff and dowie at the best,*
For half a hundred score o' 'em;   *Their allegros and a' the rest,*
They're douff and dowie at the best   *They canna please a Highland taste,*
Douff and dowie, douff and dowie   *Compar'd wi' Tullochgorum.*[9]

---

* It was said of Jamie Allan of Forfar that his 'Wondrous length of arm' required a bow an inch longer than that used by 'ordinary' players. (Henry Dryerre. *Blairgowrie and Strathmore Worthies*, p. 431.)

Robert Fergusson in his 'Daft Days' writes along the same lines:

Fiddlers! your pins in temper fix   *For nought can cheer the heart sae weel*
And roset weel your fiddlesticks,   *As can a canty Highland reel;*
But banish vile Italian tricks   *It even vivifies the heel*
From out your quorum,   *To skip and dance;*
Nor fortes wi' pianos mix—   *Lifeless is he wha canna feel*
Gie's Tullochgorum.   *Its influence.*[10]

In 'The Cotter's Saturday Night' Burns, too, meant no more than this when he claimed that beside the psalm tunes of Scotland (by no means in the national idiom, but attached to Scotland by sentiment) 'Italian trills' were 'tame'.

Of the influence of the violinist's technique on the compositions of at least one composer of reels and strathspeys there is no doubt. That composer is James Scott Skinner (plate 27). Here, for the most part, is music at which the traditional fiddler of former days would balk, yet it unquestionably is exciting music in the Scottish rhythms, if not modal idiom. It is true, however, that some purists regard Skinner with suspicion, for his phrasing and ornamentations are a product of bowing technique. The chromaticism, too, of so many of his compositions is also a product of his training, and, of course, of the musical 'ear' of his time.

The traditional fiddler did not know the secret of the big sound procurable by the violinist. Nor did he need it, of course, until he was playing for a dance in a bigger space than his sound could fill. His art lay in his grasp of the idiom of his music, that quality which cannot be transmitted to the printed page, so subtle indeed that it would seem that the very heather on the hills, the sheep by the corrie and the peat-stained water leaping white over the linn, must communicate some essential flavour. No amount of formal training can supply this: it is a fact of Scottish music as it is of the folk or national music of any people. Its secret nuances can only be absorbed from the main stream of tradition itself.

The fiddler learned his tunes by ear and only a few could pick a tune from the book. This aural transmission of tunes led, of course, to the currency of as many versions of them as there were fiddlers. In the introduction to the second part of Gow's *Repository*, Nathaniel Gow writes, 'In every part of Scotland where we have occasionally been, and from every observation we were able to make, [we] have not *once* met two professional musicians who play the *same* note of *any* tune.' It was hoped that the publication of what the collectors believed was the best version of a tune would be a boon to the musician; it certainly has been a boon to posterity.

Scott Skinner had something to say on the subject of native art in a manual of his technique which he left us. He believed that many prominent contemporary fiddlers 'could have soared even higher with good sound training in manual equipment and still remembered to render their country's music by the light of nature'.[11] He was probably right, but of course he would have agreed that any loss of character of the music would be less desirable than poor technique. The subtle tricks of nuance 'stopping' and 'trebbling' which are part of the craft of the traditional fiddler are indispensable, but the advantages of tutored skill need not be incompatible, and it may well be that Niel Gow, for instance had discovered some of its secrets. K. N. Macdonald includes a note on Scott Skinner's technique in his Skye Collection, 1898.[12] There was what Skinner called the 'straight slur', (♩. ♪) performed by lifting the bow smartly off the strings, both notes being taken in one up or down bow, the short note being taken with the end of the bow. In his publications, he indicated the mode of attack by such symbols as the 'arrow' ( ) to indicate that the first note is to be taken down and the other three all up, taking care to re-emphasize the third note. The 'loop' ( ) was used only at the termination of a strain, the bow being dragged along generally in a down bow. In playing strathspeys, the D's, A's and E's were to be played 'double', i.e. with the open and the adjacent closed strings together, for greater effect. When closing a tune, the chord of the key was to be given 'as many strathspeys and reels do not end of the key but on the 5th'.

In the performing of a number of tunes in series, as is demanded by the Highland Reel, a crucial contribution to musical interest and to the dance can be made by the judicious variation of keys. This applies to all extended music as every musician knows. A change of key along with change of tune has a refreshing impact on the senses. Apart from this, it is of no advantage to the traditional musician to have command of a number of keys. Many of the tunes in his repertoire are in familiar modes, and most self-taught exponents of Scottish music—on various instruments—confine themselves to those keys which they find easiest to handle. Skinner remarks that A and D major were 'the most effective and popular'. It may be significant that these are the keys closest to the scale of the great pipe. The printed collections of fiddle music suggest that the 'flat' keys were favoured by Marshall and Gow although more recent editors transcribe many of these into the nearest 'sharp' key.

Scott Skinner had a very decided opinion about the character of various keys. The distinction between major and minor is evident, as between one mode and another; but are there differences in tonal character of a given mode depending upon the pitch of its tonic?

There is the slender possibility of a scientific justification for this idea in the case of a string instrument; but psychological considerations are probably much stronger. In any case, Scott Skinner's description of what he considered the character of various keys is of some interest:

C—bold and piercing
A minor—sad and plaintive
G—plenty of body
E minor—sterile, thin
D—splendid body
B minor—rather sad
A—the fiddle key

F♯ minor—exquisitely harrowing
E—brilliant but lacking in body
F—thinnish
B flat—velvet, very rich and fine
E flat   } weird, fascinating
C minor } and beautifully sad.[13]

On the subject of technique, a correspondent quoted among notices in Skinner's *Logie Collection*, 1888, has this to say of a Skinner performance:

From my own experience of violin playing, I will say, without fear of contradiction, that as a classical player his execution in bowing and fingering is excellent, and that he produced a superior tone. His dexterous staccato upbow gives a telling effect in rapid scale and arpeggi. The ease and the grace with which he glides from the nut to the top of the fingerboard, and *vice versa*, on all strings, seems, to the mind of the ordinary listener, unsurpassable. His double stopping in some very intricate passages was truthfully executed. He did not even descend in my estimation in his trick performance à la Paginini. He has evidently made the left hand pizzicato and harmonic playing a study, which enables him to give an effective rendering of the bird-like sounds . . .

The *Forres Gazette* reports the 'Brothers Skinner' at the Mechanics Hall—'unrivalled in Scotch music, and playing Strathspeys and other dance music with a swing and a length of bow which have never been equalled since the days of Donald Grant of Cromdale'. A favourite *pièce de resistance* on these occasions was 'Auld Robin Gray'.

As regards performance, one authority tells us that strathspeys should be begun softly, with controlled spirit and ended loudly and vigorously.[14] Doubtless this was not intended to apply to dance accompaniment.

It is a pity that we have no sound recordings of the performances of the famous fiddlers of the past. Skinner alone of that number has been recorded, his earliest being made in the days of the cylindrical records and the latest in 1925. For the earliest records he used a violin fitted with a soundbox and horn for amplification. This was called a 'Stroh' fiddle and the particular instrument Skinner used is now in the possession of John Junner of Banchory, who himself has recorded some of the outstanding Scottish fiddlers of today for his private collection.

The stock-and-horn (*hornpipe or piobcorn*)

In the *Complaynt of Scotland*, two of the instruments played by the shepherds were—'ane pipe maid of ane gaet (goat) horne' and the 'corn pipe'.

The first is a horn with a reed, the second is a reed pipe with a horn-end. This reed pipe and horn was called the stock 'n horn (plate 9) in Lowland Scotland and piobcorn (pibgorn or piccorn) in the Gaelic-speaking regions. *Piob* (Gaelic), *pib* (Welsh), *pipeau* (French), are *pipe* in English and similarly *corn* is horn. The English name, of course, is hornpipe.

In a letter to George Thomson, 19th November 1794, Burns writes:

> Tell my friend Allen (for I am sure that we only want the trifling circumstance of being known to one another to be the best friends on earth) that I much suspect he has, in his plates, mistaken the figure of the stock & horn.—I have, *at last*, gotten one; but it is a very rude instrument.—It is composed of three parts; the stock, which is the hinder thigh-bone of a sheep, such as you see in a mutton-ham: the horn, which is a common Highland cow's horn, cut off at the smaller end, untill the aperture be large enough to admit the 'stock' to be pushed up through the horn, untill it be held by the thicker or hip-end of the thigh-bone; and lastly, an oaten reed exactly cut & notched like that which you see every shepherd-boy have when the corn-stems are green & full-grown.—The reed is not made fast in the bone, but is held by the lips, & plays loose in the smaller end of the 'stock'; while the 'stock' & the horn hanging on its larger end, is held by the hands in playing.—The 'stock' has six, or seven, ventiges on the upper side, & one back-ventige, like the common flute.—This of mine was made by a man from the braes of Athole, & is exactly what the shepherds wont to use in that country.— However, either it is not quite properly bored in the holes, or else we have not the art of blowing it rightly; for we can make little of it.[15]

This account gives us an excellent idea of the stock-and-horn as it was known in the Scottish countryside, and particularly in the Central Highlands. Another description of the 'original genuine Scottish pastoral pipe' is given by the editor of Dr Pennecuik's works in 1815: '. . . the *stock-in-horn*, consisting of a cow's horn, a boor-tree stock, with stops, in the middle, and an oaten reed at the smaller end for the mouthpiece'. The boor-tree or bourtree is the elder. In 'Colkelbie's Sow', the fifteenth-century poem, we read of 'the pype maid of a borit bourtre' as the instrument of cowherds.

In the same poem the rustics set out with *stoc horns* blowing. This, however, is probably the open cow horn. Leyden writes that the *stock and horn* was formed in such a way that the parts could be easily separated, so that the horn could be used as a bugle, and the pipe as a simple pipe or whistle.[16] Jamieson describes it thus in his *Etymological Dictionary of the Scottish Language*, 1818: 'A musical instrument composed of the stock, which is the hinder thigh-bone of a sheep: the horn, the smaller end of a cow's horn, and an oaten reed.'

In his *House of Fame* Chaucer writes:

> *And many flowtes and liltynghorne,*
> *And pipes made of grene corne,*
> *As has thise little herde-gromes*
> *That kepe bestis in the bromes.*[17]

His 'liltyng horne', or the 'lilt pipe' of the Scots fifteenth-century poem 'The Howlate',[18] are doubtless other names for our stock and horn, although Chaucer uses the word 'hornpipe' in his translation of the *Romaunt de la Rose*:

> *. . . Yet wolde he lye*
> *Discordaunt ever fro armonye,*
> *And distoned from melodie,*
> *Controve he wolde, and foule fayle,*
> *With Hornpipes of Cornewaile.*

In this, Chaucer has translated *chalemaulx de Cornoaille* as 'hornpipes of Cornewaile' and this in turn has been interpreted as 'hornpipes of *Cornwall*' by later readers. *Cornoaille*, however, is a district in south-west Brittany just as it is the name of the place of origin (Cornwall) of the Britons who settled there. We would expect the culture of Brittany to bear affinity to that of Cornwall and that the confusion of *Cornoaille* with Cornwall would therefore lead to no serious error. However, there is no trace of popular use of the hornpipe in Cornwall, although we shall see that it was certainly a familiar instrument in Wales.

The *chalumelle*, however, described as an instrument of the clarinet family by most authorities, was popular in France, and the *corne challumelle* is mentioned in an early French poem by Merciai—'Les Vigiles de la mort du Roi Charles Septiesme.'[19] This to all appearances seems equivalent to the hornpipe, but *chalumeaus* and *chalumele* are distinguished in the *Romaunt de la Rose*, viz.:[20]

> *Puis met en* cimbales *sa cure;*
> *Puis prent* freteaus, *e refretele,*
> *E chalumeaus, e chalumele, . . .*
> *E tabour e fleüte e timbre,*
> . . . .
> *Puis prent* sa muse e puis travaille
> *Aux estives de Cornoaille,*

Chaucer, therefore, cannot be quoted as an authority testifying to the association of the hornpipe with Cornwall.

Nevertheless the hornpipe appears to have had fairly wide currency in sixteenth-century England, not only as an instrument, but as a country dance and as a class of tune. It is pleasant to read of that period in Edmund Spenser's *The Shepheard's Calendar*, 1579:

> *Before them yode a lustie tabrere,*
> *That to many a horn-pype playd.*
> *Whereto they dauncen eche one with his mayd.*
> *To see those folks make such jovysaunce,*
> *Made my heart after the pype to daunce.*[21]

And this from Scotland, in Allan Ramsay's *Gentle Shepherd* (plate 4) over a century later:

> *When I begin to tune my stock and horn,*
> *Wi a' her face she shows a cauldrife scorn—*
> *—Flocks, wander where ye like, I dinna care,*
> *I'll break my reed, and never whistle mair'* [22]

There are many other references in Spenser's pastoral poem, particularly to the oaten reed or oaten pipe, or what Shakespeare calls 'oaten strawe', the most basic of the reed instruments of the countryside, from which, it seems certain, all other reed instruments have been derived. If the slender oaten reed is made to form a removable mouthpiece to a stalk of larger bore in which finger holes are cut to form a scale, we have a superior reed pipe, and doubtless it was a pipe of this kind which Leyden in *The Complaynt of Scotland*, 1801, says had a compass which varied with the ingenuity displayed in its formation, and that in the Highlands he had heard produced from it tones which he had more than once mistaken for those of the bagpipe.

Horns, too, are basic, and have an archaeological advantage over the oaten reed in that they can survive in old tombs. They have been found in tombs identified as megalithic, Iron Age and Bronze Age, along with bone pipes of the kind forming the stock-and-horn described by Burns above, not only in the British Isles, but all over Europe. The medieval Scots blew horns of different tones when going into battle and doubtless some of these were reed horns.

We know that the Anglo-Saxons had a *swegel-horn*, i.e. a 'shinbone' and horn, and a similar instrument of deer bone is in the National Museum of Ireland, Dublin.[23]

Several examples of hornpipe are reported to survive: two in the Royal College of Music, London; three from the eighteenth century in the Welsh Folk Museum, St Fagans; and one in the collection of the Society of Antiquaries, London. As early as 1775, Daines Barrington wrote of a specimen of the pibcorn from Anglesey where it was then in some use, although he tells us it was scarcely used in any other part of North Wales. He added that 'the tone, considering the materials of which the Pib-corn is composed, is really very tolerable, and resembles an indifferent hautbois'.

It was from 18 to 20 inches long, the stock was of reed with six finger holes in front and a small thumb hole at the back, a bell-mouth of horn and a mouthpiece of horn.[24] Some, according to the surviving examples, had a wooden stock, of square section, which, according to Edward Jones was a type restricted to Anglesey.[25]

Jones also mentions a Welsh instrument of allied form—'a sort of pipe used in some parts of South Wales, called *cornicyll* (from cornig, a diminutive of corn), which has a concealed reed on the same principle as the pibcorn, and the mouth-piece screws off in order to introduce the reed; in other respects the instrument is made like a common clarinet'.[26]

The two types of reed, the 'beating reed' (clarinet style) and the 'double reed' (oboe style) have both been used in the hornpipe, although the clarinet type was probably the original. The use of a mouthpiece chamber to enclose the reed protected it, and may have made a little easier the maintaining of a steady blast while breathing with the nostrils, a trick known to many bagpipers who use a practice chanter.

In the Middle East and Southern Asia, a gourd is sometimes used as a mouthpiece chamber, and there are often two pipes, one of which in some forms serves as a drone, and sometimes an inflated skin bag takes the place of the gourd—a bagpipe! The variety of instruments of this class is very great in India, as a cursory study of Indian wind instruments—the *toomeri, poongi, magoodi*, and others—will show, but the Arabs have almost as many.

In the British Isles, the regions of greatest concentration of the hornpipe appear to have been Wales, Lancashire, South Scotland and Ireland. There can be no doubt that it was familiar in many parts of the Highlands, although its traditional association with herd boys or herdsmen explains why it appears more a part of the domesticated Scottish environment— much of which was Gaelic-speaking along the Highland line in the eighteenth century—than that of the 'sylvan' Scots, as John Major so aptly described them.[27]

The hornpipe has given its name to a class of dance music and a class of dance in which attention is concentrated on stepping out the rhythm. The use of the word in these senses is clearly an English contribution, although the classes of music or dance of which it is used are not all necessarily English. The Scots and Irish have simply adopted the word, apparently because they had no word of their own for step-dance.

The bagpipe

The idea of inserting a reed pipe into a leather or skin bag acting as a reservoir of air is very ancient. This is the 'pipe maid of ane bleddir and o ane reid' of the *Complaynt*. The bag was inflated through a blow pipe by mouth or by bellows.

The addition of a further reed pipe (or pipes) to the bag, devised to
roduce a sustained note (or notes), produces what was called in the
omplaynt 'ane drone bagpipe'. A great variety of similar instruments of
iis class is to be found in India and in the Middle East.

There are several suggestions of evidence of the bagpipe in the Middle
ast and Greece as early as the eighth century B.C.[28]; but the earliest
ertain allusions to an instrument of this class occur in 100 A.D., with
ference to the Roman emperor Nero. One is from the hand of Suetonius,
ie Roman historian, who writes of Nero that towards the end of his life
e 'took a public oath that if he managed to keep his throne he would
:lebrate the victory with a music festival, performing successively on
rater-organ, *choraulam et utricularium*'.[29] The tibia utricularis of the
.omans was a 'pipe' and 'leather bag', unquestionably the 'bagpipe'! A
:reek contemporary of Suetonius, Dion Chrysostomos, provides the
:cond comment on Nero and the bagpipe: 'Besides, they say that he
>uld paint and fashion statues and play the pipe, both by means of his
ps and by tucking a skin beneath his armpits.'[30]

Obviously, if the Celts did not themselves bring the bagpipe to Britain,
iey could have made acquaintance with it through the Romans. But it is
ot until the thirteenth century that we encounter any pictorial presenta-
ons—as distinct from bas reliefs—of this immensely popular instrument
1 Britain. One of the earliest of these is the device of a pig playing on a
agpipe, forming part of the illumination of an initial letter in an Irish
ipographical history, *Dinnseanohus*, dated 1300, in the British Museum.[31]
'his MS. describes the Irish kerne who accompanied King Edward to
.alais in 1297.

The most notable early Scottish representations of the bagpipe occur
mong the frescoes at Melrose and Rosslyn Chapel. These also are from
ie thirteenth century. If tradition is correct—and that is not unlikely—the
rst music that the infant Christ heard was of the shepherd's bagpipes, yet
1 some of the lurid medieval paintings depicting Hell, the bagpipes find
. place. The evidence is irrefutable that His Satanic Majesty himself pre-
:rred the bagpipe above all other instruments and when, in 'shape o'
east' in a 'winnock-bunker' in 'Alloway's auld haunted kirk'—

> He screw'd the pipes and gart them skirl,
> Till roof and rafters a' did dirl' [32]

—he was in his musical element, and of course he had centuries of
ractice behind him. This is an embarrassing association which genera-
ons of pipers have had to live down and which provides a good indica-
on to us, if we did not know of it otherwise, of the place of the bagpipe
1 the social life of the people. Chaucer's miller in the Canterbury Tales
:d the pilgrims with a bagpipe, and other thirteenth- to fifteenth-century
:ferences could be cited from Lowland Scotland and England, and have

been quoted elsewhere in these pages; but as late as 1625, William
Browne, an English poet, could write:

> As I have seene the Lady of May
> Set in an arbour (on a holy day)
> Built by the May-pole, where the jocund swaines
> Dance with the maidens to the bagpipes straines,[33]

and later in the same century we read of a scene in London: 'some were
dancing to a *bagpipe*; others whistling to a Base Violin, two Fiddlers
scraping Lilla burlero, My Lord Mayor's Delight, upon a couple of
Crack'd Crowds'.[34] But by this time the bagpipes were rapidly receding
from the English scene and the field was more and more being left to the
Great Highland Pipe, until today it comes as a surprise to many to realize
that the bagpipe was not always solely associated with Scotland!

As regards the English bagpipes, certain counties seem to have cultivated their own varieties: Lincolnshire, Worcestershire, Yorkshire,
Nottinghamshire, Lancashire and Northumberland are all mentioned in
this connection. Shakespeare refers to a 'Yorkshire bagpiper' and 'the
drone of a Lincolnshire bagpipe'.* Judging from inscriptions and sculp-
tures and evidence of this sort, drones do not appear on the simple
'bleddir and ane reed' until the thirteenth century in Britain.

The disappearance of the bagpipe began in the south and moved north-
wards until only the Scottish and North of England varieties remained by
the late eighteenth century. By this time the drone bagpipes predominating
in Scotland were the Great Highland Pipe or Piob Mór (plate 11), which
was mouth-filled, and a smaller version of the same, used for dance music,
which may in some cases have been bellows-blown. There were also what
were known as the Lowland or Border pipes. The border pipes were
bellows-blown with three drones emerging from a single stock (plate 14).
The scale of the chanter is said to have been the same as that of the piob
mór, although this has not been convincingly investigated. The drones
were of three forms—one, tuned as for the piob mór, another likewise but
with one of the drones tuned to the dominant between the tenor and bass
drone; and yet another with three drones in octaves, starting with the
lowest chanter note.

There was also a smaller version, the largest drone being a mere ten inches
as opposed to about twenty-four inches in the above. All of these varieties
of bagpipe found in the Scottish Border country had 'open' chanters.[35]

The Irish had a mouth-filled and a bellows-filled bagpipe. The latter
survived into the nineteenth century and were called the 'Union' Pipes, a
corruption of the Gaelic—*uillean*—meaning 'elbow'. Clearly a similar
corruption, as Flood[36] suggests, explains the 'woolen' bagpipes referred

* 1 Henry IV, I, ii. Some commentators suggest that this was a facetious allusion to the
croaking of frogs in the Lincolnshire fens.

to by the English writer Richard Stanihurst in 1575. Another mouth-filled bagpipe was introduced in 1912 to Irish pipe bands, for military purposes, and today they often use the Scottish piob mór or Highland bag-pipe which has been the most enduring bagpipe of the British Isles, thanks to its special place in the culture of the Gael and to its military use.

Apart from the differences in tone and technique which exist between the main styles of bagpipe, there are differences in tonality and compass, and not only between one style and another, but within a given style at various stages of its evolution. The bagpipes of the British Isles—with the exception of the Northumbrian pipes—have double-beating reeds in the chanter and single-beating reeds in the drones.

The Northumbrian 'smallpipes'

The endearing Northumbrian 'small'-pipes, or 'smallpipes' as it is usually written, is the smallest of the British bagpipes, bellows-blown and fitted with adjustable-pitch drones. The bag is held under the left arm and the bellows is usually strapped to the right forearm exactly in the manner and form of the French *musette* of which the smallpipes can be regarded as an English version. The chanter is of uniform bore, and not tapered as in the case of the Highland bagpipe, and its sound is sweet, very similar in quality to that of the *Uillean* pipes. The chanter, unlike that of the piob mór, is closed and of uniform bore, although it is said that both chanter and drones were open-ended prior to the eighteenth century.[37]

Early in the eighteenth century, the Northumbrian pipes differed little from the *musette*, the minature bellows-blown bagpipes which, after Hotteterre's improvements (*c.* 1650), became very popular with ladies of the court of Louis XIV. Both had four drones and double-beating reeds throughout. The drones were enclosed in a cluster within an ivory cylinder and all solid parts were of ivory. The *musette* had a gaily embroidered bag and its drones were bedecked with coloured ribbons, whereas the Northumbrian instrument had a plain woollen cover over the bag and no special adornment. The drones were tuned by means of buttons sliding through slots cut in the enclosing cylinder; but by the end of the eighteenth century, the drones of the Northumbrian pipes were divested of the cylinder.

During the nineteenth century 'improved' versions of the smallpipes were introduced until there were eighteen stops fitted to the chanter and six drones, so that they could be tuned to any major or minor key. Later, four drones and a chanter with seventeen stops became general. This gave the Northumbrian pipes a flexible chromatic scale of two octaves. The four drones are used three at a time, two are tuned to G an octave apart spanning 'middle' C, and the other to D. In the older instruments, the compass extended an octave—and possibly a note or two more in some varieties—upwards from G, second line of the treble stave. The scale was G. The endowment with chromaticism has been no advantage to the instrument; indeed it did harm in the same way as it would do to the Highland pipe, destroying its distinctive character and ancient flavour.

The character of the Northumbrian pipes can be described as domestic. Its tone quality has been described as 'cheeping' and 'chirpy', and W. Gillies Whittaker wrote:

> It wins the hearts of all hearers, it insinuates itself into the mind, it produces a feeling of quiet contentment. I have often watched the faces of audiences listening to the small-pipes; gradually every face relaxed into a smile . . . The player may smoke while playing. Possibly this circumstance has helped to make so many pipe tunes light-hearted . . . I shall never forget Mr. Clough, jun. . . . playing 'Bonny at morn' to me. He tuned his drones in a new way, and though I had known the lovely mournful melody intimately for many years, arranged it in various ways, taught it, sung it, and conducted it chorally, it seemed like something utterly different from what I had known and it moved me profoundly, haunting me for many a day and night afterwards.' [38]

The music of the smallpipes is markedly distinguished from that of other pipes by the way a note can be started and stopped cleanly and sharply at will and even reiterated indefinitely. This is made possible by the closed chanter; when all the finger-holes are closed there is no sound. In the case of the Highland and other pipes, the chanter is open, so that there is always sound as long as there is air in the bag. It is not possible to reiterate a note on an open chanter without the note of the open chanter intervening. The performer on the piob mór or Great Pipe achieves the impression of reiteration by interposing 'burls' or flourishes between the repeated notes and thus makes a virtue of necessity with fascinating effect. Staccato playing, therefore, is natural to the smallpipes but not to the Great Pipe, giving even a rapid cascade of notes clean, brilliant articulation, like showers of droplets from a fountain.

These characteristics of the smallpipes lead to the extensive used of arpeggios and the treatment of every tune as a subject for variations contrasting staccato and legato runs. On another instrument the variations may sound elementary and even puerile, yet the effect can be enchanting on the smallpipes. This, no doubt, has led to most smallpipes tunes being in compound time: 9/8, 6/8, 3/4, 12/8, 6/4. Also, from a habit of fingering, intervals of a third are greatly favoured. A common example of this is 'The Keel Row', undoubtedly a smallpipes tune. Intervals of a sixth are also popular and a large number of the tunes, in common with Scottish folk music in general, do not end on the tonic.

A characteristic specimen of smallpipe variations is 'Jockie stays long at the Fair' [100], from Peacock's collection: [39]

Quickly

[100]

John Peacock's *Collection*, c. 1810

Perhaps it may be asked what Northumbrian music has to do with Scotland. In answer to this, it need only be pointed out that the Scottish-English border was not a 'sound barrier', either in music or in language. It is certainly curious, however, that a Northumbrian musician visiting Edinburgh in the early nineteenth century found that the smallpipes were new to Gow (our informant writes Niel but it was more probably Nathaniel or his son Neil) and even more curious that the erudite antiquarian Robert Chambers who is often quoted in these pages, and who was born in 1800 and raised in Peebles in the Borders, 'did not know the Northumbrian pipes and airs' in 1856.[40]

The Highland bagpipe

The Piob Mór, or Great Pipe, or Great Highland Bagpipe (plate 11) as it is variously called, is probably so named from its loudness, arising from the bore of its drones and the size of its reeds, relative to those of other bagpipes. As mentioned previously, it has an 'open' chanter, i.e. when the holes are completely covered, there is sound (the chanter note) which thus cannot sharply be cut off as in the smallpipes, and the bag is mouth inflated. The nine degrees of the chanter are roughly: G A B C D E F G A. Only G, A and E can be said to sound identical to the corresponding notes on the piano, although the series sounds acceptably close to the same on the piano (or 'well-tempered' series) with the exception of D and top G which are markedly sharp.

The results of modern experiments have established the following general results with reference to the 'well-tempered' (piano) scale:

A, very slightly flatter than A
G, much sharper than G
F, slightly flatter than F$\sharp$
E, approximately the same as E
D, much sharper than D
C, much flatter than C$\sharp$
B, slightly flatter than B
A, same as A
G, approximately the same as G

Is this series of sounds intended to comprise a single diatonic scale, or is it a keyboard embracing a system of scales? The late Donald Main was an eloquent proponent of the latter suggestion; he specifically postulated a system of four-note scales, which he called 'pentatonic sequences' and which he maintained were the tonal basis of pibroch.[41] His arguments have not yet been adequately examined.

As it happens, the chanter 'keyboard' accommodates very well the Mixolydian Mode (with A as tonic) and the scale of D major, really what we could call the plagal scale of D major (i.e. we would have the scale of D major if the lower notes of the chanter series were raised one octave). It also reasonably accommodates the scale of A major and by eliminating C and F we can obtain the pentatonic scale GAB-DE-G.

The piob mór has three drones: two tenor drones tuned to A, an octave below the second degree of the chanter, and one bass a double octave below. Thus we do not have a chord of drones, but a reinforced A. Frequency analysis has shown that the bass drone has a strong second harmonic giving the effect of a fifth, i.e. E, and the tenor drone a strong first harmonic at the pitch of the Chanter A.[42]

Tuning to two As and a D, or two Ds and an A, has been known in the past, and Arthur Geddes has pointed out that by tuning the drones to B, the instrument is free to play music in the Aeolian Mode (B minor) [43] (starting on B—l td r mf s (l)) which he claims extends the piob mór's usefulness in the accompaniment of song in that mode. There is no reason to doubt that he experimented with this, but most pipers would find it not only impractical but aurally objectionable. The use of the piob mór on such 'casual' music is of course an abuse.

On the face of it there seems something perverse in clinging to the 'imperfections' of the Highland bagpipe when by increasing the number of stops, altering the system of boring and devising a means of altering the drones—as with the Northumbrian pipes—it would conform more closely to our conception of tonality. But if the instrument were altered in this way it would lose its whole being. Whatever 'well tempered' ears may say of its effects, its tonality becomes intelligible with familiarity and is perfect in that music which is specifically composed for it. This music is called Ceòl Mór (great music); the other, the marches, strathspeys, reels, and song tunes—Highland as well as Lowland—is Ceòl Beag (little music) and for the most part, not being composed for the bagpipe, is performed on the instrument only with many compromises to compensate for the lack of range and chromaticism. 'For the most part', because there have been many tunes in this category, particularly jigs, composed by pipers specially for their instrument.

The piob mór did not always have three drones. An old bagpipe formerly in the possession of J. & F. Glen, Edinburgh, had two drones emerging from a common stock which bears the letters 'R. McD.' above the inscription of a galley, and the date 1409 in Roman numerals (plate 10). Another old instrument with one drone belonging to Macdonald of

Kinloch-Moidart is said to have led the Macdonalds into battle at Bannockburn.[44] The bass drone is said to have been added in the eighteenth century, but perhaps it would be more correct to say the 'third' drone, for possibly the original and the source of the term 'Great Pipe' was the bass drone, as may be inferred from the allusion in Tans'ur's *A New Musical Grammar*, London, 1753: 'There is generally three pipes, viz. the Great Pipe or Drone, and the Little Drone—each tuned in concord to the other, and the chanter or small pipe, which is about 15 inches long, with 8 holes like a Flute. They all have reeds in their tops, and make a fine Harmony; especially if they have a flat chanter, in the D pitch.' Also, in an Irish engraving of 1581 (plate 13), showing a piper leading some warriors, the bag is almost as long as the piper's torso and is held in front between his arms [45]; but of importance here, there are two drones as in the instrument described in Tans'ur's *Grammar*, and one is decidedly larger than the other.

Joseph MacDonald, a native of Sutherland, whose valuable treatise, *A Compleat Theory of the Scots Highland Bagpipe* was written in the second half of the eighteenth century,[46] tells us that in his time the 'North-country' pipes all had three drones, those in the Isles two. The reason given by the Islesmen 'for laying aside the use of the Great Drone' was that it was too loud for the chanter. This, in MacDonald's opinion, was 'frivolous and unfounded', as the fault could easily have been rectified by weakening the reed of the Great Drone. The Great Drone, in his view—and most will agree with him—added vastly to the grandeur of the pipes both in sound and show.

W. L. Manson, in his *Highland Bagpipe*, an oft-quoted authority, goes so far as to declare that 'the bagpipe had originally but one drone. A second drone was added about 1500 and a third about 1800'.[47] This last date is refuted by Joseph MacDonald's remarks alone. A picture of the piper to the Laird of Grant, dated 1733 (plate 1), shows three drones on his bagpipe and this seems to be the earliest pictorial record of a mouth-blown bagpipe with three drones. There is a dearth of information on this point prior to the eighteenth century, although there is ample evidence of bagpipes with two, or one drone, or even without drones at all from early medieval times in Britain and on the Continent.

The tonality of these instruments is a matter of conjecture. Most, we can safely assume, adhered to the common folk modes. The Scottish piob mór may have a unique tonality, as we have already observed, a tonality which has significance in the art form of Pibroch, an art form which belongs peculiarly to the piob mór. The function of the drones is integral to Pibroch, and it is therefore of interest to consider the bagpipe which may have been used by the MacCrimmons and their pupils at their piping school in Skye when it first attracts our notice late in the sixteenth century. Here, again, however, there is no direct evidence to help us.

How many drones had the MacCrimmons on their pipes? Possibly two. Was the bass drone one of them? Again, noting the West-Highland aversion to the Great Drone this would seem unlikely, but MacDonald does not say that they rejected its introduction; he says only that they 'layed it aside'. It is worth noting that at Dunvegan in 1773 at the daily recital of bagpipe music, Dr Johnson 'used to stand for some time with his ear close to the *great* drone'!

Duncan Fraser writing in 1907, remarks that 'in my young days the Inverary Gipsies, who were—many of them—great pipers, never used any but a one-drone or two-drone Bagpipe'.[48] I myself can add to this that I have recently listened to a tinker in that very town play a three-drone bag-pipe with but one drone in operation, and on another occasion only two. James Logan states in a footnote that 'The absurd term "pair of pipes", perhaps arose from many of the poorer sort having formerly but two drones. It may be observed, pipers often have but two that are furnished with reeds.'[49]

The Edinburgh Gaelic Society found it necessary in the early years of the nineteenth century to make a regulation requiring all pipers at the competition of piping to employ three drones. Apparently many had hitherto competed with only two. The two-drone piper has some advan-tage in the matter of tuning his drones—an essential particular—and of course in the amount of air required to sustain the whole chorus.

I have already alluded to the existence of small replicas of the piob mór, and what I have said is supported by Joseph MacDonald:

Though the Reels and Jigs, peculiar to the Pipe, are in large Com-panies as at Weddings, etc. playd to good Effect on the greater Pipe, yet they have besides, thro' the Highlands in general, a smaller Bagpipe, Compleat, the same in form and apparatus with the greater, differing only in size, and used for Dancing Music alone, altho all other Music peculiar to the Instrument may be also played on it as truely, though not so grandly, as on the large Pipe.

There is certainly evidence, 'verbal' evidence shall we say, of a bellows-blown pipe in the Highlands, but no example has survived. The 'half-set' piob mór, and chamber pipes, were sold in the nineteenth century, and in fact may be purchased today, but bellows-blown versions are no longer seen.

It is most interesting to note MacDonald's reference to 'Reels and Jigs *peculiar to* the Pipe' in the above quotation.

It is assumed that the great pipe, referred to in some burgh records, is the Highland pipe, and possibly it is. Why is it not called the 'Highland' pipe? For instance, a charge was laid against a piper in Perth in 1623 for playing on 'the *great*-pipe'; and even on the Borders, in Hawick, in 1700, Thomas Beattie the town piper was censured for 'his night revelling in going upon the fairs, night playeing with the *great* pype through the haill towne in company of some drunken persons . . .'

The term pìob mór, as we have seen, is indeed the Gaelic name for the Highland Pipe. But although Alexander Hume, the poet, refers to 'Highland' pipes in the year of the Armada, the fact that burgh records and the like distinguish only what they called the Great Pipe, means that it was apparently not associated by them peculiarly with the Highlands. Such a name as the Great Pipe, however, does imply the existence of a smaller pipe—or pipes—and, of course, we have identified some of these.

Lowland or Border pipes

Leyden makes some unexpected comments on bagpipe music in the Borders (*c.* 1800). He tells us that

the Borders, particularly the middle and west Marches, possessed a peculiar style of music, well adapted to the bagpipe, the wild and ferocious expression of which, corresponded to the fierce and energetic character of the Border clans. The original airs of the *Gathering songs* and Historical ballads have no inconsiderable resemblance to the martial tunes of the Welch, Irish, and the Scotish Highlanders, and formed the favourite music of the Border pipers; among whom the perfection of the art was supposed to consist in being able to sing, dance, and play on the bagpipe at the same time. I recollect to have heard different pipers applauded for this excellence. With the town pipers, there is the utmost reason to believe that many ancient airs have perished. The last piper of Jedburgh, whom I have often heard play on the bagpipe in infancy, always affirmed that he was acquainted with some ancient airs unknown to every other person. I only recollect *The Hunting of the Fox*, which from its uncommon expression and the irregularity of its modulation seemed to have a strong resemblance to a Highland Pibrach.[50]

This Border music of which Leyden writes may or may not have been 'Border' in origin. 'The Hunting of the Fox', for instance, in all likelihood is the same as 'The Fox Chase', a well-known and favourite set of variations among Irish pipers in the nineteenth century. This composition, which is to be found in *O'Farrell's Pocket Companion for the Irish or Union Pipes*, *c.* 1806, has been attributed to Edward Keating Hyland, a celebrated blind piper who lived at the end of the eighteenth century. The resemblance to pibroch would arise from the variations form.

Leyden was referring to the bellows pipe of the Borders—when we talk of singing while playing the bagpipe we are considering a bellows pipe—and one suspects his imagination has run away with him when we read the phrase 'wild and ferocious expression' with reference to a bellows pipe, or, indeed any pipe of lesser power than the pìob mór itself. But the larger bellows pipe of the Borders was used for military purposes in its time. It saw something of a revival, W. Gillies Whittaker tells us, in the years prior to World War I, with Boy Scout troops and the Officers' Training Corps in some Border regions.[51]

Alexander Campbell, poet and editor of *Albyn's Anthology*, left an MS. journal in which he records some information about famous Border pipers which he received during a visit to Roxburghshire in 1816 from Sir Walter Scott's uncle Thomas Scott, at Monklaw, himself an enthusiastic performer.[52] In this he notes that Geordie Syme was the best piper of his day, which recalls the caption under Syme's likeness in Kay's *Portraits*:

> *This represents old Geordie Sime,*
> *A famous piper in his time.*[53]

He was one of those who knew the art of pinching the back hole of the chanter of the Border pipes to produce the high octave, as did his contemporary Donald Maclean of Galashiels, who in consequence enjoyed the distinction of being the only man who could play the then popular 'Sour Plums of Galashiels' [101].

[101] SOUR PLUMS OF GALASHIELS
G. F. Graham, *Songs of Scotland*, 1848

John Hastie, piper of Jedburgh (whom we have already noticed), was
said to be the first performer who introduced what Thomas Scott described
as 'those tunes now played in Teviotdale on the bagpipe'. Hastie's
instrument, as we have seen, was the bellows bagpipe. He was decidedly
of the opinion, widely shared by his piping contemporaries, that the
Border bellows-bagpipe was of Highland origin or at any rate from the
North-East coast. Campbell stated that this was a remarkable fact, not
generally known, and difficult of belief.*

The earliest pipers of the Border, said Scott, were of the tinker family of
Allen, born and bred at Yetholm in Roxburghshire. James Allen, who
died in 1808 at the advanced age of eighty, was piper to the Duke of
Northumberland, and was, it is said, the best performer of his time of the
'loud' and 'small' bagpipes. That is, presumably, the large and small
bellows pipes.

Other pipers thought worthy of notice were Walter Forsyth, father and
son, of Roxburgh; three generations of Thomas Anderson, at Kelso; and
Robert Hastie, who succeeded his uncle John, at Jedburgh, about 1731.

It is touching to read Sir Walter Scott's account of his aged uncle
Thomas on his deathbed having his son James play over to him the air
'Sour Plums of Galashiels' [101] to make sure that he was leaving him in
full possession of it.[54] This was in January 1823.

Heir to the clarsach

In the Highlands, the piob mór enjoyed a unique prestige, being revered
as an instrument of state in the manner of the clarsach (plate 5) and falling
heir to the clarsach's regal mantle; it was not associated with the lyric
music of the Gael, except, as we have seen, through puirt-a-beul. In view
of this and the fact that it claimed to itself an art form of its very own—
piobaireachd—it is easy to understand the singular place of the piob mór
in the culture of the Highlands. The same instrument was presented in a
different guise in Lowland society where traditionally bagpipes played a
lyrical role. There it was divested of its aristocratic mien and pressed into
more humble service accompanying the dancing at country fair and kirn-
feast, without any thought of propriety.

Dr Johnson, on his famous tour in 1773, remarked that the bagpipe
was falling into oblivion, but that some of the principal families such as
MacLeod, and Maclean of Coll, still kept a hereditary piper. It is striking
that these two important chiefs also retained a harper in their establish-
ments until that very century. The hereditary office of piper has long since
disappeared, but the family piper has prevailed among some of the
nobility to this day, and was re-introduced to the Royal House by Queen

* There may be accidental confusion, here, with the 'North East Coast' of England.

Victoria. As remarked by Dr Johnson, however, a decline in piping was noticeable at the end of the eighteenth century and was no doubt caused by emigrations from the glens to the cities and the colonies, even more than to the proscription of the bagpipe together with other symbols of the culture of the Highlander under the Disarming Act, which was in force from 1747 to 1782. A way of life has been disturbed, and the Gaels of the towns instituted in 1778 the first of their clan or Highland societies, the Gaelic Society of London, and established an annual piping competition at Falkirk in 1781 (held in Edinburgh from 1783) to foster an interest in the instrument and preserve its music.

This competition was a mecca for those visitors to Scotland whom we would now call tourists. Mendelssohn was accompanied there by Finlay Dun, a noted teacher of music in the city, who tells us that the famous composer took a 'lively interest' in the music.[55] This could hardly be said of Sir John Carr who, after three hours of polite attention, 'left with the same sensations with which I should have quitted a belfry on a royal birthday'.[56] Mendelssohn departed with ideas for his 'Scotch' Symphony and was inspired by his subsequent visit to the Hebrides to compose the first really great orchestral 'sea music'. This more or less marks the great difference between the Continental and the English attitude towards Scotland at that time, a difference well illustrated by the way in which Macpherson's *Ossian*, and the works of Scott and Byron in their hey-day, enjoyed a much greater vogue on the Continent than they did in England.

To return to piping, however, and to mark the changes of fortune with regard to it, I can do no better than quote Henry Cockburn on the occasion of his meeting Angus Cameron of Ballachulish in 1819 [57]:

Angus was the best piper in his day, and when only eighteen, gained the competition prize at Edinburgh. But he had the misfortune to marry what was called 'a leddy'—a very good wife, I hope, but who thought the pipes below her dignity, and so fiercely discouraged them, that at last she has compelled her spouse totally to abandon the source of all his glory. On one occasion, when he was delighting a crowd of admirers, and would not take a gentle hint, she stepped forward with a knife and stabbed the bag.

Though giving great praise to old rivals, and to young aspirants, he bemoaned the general decline of the art, for he said that there was not now one single '*real*' pipe—'a man who made the pipe his business', in the whole of Appin. I suggested that it was probably owing to the want of country militia regiments, for the Highland colonels used to take their pipers with them. But he eschewed this, saying that we had plenty pipes long before the militia was heard of. I then suggested the want of training. 'Ay! There's a deal in that, for it does tak education: a deal o' education.' But then, why were they 'no educated'? So he hit it on the very head by saying it was the decline of chieftains, and their castles and gatherings. 'Yes', said I, 'few of them live at home now.' 'At home! ou, They're a' deed! an they're a' puir! An they're a' English!'

The decline in piping standards by the early part of the nineteenth century is remarked by both James Logan in his *Scottish Gael*, 1831, and and J. G. Dalyell in his *Musical Memoirs of Scotland*, 1849. Present pipers, they believed, were inferior to their predecessors and were getting worse. G. F. Graham, about the same time, remarks that an assemblage of a hundred pipers, such as preceded Prince Charlie into Carlisle in 1745, would be a surprising phenomenon in 1854, even at the Edinburgh competition.[58]

Some measure of the improvement since that time can be offered by considering how familiar is such a spectacle now-a-days at tattoo and Highland games, and not only in Scotland, but in many Commonwealth countries. We can hope that the Glasgow College of Piping and the military School of Piping at Edinburgh Castle, combined with the growth of a more scholarly interest in the piob mór will lead to a renaissance of the great art of Ceòl Mór, the 'great music'. Then with John Cotton in the twelfth century we can say with new feeling that the bagpipe is superior to all other instruments, because it simultaneously 'employs the human breath like the tibia, and the hand like the viol, and the bellows like the organ'.[59]

CHAPTER 9

The Sweetness of a Scottish Tune

In July 1666, Pepys tells us, he heard one of Lord Lauderdale's servants play some Scottish tunes on the violin: 'several, and the best of their country, as they seem to esteem them by their praising and admiring them: but Lord! the strangest air that ever I heard in my life, and all of one cast'.[1] This suggests to us one way in which Scottish tunes were introduced into London as well as indicating that there was something peculiar about them to English ears. As we have noted on page 53, John Dryden some thirty years later referred to the 'sweetness of a Scottish tune'. Then in 1776 Sir John Hawkins, the music historian, writes: 'All men know that the style and cast of them [i.e. Scottish tunes in general] is unaccountably singular', and refers to an Italian writer of the sixteenth century, Alessandro Tassoni, who wrote that King James 1 . . .

> not only composed poems set to music, but also of himself invented a new, melancholy, and plaintive style of music different from all the other. In which he has since been imitated by Carlo Gesualdo, Prince of Venosa, a distinguished musician.

Tassoni also said that Gesualdo 'imitated and improved that melancholy and plaintive kind of air which distinguishes the Scots melodies, and which was invented about the year 1420 by James the First of Scotland.'[2]

We know, of course, that James was an accomplished musician and was doubtless very familiar with the music of his subjects, especially that music which so distinguished the Highlanders and Irish, of which Giraldus writes, as well as the music of the Church. Perhaps some Italian visitor to the Court, not having heard Scottish traditional music before, imagined that the king who could play it so well had in fact invented it. However, it is not a surprise to be told that a study of Gesualdo's music reveals no characteristics which would warrant Tassoni's remarks.[3] It is absurd to imagine that Scottish folk song owes its cast to any one person, still less David Rizzio, Queen Mary's secretary, who was an accomplished lutenist and singer, and who likewise has been credited by romancers with the creation of this idiom.

It seems as though some people have found it difficult to believe that such beauty could flourish in the rude and stony cultural soil of Scotland. Thomson, in the first edition of his *Orpheus Caledonius* [1725], marked seven tunes as composed by Rizzio—'The Lass of Patie's Mill', 'Bessie Bell', 'The Bush aboon Traquair', 'The Bonny Boatman', 'An thou were my ain thing', 'Auld Bob Morris', and 'Doun the Burn Davie'. What led Thomson to do this was never brought to light but he removed this attribution of authorship from his second edition in 1733. There has been some kind of tradition here which could much more feasibly have arisen from some collection of Scottish songs compiled by Rizzio. It would be very natural for him to set down some of the indigenous airs of his new home as they took his fancy. Perhaps, too, he would be tempted, as others have been since then, to 'improve' them. All this is feasible, but there is no evidence other than this troublesome 'tradition' to support the idea.

The Scottish idiom

We can be certain, however, that no single person created the idiom or style of the music of Scotland or of any other nation. Probably the first attempt to isolate the distinguishing characteristics of Scottish music was made in 1721 by Alexander Malcolm of Edinburgh in a learned treatise [4] and referred to by Hawkins. It is very abstruse, and as Colin Brown says, 'as far from the point as possible'.[5] Then came Finlay Dun's 'Analysis of the Scottish Music' (appended to Dauney's *Ancient Scottish Melodies*),[6] in which he considered the following apparent characteristics of Scottish music:

1. Sudden transitions from the scale of one key to that of another one degree higher or lower, e.g., 'Adew Dundee' and 'John Anderson my Jo'.
2. Alternation of the major with its relative minor; the melody moving to and from these keys to the exclusion of every other, and not infrequently at regular distances, e.g. 'Poortith Cauld', 'Wandering Willie', 'Bonny Mary', and 'Alas that I cam ower the moor'.
3. Many of the airs modulate out of the scale of the principal key into the scale of another key, not as a substituted key but as a principal key, bearing for the time, its own scale; e.g. 'The Flowers of the Forest' and 'Waly, Waly' where the minor seventh of the major scale is introduced, thus temporarily removing the sense of the principal key. In both examples the modulation is made into the fourth degree of the principal key.
4. Two frequent recurring traits of melody shared by Irish music are:

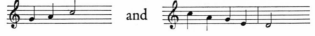

5. Although closure on the key note of the melody is usual and common in European music, Scottish melodies frequently end on other degrees of the scale; commonly the second, third, fifth, sixth, seventh and eighth. The most remarkable are those on the second, sixth and seventh; those on the fifth are rare.

Modality

The above observations refer to certain melodic clichés of Scottish music; but they make little of its scales (or modes). Finlay Dun recognized that the traditional Scottish airs were composed in the old ecclesiastical modes but in his time it was not widely appreciated that the ecclesiastical modes are the scales predominantly encountered in European folk music in general. Next to these come the so-called pentatonic ('five-note') modes.

Some comments on these modes, or scales, may be welcomed by many of the readers of this book; there are, however, numerous erudite works on tonality in which the subject is treated more thoroughly.

In modern times, the most familiar European scale is that which runs (in sol-fa)—d r m f s l t d. This is what we call the 'major scale'; it is the old ecclesiastical mode known as the Ionian. It is a seven-note 'heptatonic' scale and it has two semi-tone intervals within it—m f and t d. Keyboard instruments, such as the piano are designed so that this mode—the Ionian or major—can be produced with a variety of pitches serving as the tonic or 'doh' of the scale. Thus beginning on D or A or E, etc., we can produce the major mode with D or A or E serving as the tonic. We familiarly refer to these as different 'scales'—D major, A major, E major—but they are in fact all the same scale—the major—differing only in the pitch of the tonic. The black keys of the piano are introduced to facilitate this.

Consider, then, the major scale beginning on C. The series is C D E̅ F̅ G A B̅ C̅; the intervals E F and B C are semitones. Keeping to these notes and beginning on D we have—D E̅F̅ G A B̅C̅ D (or r-m̅f̅-s-l-t̅d̅-r′), which is another scale, the Dorian mode.

By keeping thus with each of the notes in this series in turn (i.e. keeping to the piano's white keys) we can produce seven scales; these are distinguished one from the other by the positions of the two semitone intervals within the scale:

Ionian (major)	C D EF G A BC
Dorian	D EF G A BC D
Phrygian	EF G A BC D E
Lydian	F G A BC D EF
Mixolydian	G A BC D EF G
Aeolian (minor)	A BC D EF G A
Locrian	BC D EF G A B

These are the principal scales on which was composed that great body of Christian Church music from the sixth century into medieval times. In the course of time, for reasons which have largely to do with the requirements of harmony, two of these scales predominated—the Ionian and the Aeolian. The Ionian is what we call the major scale and the Aeolian the minor scale. If we set out the ecclesiastical modes with reference to the same tonic (see below) it may be noticed that three of the modes can be reduced to the major and three to the minor, by sharpening or flattening only one note! This gives us a further hint as to the forces tending to favour the domination of the major and minor scales.

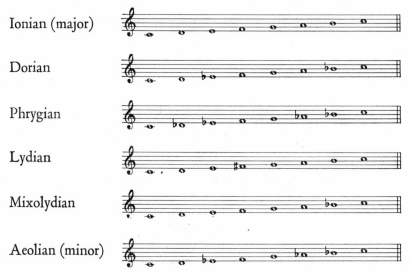

Ionian (major)

Dorian

Phrygian

Lydian

Mixolydian

Aeolian (minor)

More primitive than the ecclesiastic modes are those which omit the semitone intervals altogether, leaving five notes instead of seven. These are called the 'pentatonic' scales or modes. It is commonly thought that there is only one pentatonic scale; but authorities on the subject recognize five; five scales differing, one from the other in the position of the two gaps of $1\frac{1}{2}$ tones present in them. Here they are in their most common order, as set out by Bertrand H. Bronson: [7]

       1. drm—sl—d′

       2. rm—sl—d′r′

       3. m—sl—d′r′m′

       4. sl—d′r′m′—s′

       5. l—d′r′m′—s′l′

The pentatonic scales are essentially a combination of a group of three notes a tone apart, and a pair of notes a tone apart; the group and the pair being separated by an interval of $1\frac{1}{2}$ tones. In a complete span of the scales there are thus two 'gaps' of $1\frac{1}{2}$ tones—hence the term 'gapped scales' which is their other name. On the white notes of the piano, the gaps correspond to the omission of F and B, or E and B, or F and C. If these gaps are strictly maintained in a tune, it is said to be pentatonic.

Scale (1) is strongly major in feeling. Scottish tunes in scale (4) are rare and those in scale (5) are plentiful.

To determine the mode of a tune, it is a good start to accept the final note of the tune as the tonic. The tonic ending is to be expected in most tunes since it is natural to close on the 'home' note of the mode. Unlike the bulk of European folk music, unfortunately, Scottish tunes have a perverse habit of not closing on the tonic, a characteristic which may well arise from repeating the tune over and over for dancing.[8] However, the next step is to observe whether or not there are 'gaps' in the series of notes used in the tunes and hence whether it is pentatonic or not. Sometimes there is only one gap maintained, in which case the scale is regarded as hexatonic, i.e. a six-note scale. If both gaps are filled, then we have a heptatonic, i.e. a seven-note scale, of which the ecclesiastical modes are examples. A heptatonic scale established, it remains only to examine the 2nd, 3rd, 6th and 7th notes of the scale to determine the mode. If all are minor (see musical example, p. 204), the mode is Phrygian. If only the 7th is minor, the mode is Mixolydian, and so on.

The structure of the pentatonic scales follows from the natural laws of vibrations; they are easy to sing and are regarded as essentially vocal scales. People accustomed only to pentatonic music have great difficulty in distinguishing the semitone introduced when a gap is filled. The heptatonic scales, on the other hand, are associated with the introduction of fixed scale instruments such as the harp or flute. The hexatonic lies between the two as though it were a vocal scale developed by a people somewhat familiar with heptatonic instrumental music.

Pentatonic survivals

With this information in mind, the distribution of surviving pentatonic music is very revealing. For instance, in India, E. C. Curwen has pointed out, pentatonic scales seem to be mainly associated with the pre-Aryan population, in the Himalayas and Bengal especially. but Hindu music is heptatonic as is that of Persia, the Middle East and, of course, Europe, whereas most music from the Far East is pentatonic. Turning again to Europe, there is a markedly strong pentatonic tradition in the Hebrides, but even more notably pentatonic is the music of Lapland. Surveying this picture, it appears that the Indo-European and Arabic language region forms an 'Island of heptatonic scales in an ocean of pentatonic' which lends great force to the view that the heptatonic system spread at the expense of an earlier pentatonic system. Applying this to the British Isles, it seems most probable that the pentatonic system belonged to the pre-Celtic descendants of megalithic stock, and that the heptatonic system, along with the instruments which inspired it, came with the Celts.[9] Malcolm Macfarlane deduced similar conclusions many years previously, from a study of Gaelic music.[10] Curwen states further:

> While the survival of a pentatonic musical tradition in Scotland, and to a less extent in Ireland, indicates the persistence of a conservative pre-Celtic element in the population, corresponding to the historical Picts, and ultimately derived from the megalithic culture, nothing could better illustrate Fox's insistence on the continuity of culture in the 'highland zone', its conservatism, and its tendency to absorb and modify immigrant cultural elements, while remaining at heart ever the same.

There is no doubt that from geographical considerations alone, the Hebrides and Western Highlands have enjoyed considerable isolation, except perhaps from the Vikings. But in the islands, particularly, the tenacity of ancient custom has been such that the general manner of life, until very recently, was that of the early Iron Age. We can surely expect to discover in a region of this nature a corresponding survival of very ancient culture. With this in mind, it is very interesting to note the high incidence of pentatonic music in the Hebrides and the comparatively high percentage of this which has a compass of less than five notes. Nothing like an exhaustive statistical study has been made, but Curwen's limited survey has revealed extremely plausible and enlightening figures.

One conclusion reached from this study confirms observations made by other scholars over the past century, namely, that the pentatonic tradition is very strong in Scotland, fairly strong in Ireland and very weak in Wales and England. Within Scotland itself the prevalence of pentatonic tunes tapers off in all directions from a maximum in the West.

If it were possible to say that because a particular air is pentatonic or modal it is therefore ancient, we would have no problem in determining the antiquity of Scottish tunes. The taste for these scales, however, shows through many of the products of composers of Scottish song and dance music of more recent date. The tradition is there.

Cecil Sharp noticed that the majority of English folk-tunes, about two-thirds, were in the major (Ionian) mode, the remaining third being fairly evenly divided between the Mixolydian, Dorian and Aeolian modes, with perhaps a preponderance in favour of the Mixolydian.[11] The large proportion of Ionian tunes is not necessarily due to modern influence, for it was so popular with the common people that the Church called i *modus lascivus* and prohibited its use for sacred ends. The remarkable early folk round 'Sumer is icumen in' is set in this mode.

It has been observed that a tune may be changed in mode in the course of oral transmission, although persisting predominantly in a favourite mode. This easily arises from the small differences subsisting between adjacent modes. The Ionian or Mixolydian, for instance, differ on the 7th tone. The removal of the 7th leaves a hexatonic scale which is as closely related to the Ionian as it is to the Mixolydian. Likewise the Mixolydian and the Dorian differ only in the 3rd. The removal of the 3rd leaves a hexatonic scale which is equally related to both, and so on for other pairs of modes.

Then the removal of both semitones from each mode leaves a pentatonic scale. If, for instance, we remove the 4th as well as the 7th from the Ionian, the resultant pentatonic scale can be embraced in all its notes by the Ionian, Mixolydian and Lydian, and that pentatonic scale itself is a common denominator with the other pentatonic scales.[12]

Very frequently in Scottish music we encounter tunes which would be purely pentatonic were it not for the occasional filling of one of the gaps with a passing note. The question arises as to whether this establishes a hexatonic scale for these tunes or whether the filling of a gap in this way is really only accidental and should be ignored. Obviously, each of the five pentatonic scales can be turned into two different hexatonic scales by the introduction of the missing note in either gap, which gives us quite a range. Well-known tunes like 'Invercauld's Reel' (O Tibby I hae seen the day), Whistle o'er the lave o't' and 'Ca' the Yowes', are 'virtually' pentatonic or hexatonic.

Debatable tonality of Scottish tunes

The selection of examples of tunes in particular modes from printed sources is fraught with hazards. First, one must be satisfied that the tune has not been adulterated by its editor or arranger. Then a great number of Scottish tunes are of debatable tonality in any case, except when they are clearly pentatonic or clearly end on the tonic of the mode.

The harmonized versions of Scottish, indeed of British folk songs, which began to be published in the eighteenth century tended to reduce all tunes to major or minor and destroy any modal character. In the first place, the modal nature of the music was imperfectly understood, and in the second place few arrangers had much idea of how to harmonize a modal melody, the essential principle of which is to keep exclusively to the notes of the mode. In any case, it was very tempting to tamper with the original tunes to suit the predilections of ears conditioned to major and minor conventions.

Finlay Dun perceived this early in the nineteenth century and wrote in

his appendix to Dauney that it could be proved that such changes ha
been made on tunes by comparing the various versions of them publishe
in different collections. 'Through mistaken attempts at refinement an
modernization, many of our melodies have already been almost entirel
deprived of their national and characteristic form; and should suc
attempts be continued, it is not difficult to forsee that a period may arriv
when the music of Scotland may be so completely blended and incor
porated with that of other countries, as to lose all title to a distinctive an
national character.'

One can respect the practice of eighteenth-century Edinburgh ladies i
singing their native songs without accompaniment, and as Henr
Mackenzie tells us, 'they scarce admitted of counterpoint, or any but
slight and delicate accompaniment' [13] and that doubtless on the spinet o
harpsichord.

The Gael, enjoying as he does a more tenacious oral tradition, has pre
served the tonality of his songs longer than has the Lowlander. Whe
Marjorie Kennedy Fraser set out to collect and preserve some of thes
treasures and to communicate them to the world, she arranged them a
drawing-room songs with full harmonic accompaniment in accordanc
with the tastes of the Victorian South. Some of her productions, judged a
art-songs in the Germanic tradition, are extremely pleasing and perhap
we should be glad that beautiful melodies and themes of Scotland's isle
have been preserved even in this unnatural guise, for in artistic hands the
remain very beautiful. To the Gael, however, and to those who throug
familiarity with Scottish songs have acquired an ear for the bitter-swee
quality of the original modes, such arrangements are just as velvet com
pared with peat-smelling tweed. The cultivated musician is already pre
pared to recognize this but the popular ear has been dulled.

Strictures of a similar kind have been applied to Irish music: 'Th
peculiar tonality of many of the Irish airs', wrote G. F. Graham abou
1840, 'has been altered by different arrangers . . . to force them into
union with the modern system of harmony and accompaniment. Conse
quently the originality of the airs has been destroyed, and only a bad an
heterogeneous compound produced.' [14]

The translation of Gaelic lyrics into English—or Lallans—usuall
leads to modifications in the rhythm of the airs. Macfarlane noted in hi
'Studies' that the alteration of musical accent and the introduction o
what he called 'slurs' to tunes which had originally been the vehicle o
Gaelic words could identify the Gaelic origin of tunes. By this procedur
he showed that the tune 'Gilderoy', for instance, was of Gaelic origin. It
title, of course, 'Gilleruadh' (red-haired youth) itself suggests a Gaeli
association, but it had nevertheless been claimed as a song of a 'characte
essentially English'.[15] Music has no linguistic barriers, but the cadenc
and phrasing of the tunes of songs are influenced by language.

The undying tradition of the Celt

t was a matter of record by Macfarlane before the era of radio and gramo-
hone that an illiterate English labourer from the heart of the English
gricultural counties could be found singing songs, learned from illiterate
orefathers, which are occasionally claimed by the Irish or Scots or both.
or instance, the song 'Belfast Mountains' is claimed by one authority as a
ussex song but a variant of it appears in Petrie's [16] great collection of Irish
irs with the title 'The Belfast Mountain'. And another, 'The Gallant
'oachers' which has a refrain 'Van Diemen's Land' is likewise found in
imilar guise in Petrie under the title 'Van Diemen's Land'. Furthermore,
oth of these airs are in a style recognizably common in Gaelic songs. The
ine 'John Anderson my Jo' is found in Wales to Welsh words, in
reland and Scotland to Gaelic and English words, it is said by Macfar-
ine to have been found in Sweden, and it survives in America in the
orm of 'When Johnnie comes marching home'. Variants of the air
Gilderoy', already mentioned, are very numerous and widespread in the
Fritish Isles, including the beautiful Gaelic air 'Mairi Ban Og'.
   The amount of Gaelic song music, both Scottish and Irish, set to
allans or English words in the Lowlands of Scotland is very great; but
ie amount of Lowland or, what is somewhat less ambiguous, English
ong music, to Gaelic words is negligible. A striking peculiarity pointed
ut by Macfarlane is the surprisingly small amount of Irish song music in
Faelic Scotland. The movement of tunes from the Gaelic-speaking
eoples, both Scots and Irish, to the English speaking has been greater
ian in the reverse direction and several reasons can be given for this; but
/e shall not discount the persistence of Britain's Celtic ancestry in the face
f alien intrusions.
   In his book on Scottish music, published after the above was written,
'rancis Collinson writes:

There has, it is true, been a small amount of desultory borrowing of
song airs from the opposite language culture by both sides (Lowland
and Gaelic); but this has been at the literary rather than at the folk level.
the borrowing of Gaelic tunes for Lowland songs has been the work of
a relatively small number of song-writing poets, of whom Allan
Ramsay, Robert Burns, Lady Nairne and Sir Walter Scott have been
the leading figures.[17]

He is a bold man indeed who shall maintain that a great many of the
ines set to Lallans words before these poets came on the scene at all had
ot seen prior use with Gaelic words or as instrumental dance tunes in the
Faelic-speaking regions, regions which embraced many parts considered
Lowland today.
   However, we have touched on many aspects of this subject in the fore-

going pages and noted the varying incidence of the modes of folk song
throughout the country. This in itself is an indication of variation, for the
character of a melody is to some extent derived from the mode in which it
is cast. But it is not in the modal or pentatonic qualities alone that the
distinguishing characteristics of Scottish airs lie. The final identifying
peculiarities must lie in certain rhythmic and melodic clichés. The
rhythmic characteristics so closely associated with the dance rhythms as
they are, have been dealt with. Of melodic clichés, those identified by
Finlay Dun have also been presented. Some others apparently derive from
the fact that the following triads are embraced by the chanter of the piob

mór:

A very characteristic cliché is for a melodic figure to be based on one of
these followed by the same or closely related figure on the triad one tone
below or above as the case may be. For example, in [102] 'The Athol
Highlanders'

[102]

Scots Guards Standard Settings of Pipe Music, London, 1954

Fiddlers often play bagpipe tunes and likewise pipers play fiddle tunes
(and vocal tunes) with the necessary modifications to bring them within
the range of the chanter. Then, not at all uncommonly, fiddlers or pianists
will in turn reproduce the adulterated versions of the bagpipe. Thus, for
instance, one can encounter a Country Dance band playing 'Whistle o'er
the lave o't' (common tune to the dance 'Seann Triubhas') as taken from
a book of bagpipe music rather than from its original fiddle version which
is not exactly reproducible on the bagpipe.

This interchange has led to the elaborate introduction of grace notes—
a necessity with the bagpipe—to the performance of strathspeys and reels,
etc., on the violin and other instruments. The employment of grace notes
is encountered too in the singing of the countryside, a natural embellishment probably derived from the bagpipe, producing something akin to an
oriental style of singing, which is very much in character.

Although it would seem that the times are not conducive to the
preservation of the traditional arts in their pristine purity, a remarkable
wealth of traditional song has been found surviving on the lips of the

Scottish country-folk. We have seen, too, the phenomenal growth of a living interest in folk song among the young of Britain and America in which Scotland's heritage of balladry enjoys a prominent place. Scores of ballad singers, girls and boys, long-haired and guitared, are a familiar part of the modern musical scene.

Yet despite periods of ascendancy and decline, music for the dance—hornpipe, jig, strathspey and reel—has never ceased to claim an enduring place in the musical allegiance of all who enjoy even a trace of Scottish blood in their veins.

Chapter 1: *The Dawn over Alba*

1 'Columcille fecit', attributed to Columba, as translated by Michael O'Curry, from an Irish MS. in the Burgundian Library, Brussels. It was given in 1866 to William Skene who published it in his *Celtic Scotland: a History of Ancient Alban*. Edinburgh, 1876–80. *Colum Cille* means 'Colum of the Churches'.

2 'Columcille cecenit', translated by Douglas Hyde in *The Three Sorrows of Story-telling* and *Ballads of St Columba*, London, 1895, and reproduced in *Lyra Celtica* (ed. Elizabeth A. Sharp), Edinburgh, 1896.

3 See John Mackenzie (ed.) Excursus of the Dewar MSS., Glasgow, 1964.

4 Eugene O'Curry. *Lectures on the Manuscript Materials of Ancient Irish History*. Dublin, 1861.

5 Poem of *Bas Oisiain*, quoted by John Gunn in the *Harp*. London and Edinburgh, 1807.

6 A. N. Garmonsway, Jacqueline Simpson and Hilda M. Davidson (trans.). *Beowulf and its Analogues*. London, 1968. An earlier rendering of 'the merry harp' as 'wood of joy' is close to the literal meaning of clarsach.

7 Reproduced (no. 32) in F. Harrison and J. Rimmer. *European Musical Instruments*. New York, 1964.

8 *Ibid*.

9 See the Pavan, 'Belle qui tient me vie', in Thoinot Arbeau's *Orchésographie*, 1588; trans. C. W. Beaumont. London, 1925.

10 Curt Sachs. *The World History of the Dance*. London, 1938.

11 *Ibid*.

12 Bruno Nettl. *Music in Primitive Culture*, pp. 21–5. New York, 1956.

13 Margaret Fay Shaw. *Folksongs and Folklore of South Uist*. London, 1955.

14 Nettl. *Op cit*.

15 Sir Thomas Elyot. *The Boke named the Governour*. Ed. Henry Herbert Stephen Craft, vol. i. London, 1883; Everyman's Library (modern spelling), 1962.

16 Charles Butler. *The principles of Musik in singing and setting with the twofold use thereof: Ecclesiastical and Civil*, Chap. 1, 'Of the Ionic Mode'. London, 1636.

17 Margaret Fay Shaw. *Op. cit*.

18 Keith Norman MacDonald. *Puirt-A-Beul*. Glasgow, 1901, 1931.

19 Alexander Carmichael. Milking Song from Barra in *Carmina Gadelica*, vol. i, no. 99. Edinburgh, 1900.

20 *The Historical Works of Giraldus Cambrensis. Topographia Hiberniae* (1185), trans. Thomas Forester, revised and ed. Thomas Wright, Book xi. London, 1863.

21 Dr Alexander Pennecuik. *Description of Tweeddale* (1715), included in his Works. Leith, 1815.

22 Robert Sempill of Beltrees. 'The Piper of Kilbarchan', in various collections, e.g. George Eyre-Todd, *Scottish Poetry of the Seventeenth Century*. Glasgow, 1895.

23 Giraldus Cambrensis. *Op. cit.*

24 Gustave Reese. *Music in the Middle Ages*. London, 1941.

25 Dr Henry G. Farmer. *A History of Music in Scotland*. London, 1947.

26 Adamnan. *Vita S. Columbae* (Life of Saint Columba), trans. and ed. William Reeves. Edinburgh, 1857; ed. J. T. Fowler. Edinburgh, 1894.

27 Joseph Ritson. *Scotish Song*, 2 vols. London, 1794.

28 William Tytler of Woodhouslee. *Dissertation on the Scottish Music*. Edinburgh, 1779.

29 John Pinkerton. *Ancient Scotish Poems*, 2 vols. London, 1786.

30 *Bannatyne MS.* (George Bannatyne) ed. in 4 vols. W. Tod Ritchie, vol. i, Scottish Text Society. Edinburgh 1934 (1928–30).

31 *Maitland Folio MS.* (Sir John Maitland, Lord Thirlestane) ed. W. A. Craigie, Scottish Text Society. Edinburgh, 1913, 1927.

32 *Ibid.* and *Bannatyne MS., op. cit.*

33 *The Complaynt of Scotland*. Ed. John Leyden. Edinburgh, 1801.

34 Gavin Douglas. Virgil's *Aeneid* (1553), Book xiii, in *The Poetical Works of Gavin Douglas*, ed. John Small, 4 vols. Edinburgh, 1874.

35 Henry Playford. *Collection of Original Scotch Tunes*. London, 1700.

36 B. H. Bronson. *The Traditional Tunes of the Child Ballads*, vol. ii. Princeton, 1962.

37 James Johnson. *The Scots Musical Museum*, vol. iv. Edinburgh, 1792.

38 James C. Dick (ed.). *The Songs of Robert Burns*. London, 1903.

39 Sempill. *Op. cit.*

40 Douglas. *Op. cit.* Prologue to Book xiii.

41 Fayrfax MS. (*c.* 1500) referred to by William Chappell. *Old English Popular Music*. Ed. H. Ellis Wooldridge. London, 1893.

42 William Stenhouse. *Illustrations of the Lyric Poetry and Music of Scotland*. Ed. David Laing. Edinburgh, 1853.

43 *Ibid.*

44 Robert Fabyan. *Chronicle* (1516). *The New Chronicles of England and France*. Ed. H. Ellis. London, 1811.

45 William Chappell. *Old English Popular Music*. Ed. H. Ellis Wooldridge, vol. i. London, 1893.

46 Anne G. Gilchrist. 'Sacred Parodies of Secular Folk Songs'. *Journal of the English Folk Dance and Song Society*, vol. iii, no. 4. London, 1938.

47 Sempill. *Op. cit.*

48 Margaret Dean-Smith. 'A 15th Century Dancing Book', *Journal of the English Folk Dance and Song Society*, vol. iii, no. 2, p. 106, et seq. London, 1938.

49 John Playford. *The Dancing Master*. London, 1686.

;0 Thomas Morley. *A Plaine and Easie Introduction to Practicall Musicke*. (London 1597.) Shakespeare Association Facsimiles, no. 14. London, 1937.

Chapter 2: Coming of Age
from Medieval times to the eighteenth century

1 *The Complaynt of Scotland* (? Paris ? 1549). Ed. John Leyden. Edinburgh, 1801.
2 Hector Boece. *The History of Scotland*. Trans. from the Latin into Scots by John Bellenden, 1533. Ed. R. W. Chambers and Edith C. Batho, Scottish Text Society. Edinburgh, 1936.
3 *Accounts of the Lord High Treasurer of Scotland*, vols. i–iv. Ed. T. Dickson and Sir J. Balfour Paul. Edinburgh, 1877–1902.
4 Prohemium from Boece, quoted in Appendix pp. 42–3, *op. cit.*, from Thomas Davidson's ed., [1536].
5 Dickson and Paul. *Op. cit.*
6 Sir David Lindsay. 'The Complaynte of Schir David Lindsay', *c.* 1530.
7 Pierre de Bourdeilles de Brantôme. *Œuvres Complètes*. Paris, 1858–95.
8 John Knox. *History of the Reformation in Scotland* (5 vols., 1584). Ed. William C. Dickinson. Edinburgh, 1949.
9 John Spalding. *Memorialls of the Trubles in Scotland and in England from the year 1624 to 1645* (printed 1792). Ed. John Stuart, Spalding Club. Edinburgh, 1850.
10 David Herd. *Ancient and Modern Scottish Songs*, vol ii. Edinburgh, 1776. The verses are reproduced as written down by the collector, but his orthography does not suggest the vernacular pronunciation. In the third verse, for instance, *sic* would have been better than *sick* and in the fourth, *rankit* than *ranked*.
11 General David Stewart of Garth. *Sketches of the Character, Manners and Present State of the Highlanders of Scotland*, 2 vols. Edinburgh, 1822; vol. ii, 3rd. ed. 1825.
12 Joseph MacDonald. *A Compleat Theory of the Scots Highland Bagpipe*. Edinburgh University Library MS. La III, 1804.
13 *Privy Council Records*, 1577–80, p. 422, in MS., General Register House, Edinburgh.
14 *The Book of Sports*, 1618; re-enacted by Charles I with a new preface, 1633.
15 Reginald V. Lennard (ed.). *Englishmen at Rest and Play, 1558–1714*. Oxford, 1931.
16 James F. S. Gordon. *Glasgow Ancient and Modern*. 'Annals from Contracts of the Kirk Session.' Glasgow, [1874].
17 Sir John Graham Dalyell. *Musical Memoirs of Scotland*. Edinburgh, 1849.
18 Sir John Hawkins. *A General History of the Science and Practice of Music*, 5 vols. London, 1776.
19 Philip Stubbes. *Anatomy of Abuses* (1583). New Shakespeare Society, Part I. 1877.
20 P. Hume Brown. *Scotland before 1700* quoting Kirk Ordinance of 1609. Edinburgh, 1893.

21 William Dauney. *Ancient Scotish Melodies from a manuscript of the Reign of King James VI.* Edinburgh, 1838.
22 Dr Henry G. Farmer. *A History of Music in Scotland.* London, 1947.
23 Gavin Tureff. *Antiquarian Gleanings from Aberdeenshire Records,* 2nd ed. Aberdeen, 1871.
24 *Ibid.*
25 *Extracts from the Records of the Burgh of Glasgow.* Scottish Burgh Records Society, 1872.
26 Tureff. *Op. cit.*
27 Robert Sempill of Beltrees. 'The Life and Death of the Piper of Kilbarchan' in George Eyre Todd, *Scottish Poetry of the Seventeenth Century.* Glasgow, 1895.
28 Rev. W. A. P. Johnman. *Bagpipes and Border Pipers.* Hawick Archaeological Society, 7th Meeting 25th October 1913; 8th Meeting 24th November 1913.
29 *Extracts from the Council Register of the Burghs of Aberdeen, Edinburgh, Glasgow.* Scottish Burgh Records Society, 1871, 1872.
30 *Ibid.*
31 John Playford. *The English Dancing Master.* London, 1651. It ran to eighteen editions, under the title, from the second edition, of *The Dancing Master.* The dates are given in the bibliography, Appendix B.
32 Robert Chambers. *Domestic Annals of Scotland from the Revolution to the Rebellion of 1745.* Vol. II, quoting John Nicoll's Diary. Edinburgh and London, 1861.

Chapter 3: 'Their Allegros and a' the rest'
Scottish music-making in the eighteenth century

1 William Tytler in the *Transactions of the Society of Antiquaries of Scotland,* vol. i. Edinburgh, 1791.
2 Sir John Lauder, Lord Fountainhall. *The decisions of the Lords of Council and Session from June 6th, 1678 to July 30th, 1712* (vol. i, p. 590). Edinburgh, 1759–61.
3 Allan Ramsay. 'The City of Edinburgh's address to the Country', in *Scots Songs.* Edinburgh, 1718.
4 Henry Cockburn. *Memorials of His time.* Edinburgh, 1856.
5 Thomas Durfey or D'Urfey. *Wit and Mirth: or Pills to purge melancholy* (6 vols.). London, 1719–20.
6 Allan Ramsay. *The Tea Table Miscellany: a Collection of the most Choice Songs, Scottish and English.* Edinburgh, 1724; 18th ed. 1792.
7 Sir John Sinclair of Ulbster (ed.). *The Statistical Account of Scotland.* Rev. William Auld on Mauchline, Ayrshire, in 1787. Edinburgh, 1791–9. Also John Galt. *Annals of the Parish.* Edinburgh, 1831.
8 Edward Topham. *Letters from Edinburgh.* London, 1776.
9 Tobias Smollett. *The Expedition of Humphry Clinker.* London and Salisbury, 1671 [1771].
10 Topham. *Op. cit.*

1 Robert Chambers. *Traditions of Edinburgh*. Edinburgh, 1868.
2 Henry Mackenzie. *Anecdotes and Egotisms*, ed. H. W. Thomson. Oxford, 1928.
3 Chambers. *Op. cit.*
4 *Ibid.*
5 S. L. F. Schetky. *Ninety Years of Work and Play. Sketches from the public and private career of J. C. Schetky . . . By his daughter*. Edinburgh and London, 1877.
6 Chambers. *Op. cit.*
7 Letter from Burns to Alexander Cunningham. Dumfries, Autumn, 1794. John de Lancey Ferguson. *Letters of Robert Burns*, vol. ii, No. 624. Oxford, 1931.
8 Alexander Campbell. *An Introduction to the History of Poetry in Scotland including the Songs of the Lowlands*. Edinburgh, 1798.
9 Sinclair. *Op. cit.* Rev. Alexander Stewart writing on Moulin, Perthshire, in 1793.
10 *The Miscellany of the Spalding Club* (ed.). John Stuart, Aberdeen, 1841–52; vol. iii, 1846.
11 Allan Ramsay. *An Elegy on Patie Birnie*. [Edinburgh, 1721].
12 Robert Chambers. *Scottish Songs prior to Burns*. Edinburgh, 1890.

Chapter 4: 'Sang abune a' sang' collections, composers and fiddlers

1 John Dryden. *Preface to Fables Ancient and Modern*, London, 1700.
2 Dr Henry G. Farmer. *A History of Music in Scotland*. London, 1947.
3 Alexander Campbell. *An Introduction to the History of Poetry in Scotland, including the Songs of the Lowlands*. Edinburgh, 1798.
4 James C. Dick (ed.). *Notes on Scottish Song by Robert Burns. Written in an interleaved copy of the 'Scots Musical Museum'*, 1908.
5 J. F. S. Gordon. *Glasgow Ancient and Modern*. Glasgow, [1874].
6 John Glen. *The Glen Collection of Scottish Dance Music*. Edinburgh, 1891 and 1895.
7 Robert Burns in a letter to George Thomson, 30th June 1793. John de Lancey Ferguson (ed.). *Letters of Robert Burns*, vol. iii, no. 567. Oxford, 1931.
8 John Glen. Biographical Sketches from *The Glen Collection of Scottish Dance Music*. Edinburgh, 1891 and 1895.
9 *Ibid.*
10 *Ibid.*
11 P. R. Drummond. *Perthshire in Bygone Days*. Edinburgh, 1879.
12 Glen. *Op. cit.* (8).
13 Edward B. Ramsay (Dean of Edinburgh). *Reminiscences of Scottish Life and Character*, 6th ed. Edinburgh, 1860.
14 Drummond. *Op. cit.*
15 *Ibid.*
16 Alexander Whitelaw. *The Book of Scottish Song*. London, 1844.
17 Elizabeth Grant. *Memoirs of a Highland Lady 1797–1827*. London, 1898.

18 Thomas Garnett. *Tour through the Highlands*. London, 1800.
19 An article, 'Neil Gow', in Littell's *Living Age*, Third Series, vol. v. Boston, 1859.
20 James Grahame. *British Georgics*. Edinburgh, 1809.
21 James C. Dick (ed.). *The Songs of Robert Burns and Notes on Scottish Songs by Robert Burns*. Hatboro, Pa., 1962.
22 Henry Cockburn. *Memorials of his Time*. Edinburgh, 1856.
23 Private communication to David Laing, quoted by William Stenhouse in *Illustrations of the Lyric Poetry and Music of Scotland*, ed. David Laing. Edinburgh, 1853.

Chapter 5: The Nineteenth and Twentieth Centuries

1 Edward B. Ramsay, Dean of Edinburgh. *Reminiscences of Scottish Life and Character*, 6th ed. Edinburgh, 1860.
2 Sir J. Graham Dalyell. *Musical Memoirs of Scotland*. Edinburgh, 1849.
3 Peter Mackenzie. *Reminiscences of Glasgow and the West of Scotland*. Glasgow, 1865–8.
4 J. F. and T. M. Flett, and F. Rhodes. *Traditional Dancing in Scotland*. London, 1964.
5 James Scott Skinner. *A Guide to Bowing*. London and Glasgow, [c. 1900].
6 Dr A. Grant. 'Strathspeys and Reels, Banffshire Composers.' *Transactions of the Banffshire Field Club*. 1920–1.
7 Alexander Lowson. *Portrait Gallery of Forfar Notables*. Forfar [1880].
8 James Thomson. *Recollections of a Speyside Parish*. Elgin, 1887.
9 *Ibid.*
10 J. Baptie. *Musical Scotland Past and Present*. Paisley, 1894.
11 Alexander G. Murdoch. *The Fiddle in Scotland*. Glasgow, 1888.
12 Flett. *Op. cit.*
13 Grant. *Op. cit.*

Chapter 6: Accompaniment to the Dance

1 Captain Simon Fraser of Knockie (ed.). *The Airs and Melodies peculiar to the Highlands of Scotland and the Isles*. Edinburgh, 1816.
2 John Strang. *Glasgow and its Clubs*. Glasgow, 1864.
3 Joseph Farington. *The Farington Diary*. Ed. James Greig. London, 1923–8.
4 *The Poetical Museum*. Hawick, 1784.
5 Thomas Wilson. *Companion to the Ballroom*. London, 1817.
6 Quoted by John Glen in *The Glen Collection of Scottish Dance Music*. Edinburgh, 1891 and 1895.
7 Sir J. Graham Dalyell. *Musical Memoirs of Scotland*. Edinburgh, 1849.
8 J. F. and T. M. Flett and F. Rhodes. *Traditional Dancing in Scotland*. London, 1964.

Chapter 7: The Elements of Scottish Traditional Dance Music

1 J. F. and T. M. Flett, and F. Rhodes. *Traditional Dancing in Scotland*. London, 1964.
2 Reproduced by William Chappell, Ed. H. Ellis Wooldridge. *Old English Popular Music*. London, 1893.
3 Sir John Hawkins. *A General History of the Science and Practice of Music*. London, 1776.
4 William Chappell. *Op. cit.*
5 William Dauney. *Ancient Scottish Melodies from a manuscript of the Reign of King James VI*. Edinburgh, 1838.
6 *Cf.* William Stenhouse. *Illustrations of the Lyric Poetry and Music of Scotland*, ed. David Laing, vol. 2. Edinburgh, 1853.
7 *Ibid*: and Isaac Cooper. *Collection of Strathspeys*, etc. Banff [*c.* 1805].
8 Curt Sachs. *The World History of the Dance*. New York, 1937.
9 James Logan. *The Scottish Gael; or, Celtic Manners as preserved among the Highlanders*. London, 1831; second ed., Inverness, 1876.
10 Francis Peacock. *Sketches Relative to Dancing*. Aberdeen, 1805.
11 Quoted by Lloyd Hibbert. 'On Instrumental Style in Early Melody'. *The Musical Quarterly*, vol. xxxii, no. 1, January 1946.
12 *Ibid.*
13 *Cf.* Sachs. *Op. cit.*
14 Henry G. Farmer. *History of Music in Scotland*. London, 1947.
15 Barclay Dun. *A Translation of Nine Quadrilles*. London, 1818.
16 Thomas Garnett. *Tour Through the Highlands*. London, 1811.
17 Thomas Morley. *A Plaine and Easie Introduction to Practicall Musicke*. London, 1597. Shakespeare Association Facsimiles, no. 14. London, 1937.
18 Charles Burney. *A General History of Music*. London, 1789.
19 Letter to George Thomson. 19th October 1794. *The Letters of Robert Burns*, ed. J. de Lancey Ferguson, vol. 2, no. 644. Oxford, 1931.
20 John Glen. *Early Scottish Melodies*. Edinburgh, 1900.
21 W. H. Gratton Flood. *History of Irish Music*, 4th ed. London, 1927.
22 Gratton Flood. *Op. cit.*
23 Burns. Letter to George Thomson, 19th October 1794. *Op. cit.*

Chapter 8: The Principal Instruments Associated with Scottish Traditional Dance Music

1 Otto Andersson. *The Bowed Harp*. London, 1930.
2 William C. Honeyman. *Scottish Violin Makers*. Edinburgh, 1898 and 1910. William Sandys and Simon Andrew Forster. *The History of the Violin*. London, 1864. Peter Davidson. *The Violin*. Glasgow, 1871.
3 David D. Boyden. *The History of Violin Playing from its origins to 1761*. London, 1965.

4   Henry G. Farmer. 'An Old Violin Tutor'. *Proceedings of the Society of Ant*
    quaries of Scotland, vol. lxv. Edinburgh, 1930–1.

5   Francis Collinson. *The Traditional and National Music of Scotland*. London, 196*

6   P. R. Drummond. *Perthshire in Bygone Days*. Edinburgh, 1879.

7   Patrick Shuldham-Shaw. 'Folk Music and Dance in Shetland'. *Journal of t*
    English Folk Dance and Song Society, vol. v, no. 3, 1948.

8   John Glen. *The Glen Collection of Scottish Dance Music*. Edinburgh, 1891 an
    1895.

9   John Skinner. 'Tullochgorum'. In *Poetry, Original and Selected*. Printed for an
    sold by Brash and Reid [1800].

10 Robert Fergusson. 'The Daft Days'. In *The Scots Poems of Robert Fergusson*. Ec
    John Telfer. Edinburgh, 1948.

11 James Scott Skinner. *A Guide to Bowing*. London and Glasgow [*c.* 1900].

12 Keith N. Macdonald. Note in *Skye Collection*. Edinburgh, 1897.

13 Skinner. *Op. cit.*

14 Andrew Mackintosh. 'The History of Strathspeys and Reels'. *Transactions of t*
    Gaelic Society of Inverness, vol. xxvii. 15th December 1910.

15 J. De Lancey Ferguson (ed.). *The Letters of Robert Burns*, vol. ii, no. 647. Oxforc
    1931.

16 John Leyden (ed.). *The Complaynt of Scotland*. Edinburgh, 1801.

17 Geoffrey Chaucer. *House of Fame*. Bk. III, 133–6. Ed. C. M. Drennan. Londor
    1921.

18 W. Tod Ritchie (ed.). *The Bannatyne MS.* (1568). Scottish Text Society, 4 vol*
    Edinburgh, 1934 (1928–30).

19 Leyden. *Op. cit.*

20 Guillaume de Lorris et Jean de Meun. *Le Roman de la Rose*. Publié par Erne*
    Langlois, Paris, 1924.

21 Edmund Spenser. *The Shepherdes Calendar*. London, 1579.

22 Allan Ramsay. *The Gentle Shepherd*. Edinburgh, 1725.

23 F. W. Galpin. *Old English Instruments of Music*. London, 1910.

24 Daines Barrington. 'Some Account of two Musical Instruments used in Wales*
    Archaeologia, vol. iii. London, 1775.

25 Edward Jones. *Musical and Poetical Relicks of the Welsh Bards*. London, 1794.

26 *Ibid. Cf.* also L. G. Langwill. 'The Stock-and-horn'. *Proceedings of the Society o*
    Antiquaries of Scotland, 84 (1949–50), pp. 173–80. J. V. S. McGaw. 'A Mediev*
    Bone Pipe from White Castle, Monmouthshire', *Galpin Society Journal* 16, pp
    85–94. J. M. Coles. 'Irish Bronze Age Horns and their relations with Norther*
    Europe'. *Proceedings of the Prehistoric Society* 29 (1963), pp. 326–56. Anthon
    Baines. *Bagpipes*. Oxford, 1960.

27 John Major. *History of Greater Britain*. [Paris], 1521.

28 W. H. Gratton Flood. *The Story of the Bagpipe*. London, 1911. Francis W
    Galpin. *A textbook of European Musical Instruments*. London, 1937. Curt Sachs
    The History of Musical Instruments. New York, 1940. Anthony Baines (ed.)
    Musical Instruments through the Ages. London, 1961; and *Bagpipes*. Oxford, 1960

29 Suetonius. *Life of Nero*. Translated by Robert Graves in *The Twelve Caesars*. London, 1957.
30 Dio Chrysostom. *Seventy-First Discourse*. Translated by H. Lamar Crosby. London, 1951.
31 Grattan Flood. *Op. cit.*
32 Robert Burns. 'Tam o' Shanter'.
33 William Browne. *Brittania's Pastorals*, Bk ii. London, 1616.
34 Edward Ward. *The London Spy*, 2 vols. London, 1698–9.
35 Collinson. *Op. cit.*
36 Gratton Flood. *Op. cit.*
37 A. L. Lloyd. Foreword to reprint of *Northumbrian Minstrelsy*. Ed. J. Collingwood Bruce and John Stokoe. Newcastle, 1882.
38 W. Gillies Whittaker. *The Folk Music of North-Eastern England, Collected Essays*. London, 1940.
39 John Peacock. *A Favourite Collection of Tunes with Variations Adapted for the Northumberland Small Pipes, Violin or Flute*. Newcastle, n.d. [*c.* 1820].
40 Lloyd. *Op. cit.*
41 Donald Main. 'What is Piobaireachd?' *Scottish Life and Letters*, no. 3. 1953.
42 S. MacNeill and J. M. A. Lenihan. 'The Scale of the Highland Bagpipe'. *Piping Times*, vol. 13, no. 6. March, 1961.
43 Arthur Geddes. *Songs of Craig and Ben*, vol. ii (p. 78). Glasgow, 1961.
44 Illustrated in Charles M. McIntyre North, *The Book of the Club of True Highlanders*. London, 1881–2.
45 J. Derricke. *The Image of Irelande* (1581). Ed. J. Small. Edinburgh, 1883.
46 Joseph MacDonald. *A Compleat Theory of the Scots Highland Bagpipe*. Edinburgh University Library, MS. 1a. iii, 804.
47 W. L. Manson. *The Highland Bagpipe*. Paisley, 1901.
48 A. Duncan Fraser. *The Bagpipe*. Edinburgh, 1907.
49 James Logan. *The Scottish Gael; or, Celtic Manners as preserved among the Highlanders*. London, 1831; second ed. Inverness, 1876.
50 John Leyden. Introduction to *The Complaynt of Scotland*.
51 Gillies Whittaker. *Op. cit.*
52 Reproduced by William Stenhouse. *Illustrations of the Lyric Poetry and Music of Scotland*, ed. David Laing. Edinburgh, 1853.
53 J. Kay. *A Series of original Portraits and Caricature Etchings*. Ed. Hugh Paton, 2 vols. Edinburgh, 1838.
54 John G. Lockhart. *Life of Sir Walter Scott*. London, 1848.
55 Finlay Dun. Appendix to William Dauney's *Ancient Scotish Melodies from a manuscript of the Reign of King James VI*. Edinburgh, 1838.
56 Sir John Carr. *Tour through Scotland in 1807*. London, 1809.
57 Henry Cockburn. *Circuit Journeys*. Edinburgh, 1889.
58 G. F. Graham. *The Songs of Scotland*: notes on 'Lewie Gordon', vol. i. Edinburgh, 1848.
59 Martin Gerbert. *Scriptores ecclesiastici de musica*, 1784. Vol. ii, facsimile ed. 1931.

Chapter 9: The Sweetness of a Scottish Tune

1   *The Diary of Samuel Pepys*, vol. ii. Ed. John Warrington. Everyman's Library London, 1964.
2   Sir John Hawkins. *A General History of the Science and Practice of Music*, 5 vols London, 1776.
3   John Macculloch. *The Highlands and Western Isles of Scotland*, vol. ii. London, 1824.
4   Alexander Malcolm. *A Treatise of Music, speculative, practical and historical* Edinburgh, 1721.
5   Colin Brown. *The Thistle: a miscellany of Scottish song*. London, [1884].
6   Finlay Dun. Appendix to William Dauney's *Ancient Scotish Melodies from a manuscript of the Reign of King James VI*. Edinburgh, 1838.
7   Bertrand H. Bronson. 'Folksong and the Modes', *The Musical Quarterly*, vol. xxxii, no. 1. January 1946.
8   Cecil J. Sharp. *English Folk Song, Some Conclusions*. London, 1907.
9   E. C. Curwen. 'The Significance of the Pentatonic Scale in Scottish Song'. *Antiquity*, vol. xiv. December 1940.
10 Malcolm Macfarlane. 'Studies in Gaelic Music', *Transactions of the Gaelic Society of Inverness*. December 1908.
11 Sharp. *Op. cit.*
12 Cf. also Bronson. *Op cit.*, and *The Traditional Tunes of the Child Ballads*, vol. ii. Princeton, 1962.
13 Henry Mackenzie (H. W. Thompson ed.). *Anecdotes and Egotisms*. London, 1927.
14 G. F. Graham. Introduction to F. Robinson's *Melodies of Ireland*. London, 1850.
15 Lucy Broadwood. 'The Collecting of English Folk-Songs'. *Proceedings Musical Association*, 31st session. 1904–5.
16 George Petrie. *The Petrie Collection of the Ancient Music of Ireland*. Dublin, 1855.
17 Francis Collinson. *The Traditional and National Music of Scotland*. London, 1966.

APPENDICES

1. The Holmain Manuscript, 1710–50

The Holmain MS. is a notebook containing six pages of instructions for Country Dances. The contents are reproduced by A. S. Carruthers in 'Some old Scottish dances' in the *Proceedings of the Society of Antiquaries of Scotland*, series 5, v. ii, and are dated by him 1710–20. Hugh Thurston in *Scotland's Dances*, 1954, considers, however, that 1730–50 is a better estimate.

Green Sleeves   The Birks of Abergeldie
Cald Kale   Lennox's Love to Blanter
Hunt the Squiril   The Old Ways of Killiecrankie
The Dusty Millar   Bathget Bogs or Pease Straw
This is not my own house   Miss Hyden
Argile's Bouling Green   Reel a Down a Mereken

2. The Menzies Manuscript, 1749

The Menzies manuscript is contained in the Atholl Collection of the Sandeman Library, Perth. It contains details of the figures of the dances, but no music.

The Menzies' rant or Reel don ne
  Marachan
O'er the watter to Charly
General Stuart's reel or The new way of
  Gil Don
The Montgomeries' rant—a strathspey
  reele
Conteraller's rant—a strathspey reele
You'r welcome, Charly Stuart
Saw you Charly coming or Fye father
  see him, etc.
He'll aye be welcome back again

Open the door to three
Cope's march
The infare or Will ye marry Kitty
The mighty pretty valley or Reel of
  Tulloch
The Priest and his books
Lady Mary Menzies's reel
Thirtieth of Aprile
Miss Clemy Stewart's reel
Mr Jack Stewart's reel
The blew ribon

3. The Bodleian Manuscript, 1740

The manuscript is inscribed 'A Collection of the Newest Country Dances Performed in Scotland written at Edinburgh by D. A. Young, W.M. 1740'. The manuscript is in the Bodleian Library, Oxford. It contains both figures and music.

Bung your Eye	6/8	A Kiss for a Half Pennie	4/4
Caberfei	4/4	The Gimlet	9/8
The Collonel	9/8	Drunken Meg Yoyng	6/8
The Braes of Balquhidder	4/4	The Miller of Drone	6/8
The Drummer	4/4	The Kingdom of Fife	9/8
A' Body Loo's Me	4/4	I'll Ne'er Leave Thee	4/4
The Drunken Wives in Pearson's		The Coronet	4/4
Close	4/4	The Lads of Air	4/4
The Ragged Sailor	6/8	The Key of the Cellar	3/2
The Cadger o' Crieff	4/4	Hakie	4/4
Down on Yon Bank	4/4	Cock a Bendie	4/4
The Holly Bush	6/8	Simon Brodie	4/4
Stick the Minister	4/4	McPhersons Rant	4/4
The Lads of Leith	6/8	Stuarts Rant	4/4
Welsh Fusileers	6/8	Castle Stuart	4/4
Mairi Allan	4/4	Duncan Mackay	4/4
Arthur's Seat	4/4	Castle Grant	4/4
Mumping Nelly	4/4	The Shire of Air	9/8

ack on the Green	9/8	Macdonald's Rant	4/4
Cromdel Hill	4/4	Lancaster Hornpipe	3/2
Up in the Morning Early	6/8	The Piper	9/8
O'er the Muir Among the Heather	4/4	Eccles's Rant	4/4
The Wood of Fyvie	4/4	Captain Ross	4/4
What Meikle Sorrow Ails You	4/4	Kate McFarlan	4/4
The Fire Side Reel	4/4		

4. The Drummond Castle Manuscript

i COUNTRY DANCES

The manuscript is inscribed 'A Collection of Countrey Dances written for the use of his Grace the Duke of Perth by Dav. Young, 1734'. The manuscript is in the possession of the Earl of Ancaster at Drummond Castle.

Whip Her and Gird Her	6/8	Kiss'd Yestreven	6/8
ack Leighton	4/4	Lucky Black's Daughter	4/4
Drummond's Rant	4/4	Highland Laddie	4/4
Athol Braes	4/4	Lennox Love	4/4
Argyle's Bowling Green	4/4	Wattie Laing	4/4
Fairly Shot of Her	12/8	You'll ay be welcome back again	4/4
Allastor	4/4	Up and Worst them all Willy	4/4
New Bigging	6/8	Because I was a bonny lad	4/4
Drops of Brandy	9/8	A rantin Highland Man	4/4
Hey to Cowpar	6/8	Countrey Kate	9/8
The Maltman	9/8	Laddie with the Yellow Coatie	4/4
We're all forsaken for want of		Tibbie Fowler in the Glen	4/4
silver	9/8	Rob Shore in Harvest	3/2
A wife of my Own	9/8	Old Age and Young	3/2
uphie McNab	6/8	Braes of Mar	4/4
My own Kind Dearie	4/4	This is not my own House	4/4
Lady Jean Hum's Reel	12/8	King of Damascus	4/4
Lady Susan Montgomery's Horn-		The Old Wife Beyond the Fire	4/4
pipe	3/2	O'er Bogie	4/4
Lams Horns	4/4	Kick the World Before you	9/8
Camstronnan's Rant	9/8	Unfortunate Jock	6/8
Lady Christian Montgomery's		Drunken Wives of Fochabers	4/4
Hornpipe	3/2	Border Reel	12/8
Drouth	6/8	Confederacy	4/4
Hey my Nanny	9/8	Drummond Castle	6/8
Kirkcudbright	4/4		

ii HIGHLAND REELS

The manuscript is inscribed 'A Collection of the best Highland Reels written by David Young, W.M. & Accomptant'.

Duke of Perth's Reel
Gairntully's Rant
Tullochgorum
Sir Alex, Mcdonald's Reel
Glenbuchet's Reel
Balmoral's Rant
Pharo's Reel
Invercauld's Reel
Gillecallum
Bridge of Turk
Caper fei
Jolly Robin
Stay and take your breeches with you
Kilmarnoch's Reel
Ochal Reel
Stewart's Rant
Everybody love me
Tres ace
Cockabendie
Edinglassie's Rant
Strathmore's Reel
Baxter's Rant

Tamavuiln
Ardkinglas's Reel
Tarnivah Reel
Stumpie
Corby Reel
Collar Reel
Beggar Reel
Cadger of Crieff
Macfarlane's Reel
Harlequin Reel
Grant's Rant
The Rake's Rant
Inverara Reel
Hatton Reel
The Wood of Fyvie
What meikle sorrow ails you
Welcome to your foot again
Four and twenty highlandmen
Fireside Reel
Merry Annie
Fettercairn Reel
Tail Todle

5. *The Gillespie Manuscript, 1768*

The manuscript is inscribed 'A Collection of the Best and Most Favourite Tunes for the Violin ... Perth. Collected and Transcribed by James 4 Gillespie M, DCC, LXVIII'. The spelling is given exactly as it appears in the MS.

i AIRS AND MARCHES

1 Lord Lenox's March
2 Duet by Mr Handel
3 Gavot by Correllie
4 Count Sax's March
5 King George's March
6 A March
7 Belisle March
8 Britons Strike Home
9 Prince Eugene's March
10 Count Brown's March
11 A March in Solomon
12 The Duke of Holstine's March
13 Skelcher's March
14 Granoe's March
15 The Edinburgh Train Band's March

16 Gavot by Mr Handle
17 Dorchester March
18 Hearts of Oak. A Song
19 Charles the 12th King of Swedene's
    March
20 Gilderoy
21 Britania
22 An Air

23 Thro the Wood Ladie. A Song
24 Air by Mr Handel
25 The Grenadiers March
26 Gavott by Chas. McLean
27 Lord Loudans March
28 Old Buffs March
29 A March in Rinaldo
30 Air by Handel

ii SCOTS TUNES

31 Gillicrankie
32 Up in the Morning Early
33 The Coalliers Daughter
34 The Yellow Haird Ladie
35 I'll Never Leve the
36 Pinkie House
37 New Highland Ladie
38 The Bottom of the Punch Bowl
39 For Lake of Gold she's left me
40 Woes my Heart that we Should
    Sunder
41 Rossline Castle
42 Lo Down in the Broom
43 The Isle of Sky. A Scots Measure
44 The Lass of Livingstone. A Scots
    Measure
45 McLauchlen's Scots Measure
46 Balginie's Bowling Green
47 My Apron Dearie
48 Bonney Jean
49 The Charmes of Lovely Peggie
50 Peggie Grives Me
51 Miss Hamelton's Delight
52 The Dutch Skiper
53 Logan Watter
54 The Lilles of France
55 Widow art thou Wakeing
56 Jack and his Trowsers On
57 She Rose and let me in
58 Saw ye na Eppie Me Enab th' day
59 Throw the Wood Ladie.
60 Kathrine Ogie

61 Eatrick Banks
62 Saw ye my Love Peggie
63 I Wish my Love were in a Mire.
    New Sett
64 Moggie Lawther
65 To Danton Me
66 John Hays Boney Lassie
67 The Lasse of Patie's Mill
68 Over the Watter to Charlie
69 Johne Cope are you Wakeing Yet
70 The Ducks dang Over My Dadie
71 Joy to Great Ceaser
72 The Merry Wives of Carlile
73 The Noble Reace of Jenken
74 My Own kind Dearie
75 Where shall Our Goodman Lay
76 Duncan Gray
77 Cock up your Bevar
78 Lumps of Pudens
79 Whisle Ore the Leve Od
80 The Flowres of the Forrest
81 Grigs Pipes
82 Black Jock
83 Jackie Latten
84 Roring Willie
85 Sandie Rea &c.
86 Comely Garden. A Reel
87 John Come Kiss me Now
88 O'er the Moor to Maggie
89 Carrick Gergues. New Set
90 Sours Plumbs of Gallowshilds
91 A Reel

iii MINUETS

92	The State Houlders Minuet	121	Prince Charles's Minuet
93	The Duke of York's Minuet	122	Italian Minuet
94	Lady Ann Dundass's Minuet	123	Princess Amelia's Minuet
95	Lady Belly Erskine's Minuet	124	Miss Monro's Minuet
96	Miss Fletchers Minuet	125	Miss Pringle's Minuet
97	Lady Rothes or Lord Mark Kers Minuet	126	Miss Porterfeeld's Minuet
		127	Prince Ch: New Minuet
98	Miss Lenoys Minuet	128	Lady Betty Cochrane's Minuet
99	Miss Bowls Minuet	129	Countess of Weem's Minuet
100	Lady Mary Powiss's Minuet	130	Jigge Minuet
101	Sir Charles Sedlys Minuet	131	Lady Peggie Stewart's Minuet
102	Virjina Minuet	132	Lady Faney Erskine's Minuet
103	Miss Carmichals Minuet	133	Lord Crawford's Minuet
101	Countess of Coventrie's Minuet	134	Lady Dundass's Minuet
105	Miss Caw's Minuet	135	Miss Mary Porterfieeld's Minuet
106	Signo Pissqualie's Minuet	136	She's Swetest when She's Naked
107	Miss Montgomrie's Minuet		or Miss Faw's Minuet
108	Miss Stewart's Minuet	137	A Minuet
109	Miss Maley Edmonstons Minuet	138	Oswalds Bass Minuet
110	Lady Banff's Minuet	139	Mary Scott
111	Mr Pitt's Minuet	140	A New Minuet
112	French Minuet	141	Lulleys Minuet
113	Mrs Bouth's Minuet	142	Bellizie Minuet
114	Lady Boyd's Minuet	143	Cukoo Minuet
115	The Neapoliton Minuet	144	Weldmans Minuet
116	Marshal Sax Minuet	145	A New Minuet
117	A Minuet	146	Scarabanda by Correllie
118	Major Erskine's Minuet	147	Germain Minuet
119	Miss Mally Montgomrie's Minuet	148	Italian Minuet
120	Miss Woffingtone's Minuet		

iv HORNPIPES, JIGGS AND REELS

149	The Flowers of the Forest. A Reel	156	The Lads of Air. A Reel
150	Make the Bed. A Reel	157	Green grow's the Rashes. A Reel
151	Love's Reel	158	Sweet Mally. A Reel
152	Burford Races. A Reel	159	Lady Sinclers Reel
153	New Hay	160	The Royal Exchange Reel
154	Inch of Perth. A Reel	161	Lady Fanie Montgomries Reel
155	Up the Moor Amongest the Heather. A Reel	162	Lady Hariot Hope's Reel
		163	The Soldier Ladie. A Reel

164 A Reel
165 The Duke of Athol's Blew Britches
166 The Duke of Perths Reel
167 Miss Blairs Reel
168 A Reel
169 Sir Alexr Mcdonald's Rant
170 Lasses of Dunce. A Reel
171 Suky Bids Me
172 Shan Trowes
173 For Lake of Gold Jige
174 Linkem Dodie. A Reel
175 The Pretty She. A Strathspey
176 Strathspey Reel
177 Wanton Towdie. A Reel
178 Prince Charlie's Delight
179 Green Slives
180 Jack's Alive
181 Geld him Lasses. A Hornpipe
182 I'll lay no more with my Mother
183 Carouse and be Merry
184 O If I had such a Lassie as this
185 Daniel Couper
186 Rigadown
187 King Charles Jige
188 Unfortunate Jock
189 I'll Kick the World Before Me
190 Boll of Bear
191 Dustie Miller. A Hornpipe
192 If the Kirk would lett me be
193 The Birks of Abergeldie. A Reel
194 Cammron's got his Wife Again.
     A Reel
195 The Highland Hill's
196 Keep the Country bonny Lassie.
     A Reel
197 Peas Straw. A Reel
198 The Ranting Highlandman. A
     Reel
199 Hopetoun House. A Reel
200 Wellcome Home my Dearie
201 Invercald Reel. A Strathspey
202 Highland watchs farewell to Ireland
203 Lick the Ladle Sandie. A Reel
204 Struan Robertsons Rant

205 Reel of Tulloch
206 Will you go to Sheriff Moor
207 Peggie's Wedding
208 Kiss the Lass ye like best. A Reel
209 Ye'll ay be Wellcome back again
210 New Christmass
211 Garick Reel
212 Merry Dancers
213 Merrly Dance the Quaker
214 Bring hir ben and Bore hir beller
215 Sing Tantarah Raragh Rouges all
216 A Trumpet Jigge
217 I wish you would marrey me now.
     A Reel
218 Russians Rant. A Strathspey Reel
219 Breas [Braes] of Angus. A R[ee]l
220 Lady Jean Hoom's Reel
221 The Boney wi thing. A Reel
222 I've got A Wife of [my] Own. A
     Reel
223 The Free and Accepted Mason
224 Lochyell's Rant. A Strathspey
225 The Lass of Elgin A Reel
226 The Marques of Granby's Delight
227 Hornpipe
228 A Strathspey Reel
229 My Wife's a Wanton wi thing
230 My Minnie ['s] Ay Glowran O'er
     Me
231 Carrick Fergues. An Irish Reel
232 Love in a Vilage. A Reel
233 Bernards Well. A Reel
235 Hallow Fair. A Reel
235 Lord Kellys Reel
236 Lord Kinairds Reel
237 Jannie dang the Weaver. A Reel
238 I'll Make you be fain to follow me.
     A Reel
239 O'er the Moor among the Hedder.
     A New Set. A Reel
240 Cameronians Rant
241 Campbells are Coming Oho
242 Short Apron
243 Blair Drummonds Reel

6. Hornpipes composed by John Ravenscroft
from Sir John Hawkins, *A General History of the Science and Practice of Music.*
5 vols. London 1776

JOHN RAVENSCROFT.

B. BIBLIOGRAPHY

1. Principal References of Books and other Works

Other books are referred to in the Notes on the Text, pages 213 to 222

ABERDEEN. *Extracts From the Records of the Burgh*, 1643–1747. Burgh Records Society. Edinburgh, 1872.

Antiquarian Gleanings from Aberdeenshire Records, 2nd ed., Aberdeen, 1872.

Acts of the Parliament of Scotland. Edinburgh, 1844.

Accounts of the Lord High Treasurer of Scotland, vols. i–iv. Ed. T. Dickson and Sir J. Balfour Paul. Edinburgh, 1877–1902.

ANDERSON, DAVID. *Ballroom Guide*. Dundee, 1886, 1891 and 1894.

Universal Ballroom Guide & Solo Dance Guide. Dundee, 1900, 1902.

ARNOT, HUGO. *History of Edinburgh*. Edinburgh, 1779.

'Ayrshire at the Time of Burns'. Ayrshire Archaeological and Natural History Society, 1959.

'Bagpipes and Hurdy-Gurdies in their Social Setting'. Bulletin of Metropolitan Museum of Art. New York, Summer 1943.

BAINES, ANTHONY. *Bagpipes*. Oxford, 1960.

(ed.) *Musical Instruments Through the Ages*. London, 1961.

BAPTIE, J. *Musical Scotland Past and Present*. Paisley, 1894.

BRAND, JOHN. *Observations on the Popular Antiquities of Great Britain*. London, 1849.

BRONSON, BERTRAND HARRIS. (ed.) *The Traditional Tunes of the Child Ballads*. Princeton, vol. i, 1959; vol. ii, 1962; vol. iii, 1966.

BROWN, COLIN. *The Thistle: A Miscellany of Scottish Songs*. London [1884].

BROWNE, P. HUME. *Scotland Before 1700*. Edinburgh, 1893.

BRUCE, J. COLLINGWOOD and STOKOE, JOHN. *Northumbrian Minstrelsy*. Newcastle, 1882.

BUKOFZER, MANFRED F. *Studies in Medieval and Renaissance Music*. New York, 1950.

BURNEY, CHARLES. *A General History of Music*. London, 1789.

Burns Chronicle (Annual).

BURNS, ROBERT. *Letters*. Ed. J. De Lancey Ferguson. Oxford, 1931.

CAMPBELL, ALEXANDER. *An Introduction to the History of Poetry in Scotland*. Edinburgh, 1798.

The Grampians Desolate. Edinburgh, 1804.

Albyn's Anthology. Edinburgh, 1816–18.

CHAMBERS, E. K. *The Medieval Stage*. London, 1903.

CHAMBERS, ROBERT. *Domestic Annals of Scotland*. Edinburgh, 1861.
  Traditions of Edinburgh. Edinburgh, 1868.
  Scottish Songs Prior to Burns. Edinburgh, 1890.
  Popular Rhymes of Scotland. Edinburgh, 1826, 1828-41.
  Autobiography and Memoir. 3rd ed. Edinburgh, 1872.
  (ed.) *Life and Works of Robert Burns*, revised William Wallace. Edinburgh, 1896.
CHANCELLOR, E. B. *Life in Regency and Early Victorian Times*. London, 1926.
CHAPPELL, WILLIAM. *Popular Music of the Olden Time*. London, 1859.
CHEAP, JOHN, *The Chapman's Library*. Glasgow, 1877.
CHILD, F. J. *The English and Scottish Ballads*, ?1893-8.
COOK, DAVIDSON. *Annotation of Scottish Songs by Burns*. Burns Chronicle no. xxxi,
  January, 1922.
CREECH, WILLIAM. *Fugitive Pieces*. Edinburgh, 1815.
CROMEK, ROBERT HARTLEY. *Remains of Nithsdale and Galloway Song*. London, 1810.
CUNNINGHAM, ALAN. *Scottish Songs*. London, 1825.
DALYELL, SIR J. GRAHAM. *Musical Memoirs of Scotland*. Edinburgh, 1849.
DAUNEY, WILLIAM. *Ancient Scotish Melodies from a manuscript of the Reign of King James
  VI*. Edinburgh, 1838.
DEAN-SMITH, MARGARET. 'A Fifteenth Century Dancing Book' (Toulouze-Sur
  l'Art et Instruction de bien Dancer [*c*. 1496]). *Journal of the English Folk Dance and
  Song Society*, vol. iii, no. 2, 1937. 'English Tunes Common to Playford's Dancing
  Master, etc.' *Proceedings of the Musical Association*, Seventy-Ninth Session, 1952-3.
  (and Nicol, E. J.) 'The Dancing Master'. *Journal of the English Folk Dance and Song
  Society*, vol. iv, nos. 4, 5 and 6, 1943, 1944, 1945.
DIBDIN, JAS. *The Annals of the Edinburgh Stage*. Edinburgh, 1888.
DICK, JAMES C. *The Songs of Robert Burns*. London, 1903.
  (ed.) *Notes on Scottish Song by Robert Burns*. Written on an interleaved copy of the
  Scots Musical Museum. London, 1908.
EDGAR, ANDREW. *Old Church Life in Scotland*. Paisley, 1886.
FARMER, HENRY G. 'Music in 18th Century Scotland.' *Scottish Art & Letters*, no. ii.
  Glasgow, *c*. 1950.
  A History of Music in Scotland. London, 1947.
FLEMING, JAMES M. *Old Violins and Their Makers*. London, 1883.
  Fiddle Fancier's Guide. London, 1892.
FLETT, J. F. and T. M., and RHODES, F. *Traditional Dancing in Scotland*. London,
  1964.
FLOOD, W. H. GRATTAN. *The Story of the Bagpipe*. London, 1911.
  A History of Irish Music, 4th ed. London, 1927.
  The Story of the Harp. London, 1905.
FRASER, A. DUNCAN. *The Bagpipe*. Edinburgh, 1907.
GAELIC SOCIETY OF INVERNESS. Transactions of Publications from 1871.
GALPIN, FRANCIS, W. *A Textbook of European Instruments*. London, 1937. *Old
  English Instruments of Music*. London, 1910.
GEDDES, ARTHUR. *Songs of Craig and Ben*, vol. ii. Glasgow, 1961.

GLEN, JOHN. *Glen Collections of Scottish Dance Music* (Notes). Edinburgh, 1891 and 1895.

   Early Scottish Melodies. Edinburgh, 1900.

GORDON, J. F. S. (ed.) *Glasgow Ancient and Modern.* Glasgow [1874].

GRAHAM, G. FARQUHAR. *Songs of Scotland.* Edinburgh, 1848.

GRAHAM, H. G. *Social Life of Scotland in the Eighteenth Century,* 2nd ed. Edinburgh, 1900.

GRANT, JAMES. *Old and New Edinburgh.* London, 1882.

GRANT, ELIZABETH. *Memoirs of a Highland Lady 1797–1827.* London, 1898.

GRAY, M. M. (ed.) *Scottish Poetry from Barbour to James VI.* London, 1935.

HAWKINS, SIR JOHN. *A General History of the Science and Practice of Music.* London, 1776.

HERD, DAVID. *Ancient & Modern Scottish Song, Heroic Ballads, etc.* Edinburgh, 1776.

HOGG, JAMES. *Jacobite Relics.* Edinburgh, 1819.

JOHNSON, JAMES. *The Scots Musical Museum with illustrations of the Lyric Poetry and Music of Scotland.* Ed. William Stenhouse and David Laing. Edinburgh, 1853.

Journal of the English Folk Dance and Song Society, 1932.

Journal of the Folk Song Society. 8 vols. 1899–1931.

KENNEDY, JOHN W. 'Our Common Riding Airs.' *Hawick Archaeological Society,* 1914.

KNOX, JOHN. *History of the Reformation in Scotland.* Ed. W. C. Dickinson. Edinburgh, 1949.

LANG, ANDREW. *History of Scotland.* London, 1892.

LOCHHEAD, MARION. *The Scots Household in the Eighteenth Century.* Edinburgh, 1948.

LOGAN, JAMES. *The Scottish Gael,* 1st ed. London, 1831.

LORIMER, R. L. C. 'Studies in Pibroch', *Scottish Studies,* 6, pp. 1–30 (1962); 8, pp. 45–79 (1964).

MCELWEE, WILLIAM. *The Wisest Fool in Christendom.* New York, 1958.

MACKENZIE, JOHN. *Sar-Obar nam Bard Gaelach.* Edinburgh, 1907.

MACKERNESS, E. D. *A Social History of English Music.* London, 1964.

MACKIE, R. L. *King James IV of Scotland.* Edinburgh, 1958.

MACINTOSH, ANDREW. 'The History of Strathspeys and Reels.' *Transactions of the Gaelic Society of Inverness,* 15th December 1910, vol. xxvii, Inverness, 1915.

MACINTOSH, JOHN. *The History of Civilization in Scotland.* Paisley, 1895.

MANSON, W. L. *The Highland Bagpipe.* Paisley, 1901.

MARR, ROBERT. *Music For the People.* Edinburgh, 1889.

MILL, A. J. *Medieval Plays in Scotland.* Edinburgh, 1924.

MURDOCH, ALEXANDER GREGOR. *The Fiddle in Scotland.* London, 1888.

NETTEL, REGINALD. *Seven Centuries of Popular Song.* London, 1956.

NORTH, CHARLES NIVEN MCINTYRE. *Leabhar Comunn nam Fior Ghael* (The Book of the Club of True Highlanders). London, 1881–2.

NORTHBROOKE, JOHN. *A Treatise Against Dicing, Dancing, Plays and Interludes,* 1st ed. 1577. Ed. J. P. Collier. Shakespeare Society Reprint. London, 1843.

O'CURRY, EUGENE. *Lectures on the MS. Materials of Ancient Irish History.* Dublin, 1861. *On the Manners and Customs of the Ancient Irish.* Ed. W. K. Sullivan. London, 1873.

O'SULLIVAN, DONAL. *Carolan, the Life, Times and Music of an Irish Harper.* London, 1958.

PETRIE, GEORGE. *The Complete Collection of Irish Music.* Dublin, 1858.

PINKERTON, JOHN. *Ancient Scottish Poems.* London, 1786.

RAMSAY, ALLAN. *Works.* Edinburgh, 1848.

REESE, GUSTAVE. *Music in the Middle Ages.* New York, 1940.

RITSON, JOSEPH. *Scottish Songs.* London, 1794.

ROBINSON, F. *Melodies of Ireland.* London, 1850.

SACHS, CURT. *The History of Musical Instruments.* New York, 1940.

SAGE, DONALD. *Memorabilia Domestica* or Parish Life in the North of Scotland. Edinburgh, 1889.

SCHOLES, PERCY A. *The Oxford Companion to Music.* Oxford, 1939. *The Puritans and Music in England and New England.* London, 1934.

SCOTTISH ART AND LETTERS—Published by MacLellan, Glasgow, 6 numbers. *c.* 1959.

SCOTTISH BURGH RECORDS SOCIETY. Edinburgh—Extracts from the Records of the Burghs of Aberdeen, Edinburgh, Glasgow. Edinburgh, *c.* 1872.

SCOTTISH STUDIES. Edinburgh University. Publication of the School of Scottish Studies.

SKENE, W. F. *Celtic Scotland.* Edinburgh, 1880.

Spottiswoode Miscellany. Ed. James Maidment. The Spottiswoode Society. Edinburgh, 1844.

STENHOUSE, WILLIAM (see James Johnson). *Illustrations of the Lyric Poetry and Music of Scotland.*

STEWART, GENERAL DAVID (of Garth). *Sketches of the Highlanders.* Edinburgh, 1822.

STODDART, JOHN. *Remarks on the local scenery and manners in Scotland during the years 1799 and 1800.* London 1801.

STRUTT, JOSEPH. *Sports and Pastimes of the English People.* London, 1801.

SURENNE, JOHN T. *The Dance Music of Scotland.* Edinburgh, 1852.

THURSTON, HUGH. *Scotland's Dances.* London, 1954.

TOPHAM, EDWARD. *Letters from Edinburgh.* London, 1776.

TUREFF, GAVIN. *Antiquarian Gleanings from Aberdeenshire Records.* Aberdeen, 1871.

TYLER, P. F. *History of Scotland.* Edinburgh, 1841.

TYTLER, SARAH and WATSON, J. L. *The Songstresses of Scotland,* 2 vols. London, 1871.

TYTLER, WILLIAM (of Woodhouslee). *Dissertation on the Scottish Music.* Edinburgh, 1779. (First printed at the end of Arnot's *History of Edinburgh,* 1779.)

WHITELAW, ALEXANDER. *The Book of Scottish Song.* London, 1844.

WHITTAKER, W. GILLIES. *Collected Essays.* London, 1940.

WILSON, THOMAS. *A Companion to the Ballroom.* London, 1817.

The Complete System of English Country Dancing. London, 1821.

2. *Significant Collections of Scottish Music in Print, 1641–1900*

Developed on the basis of John Glen's compilation in his
Early Scottish Melodies, Edinburgh, 1900

ADAMS, ALEX. *The Musical Repository.* A Collection of Scotch, English, and Irish Songs set to Music, Glasgow: printed by Alex Adams, 1799.

AIRD, JAMES. *A Selection of Scotch, English, Irish and Foreign Airs.* Adapted to the Fife, Violin, or German Flute. 6 vols. James Aird, Glasgow [1782–1803].

A Favourite Collection of Scots Tunes & Highland Airs for the Violin or German Flute. With a bass for the violoncello or harpsichord. By W. M'Gibbon, J. Oswald, and Others. James Aird, Glasgow [*c.* 1787].

ANDERSON, JOHN. *A Collection of New Highland Strathspey Reels.* For the Violin or German Flute with a Harpsichord and Violoncello Bass. Composed by John Anderson. Edinburgh, 1790.

A Selection of the Most Approved Highland Strathspeys, Country Dances, English and French Dances; With a Harpsichord and Violoncello Bass. By John Anderson [Greenock]. Edinburgh, *c.* 1789.

BAILLIE, ALEXANDER. *Airs for the Flute with a Thorough Bass for the Harpsichord.* Alex Baillie, Edinburgh, 1735.

BALFOUR, DAVID. *Ancient Orkeney Melodies.* David Balfour, London. 1885.

BARSANTI, FRANCIS. *A Collection of Old Scots Tunes.* With a Bass for Violoncello or Harpsichord. Set and most humbly dedicated to the Right Honourable the Lady Erskine by Francis Barsanti. A. Baillie, and Messrs Hamilton & Kincaid, Edinburgh [1742].

BOWIE, JOHN. *A Collection of Strathspey Reels and Country Dances . . .* By John Bowie. Edinburgh [1789].

BREMNER, ROBERT. *A Collection of Scots Reels or Country Dances.* With a Bass for the Violoncello or Harpsichord. Robert Bremner, Edinburgh. Published in fourteen numbers of eight pages each, between the years 1751 and 1761, all undated.

A Second Collection of Scots Reels or Country Dances with a Bass for the Violoncello or Harpsichord and proper directions to each Dance. R. Bremner, London, 1768.

A Second Set of Scots Songs for a Voice and Harpsichord. R. Bremner, Edinburgh [1757].

Thirty Scots Songs for a Voice and Harpsichord. The Music taken from the most genuine Sets extant; The words from Allan Ramsay. R. Bremner, Edinburgh [1757].

BROWN, COLIN. *The Thistle: A Miscellany of Scottish Songs* by Colin Brown, Glasgow, 1884.

Songs of Scotland, London [1878].

BROWN, JAMES D. *Biographical Dictionary of Musicians*: with a Bibliography of English Writings on Music. By James D. Brown. Gardner, Paisley and London, 1886.

BROWN, J. *The Musical Miscellany*: A Select Collection of the most approved Scots, English and Irish Songs set to Music. J. Brown, Perth, 1786.

BRUCE, J. COLLINGWOOD and STOKOE, JOHN. *Northumbrian Minstresly*. A Collection of the Ballads, Melodies and Small-pipe Tunes of Northumbria, ed. Bruce and Stokoe for the Society of Antiquaries. Newcastle, 1882.

BUTTON & WHITAKER. *The Seraph*. A Collection of Sacred Music. Button & Whitaker, London, 1818.

CAMPBELL, ALEXANDER. *Albyn's Anthology* or A Select Collection of the Melodies and Vocal Poetry peculiar to Scotland and the Isles. Hitherto unpublished. Collected and Arranged by Alexander Campbell, etc. 2 vols. Oliver & Boyd, Edinburgh, 1816–18.

CAMPBELL, DONALD. *A Treatise of the Language, Poetry, and Music of the Highland Clans*. With Illustrative Traditions and Anecdotes and Numerous Highland Airs. By Donald Campbell, Esq. (D. R. Collie & Son). Edinburgh, 1862.

CAMPBELL, JOSHUA. *A Collection of the Newest & Best Reels and Minuets*; with Improvements Adapted for the Violin or German Flute, with a Bass for the Violoncello or Harpsichord. By Joshua Campbell. J. Aird, Glasgow [1779].

A Collection of New Reels & Highland Strathspeys. With a Bass for the Violoncello or Harpsichord by Joshua Campbell. Glasgow, 1788.

CAMPBELL, WILLIAM. *Campbell's Country Dances* . . . new and favourite Country Dances and Strathspey Reels, for the Harp, Piano-forte, and Violin. Printed and sold by Wm. Campbell, No. 8 Dean Street, Soho. (Books 1–12, some of the tunes are marked as composed by W. Campbell.) 1790–1817.

CHAPPELL, WILLIAM. *Popular Music of the Olden Time*; A collection of Ancient Songs, Ballads, and Dance Tunes, Illustrative of the National Music of England, etc. By William Chappell, F.S.A. 2 vols. Cramer, Beale & Chappell, London, 1859.

CHETWOOD, W. R. *The Lover's Opera*. By W. R. Chetwood. J. Watts, London, 1730.

CHRISTIE, WILLIAM. (1778–1849) *A Collection of Strathspeys, Reels* . . . Edinburgh, 1820.

CHRISTIE, WILLIAM [Dean Christie]. *Traditional Ballad Airs*. Arranged and Harmonised for the Pianoforte and Harmonium, from copies procured in the Counties of Aberdeen, Banff and Moray, by W. Christie, M.A., and the late Wm. Christie, Monquhitter, 2 vols. Edmonston & Douglas, Edinburgh, 1876, 1881.

CLARK, JOHN. *Flores Musicae or the Scots Musician*. J. Clark, Edinburgh [1773].

A Collection of New Strathspey—Reels and Country Dances with a Bass for the Violoncello or Harpsichord. Composed by John Clark, Perth. Perth, 1795.

CLARKSON, JOHN. A Complete Collection of much-admired tunes, as danced at the Balls and Public's of the late Mr. Strange. Purchased and arranged for the Pianoforte, and respectfully dedicated to his scholars, by John Clarkson, Junr., Teacher of Dancing, Edinburgh [1803]. (John Clarkson Senr. died St Andrews, January 20th, 1812. He practised as a Dancing Master there and at Kirkcaldy, Cupar and Dunfermline.)

COOPER, ISAAC. *A Collection of Strathspeys, Reels and Irish Jigs*, for the Piano-Forte & Violin to which are added Scots, Irish & Welch Airs Composed and Selected by I. Cooper at Banff, London, Edinburgh, & c., n.d.

Thirty New Strathspey Reels for the Violin or Harpsichord. Composed by Isaac Cooper. James Inlach, Banff, & Rt. Bremner, Edinburgh [1783].

CORRI, DOMINICO. *A New & Complete Collection of the most Favourite Scots Songs.* Including a few English & Irish with proper Graces and Ornaments peculiar to their Character, Likewise the new method of Accompanyment of Thorough Bass. By Sigr Corri. 2 Books. Corri & Sutherland, Edinburgh [1783].

CRAIG, ADAM. *A Collection of the Choicest Scots Tunes* adapted for the Harpsichord or Spinnet and within the Compass of the Voice, Violin, or German Flute. By Adam Craig, Edinburgh [1730].

CRAWHALL, JOSEPH. *A Collection of Right Merrie Garlands for North Country Anglers.* Joseph Crawhall, Newcastle, 1864.

Tunes for the Northumbrian Small Pipes, Violin or Flute, collected by Joseph Crawhall. Messrs. Horn & Storey, Newcastle, 1877.

A Beuk o' Newcassel Songs, Joseph Crawhall, Newcastle, 1888.

CROSBY, B. *Caledonian Musical Repository,* Crosby. London, 1806, 1811.

CUMMING, ANGUS. *A Collection of Strathspeys or Old Highland Reels* by Angus Cumming, at Grantown in Strathspey. Edinburgh, 1780.

DALE'S COLLECTION OF ENGLISH SONGS. *Dale's Collection of English Songs.* London, n.d.

DALE'S COLLECTION OF SIXTY FAVOURITE SCOTCH SONGS. *Dale's Collection of Sixty Favourite Scotch Songs,* Adapted for the Voice & Pianoforte or Harpsichord. 3 vols. of 60 each. London [1794].

DANIEL, JAMES. A Collection of Original Music, consisting of Slow Airs, Strathspeys, Reels, Quadrilles, Waltzes, Hornpipes & c. Adapted for the Pianoforte or Violin and Violoncello. By a Citizen. Aberdeen . . . Published by James Daniel. n.d.

DAUNEY, WILLIAM. *Ancient Scotish Melodies* from a Manuscript of the Reign of King James VI, etc., by William Dauney, Esq., F.S.A. Scot. Edinburgh, 1838.

DAVIE, JAMES. *Caledonian Repository.* Davie. Aberdeen, Edinburgh, *c.* 1829–30.

DOW, DANIEL. *A Collection on Ancient Scots Music* for the Violin, Harpsichord, or German Flute. Never before Printed Consisting of Ports, Salutations, Marches, or Pibrochs, &C. By Daniel Dow. Edinburgh [1776].

Thirty-Seven New Reels and Strathspeys, for the Violin, Harpsichord, Pianoforte, or German Flute. Composed by Daniel Dow. Edinburgh [*c.* 1776].

Twenty Minuets, and Sixteen Reels or Country Dances for the Violin, Harpsichord, or German Flute, Composed by Daniel Dow. Edinburgh [*c.* 1775].

DUFF, ARCHD. *A Collection of Strathspey Reels & c.* for the Piano Forte, Violin and Violoncello. Archd. Duff. Dancing Master Montrose. Edinburgh, 1794.

The First Part of a Choice Selection of Minuets, Dances, etc. Archibald Duff [1811].

DUFF, CHARLES. *A Collection of Strathspeys, Reels, Jiggs & c.* with a Bass for the Violoncello or Harpsichord. By Charles Duff, Dundee *c.* 1740. (N.B. Tunes marked JMcD are composed by John McDonald, late Dancing Master, Dundee.)

DUN, FINLAY. *Orain na'h—Albain,* a Collection of Gaelic Songs with English and Gaelic Words . . . Pianoforte accompaniment . . . by Finlay Dun, Edinburgh [*c.* 1860]. (The Preface contains what may be the earliest discussion of the modality of Gaelic folk-tunes.)

DUN, FINLAY and THOMSON, JOHN. *The Vocal Melodies of Scotland* by Finlay Dun and John Thomson, 1836, revised and re-edited by Edward Rimbault Dibdin. Edinburgh, 1884.

DURFEY, T. (*Or* D'urfey, T.). *Wit and Mirth: or Pills to purge melancholy*; Being a Collection of the best Merry Ballads and Songs, Old and New. T. D'Urfey. 6 vols. 1719-20 (reprint). J. Tonson.

EDINBURGH MAGAZINE, THE. *Edinburgh Magazine*, 1785.

EGLINTON, HUGH MONTGOMERIE, Twelfth Earl of. *New Strathspey Reels* for the Pianoforte, Violin and Violoncello. Composed by a Gentleman [Earl of Eglinton] and given permission to be published by Nathaniel Gow. Edinburgh [1796].

ELLIOT, C. *Calliope: or, the Musical Miscellany*. A Select Collection of the most approved English, Scots, and Irish Songs, Set to Music. C. Elliot & T. Kay, London, 1788.

ELOUIS, J. First Volume of a Selection of Favourite Scots Songs, with Accompaniments for the Harp or Piano forte, by J. Elouis, Edinburgh, n.d. Second Volume . . . *c.* 1807. (Dedicated to the Earl of Eglinton and sub-scribed to by The Queen and thirteen others of the Royal Family.)

FLORA—*Flora*, an Opera, London, 1732.

FRASER, S. *Thirty Highland Airs, Strathspeys & c.* With a Bass for the Violoncello or Harpsichord. Consisting Chiefly of Tunes entirely New with a Few Old Tunes never before Published. Selected and Composed by Mr S. Fraser. 1795.

The Airs and Melodies peculiar to the Highlands of Scotland and the Isles . . . Edited by Captain Simon Fraser and chiefly acquired during the interesting period from 1715 to 1745 . . . (Mr. John Gow, Hanover St.) Edinburgh and London, 1816. New Edition revised by Wm. MacKay . . . containing the corrections and additions by the Compiler's son, the late Angus Fraser. (Hugh Mackenzie) Inverness, 1874.

FRENCH, JOHN. *New Strathspey Reels*. John French. Edinburgh [1801].

FULCHER, JOHN. *Lays and Lyrics of Scotland*. Fulcher. London, 1870.

FULCHER, JOHN and GLEADHILL, THOMAS S. *Beauties of Scottish Song*, Glasgow, n.d.

GAY, JOHN. *Polly*, an Opera. Being the Second Part of the Beggar's Opera. Written by Mr. Gay. T. Thomson, London, 1729.

The Beggar's Opera. Written by Mr. Gay. John Watts, London, 1728.

GIBB, A. *A New Collection of Minuets, Medlies, High Dances, Marches, Strathspey and other Reels* . . . A. Gibb. Edinburgh, 1798.

GLEN, JOHN. *Glen Collection of Scottish Dance Music*. John Glen. Edinburgh, 1891 and 1893.

Early Scottish Melodies: Including samples from MSS. and early printed works, along with a number of comparative Tunes. Notes on former annotators . . . Written and arranged by John Glen. Edinburgh, 1900.

GOW, JNO. and ANDW. A Collection of Slow Airs, Strathspeys, and Reels, with a Bass for the Violoncello, Harpsichord, or Pianoforte . . . by Jno. and Andw. Gow. London, n.d.

GOW, NIEL. *A Collection of Strathspey Reels* with a Bass for the Violoncello or Harpsichord, etc. By Niel Gow at Dunkeld [1784]. Second Collection [1788]. Third
[1792]. Fourth [1800]. Fifth [1809]. And Sixth Collection, 1822. Corri &
Sutherland, Edinburgh, The Author at Dunkeld, Gow & Shepherd, & Nathl.
Gow & Son. See also detailed list on page 249.

GOW, NIEL & SONS. *A Complete Repository of Original Scots Slow Strathspeys and
Dances*, & c., by Niel Gow & Sons, n.d. Part I [1799]. Part II [1802]. Part III
[1806]. Part IV [1817]. Gow & Shepherd, Edinburgh.

GRAHAM, GEORGE FARQUHAR. *The Songs of Scotland* Adapted to their Appropriate
Melodies. Arranged with Pianoforte Accompaniments, etc. By George F. Graham.
3 vols. Wood & Co., Edinburgh, 1848–9. Re-issued, with additional notes, by
John M. Wood, Edinburgh, 1884.

GRANT, DONALD. A Collection of Strathspey Reels, Jigs & c. for the pianoforte,
Violin, and Violoncello . . . by Donald Grant. [121 tunes, 76 original.] Elgin
[1790].

GREIG, JOHN. *Scots Minstrelsie*. John Greig. Edinburgh, 1892–95.

GROVE, GEORGE. *Dictionary of Music and Musicians*, George Grove, 1879–89. Latest
ed. London, 1954.

GUNN, ADAM and MACFARLANE, MALCOLM. *Orain agus Dain le Rob Donn MacAoidh*.
New Edition. Containing several original and hitherto unpublished melodies
collected in the Reay Country . . . by Rev. Adam Gunn and Malcolm MacFarlane.
Glasgow, 1879.

HAFFMAN, F. *Ancient Music of Ireland from the Petrie Collection*. Arranged for the
Pianoforte by F. Haffman. Piggott & Co., Dublin, 1877.

HALL, JOHN. *Selection of Strathspeys, Reels*. John Hall, Ayr, 1818.

HAMILTON, F. *The Caledonian Museum*, containing a favourite Collection of Ancient
and Modern Scots Tunes, adapted to the German Flute or Violin. Book III. [100
Airs.] . . . J. Hamilton, Edinburgh, n.d. [Hamilton died 1814.]
    A Choice Collection of Scots Reels, or Country Dances and Strathspeys, with a
Bass for the Violoncello or Harpsichord . . . printed and sold by J. Hamilton,
North Bridge, Edinburgh, n.d.

HERD, DAVID. *Ancient and Modern Scottish Songs*, Heroic Ballads, etc. In two volumes.
(David Herd) James Dickson and Charles Elliot, Edinburgh, 1776.

HOGG, JAMES. *The Jacobite Relics of Scotland*: being the Songs, Airs and Legends of the
Adherents to the House of Stuart. Collected and Illustrated by James Hogg. 2 vols.
Edinburgh, 1819 and 1821.

HORSFIELD, ROBERT. *Vocal Music or the Songsters Companion*. Editions 1772, 1775.
Robt. Horsfield, London, and Selections from the First and Second Volumes.
J. Bew, London [1778].

JACK, DAVID. *Lyric Gems of Scotland*. David Jack. Edinburgh, 1854–8.

JENKINS, GEORGE. *New Scotch Music consisting of Slow Airs Strathspeys Quick Reels
Country Dances, and a Medley on a New Plan* with a Bass for the Violoncello or
Harpsichord. Composed by George Jenkins, Teacher of Scotch Dancing. London
[1793].

JOHNSON, CHARLES. *The Village Opera*. Written by Mr Johnson. J. Watts, London, 1729.

JOHNSON, JAMES. *New Music for the Pianoforte or Harpsichord*; Composed by a Gentleman (Capt. Robert Riddell), consisting of Reels, Minuets, Hornpipes, Marches and two Songs in the Old Scotch Taste, with variations to five favourite Tunes. James Johnson, Edinburgh [1787].

   The Scots Musical Museum. Humbly dedicated to the Catch Club. Instituted at Edinburgh, June 1771. By James Johnson. 6 vols. Johnson, Edinburgh [1787–1803].

JOYCE, P. W. *Ancient Irish Music*, comprising One Hundred Airs, hitherto unpublished many of the Old Popular Songs and Several New Songs Collected and Edited. By P. W. Joyce, LL.D., M.R.I.A. M'Glashan and Gill, Dublin, 1873.

KERR, JAMES SPIERS. *Kerr's Collection of Reels and Strathspeys, Highland Schottisches, Country Dances, Jigs, Hornpipes, Flirtations & c.* arranged for the Pianoforte. Glasgow [1870].

KNAPTON, JAS. & JOHN. *The Beggar's Wedding*. A new Opera. By Mr. Char. Coffey. Second ed. Jas. & John Knapton, London, 1729.

LEBURN, ALEXANDER. *A Collection of New Strathspey Reels & c.* With a Bass for the Violoncello or Harpsichord. By Alexr. Leburn, Auchtermuchty. Edinburgh, 1793.

LOWE, JOSEPH. *Collection of Reels and Strathspeys*. Joseph Lowe. Edinburgh, 1844.

MCDONALD, JOHN. *A Collection of Strathspeys, Reels, Jiggs & c.* with a Bass for the Violoncello or Harpsichord. By Charles Duff, Dundee, c. 1790. (N.B. The Tunes marked JMcD are composed by John McDonald late Dancing Master Dundee.)

MACDONALD, KEITH NORMAN. *The Gesto Collection of Highland Music*, Keith Norman MacDonald (ed.), Edinburgh, 1895.

   Skye Collection of the Best Reels and Strathspeys. Keith Norman MacDonald (ed.), Edinburgh, 1897.

MCDONALD, MALCOLM. *A Collection of Strathspey Reels*, with a Bass for the Violoncello or Harpsichord . . . by Malcolm McDonald. Edinburgh [1788]. Second Collection [1789]. Third Collection [c. 1792]. Fourth Collection 1797.

MCDONALD, PATRICK. *A Collection of Highland Vocal Airs*. Never hitherto published. To which are added a few of the more lively Country Dances or Reels, of the Northern Highlands & Western Isles; and some specimens of Bagpipe Music. By Patrick McDonald. Corri & Sutherland, Edinburgh [1784].

MACFARLANE, MALCOLM. (See Gunn, Adam and MacFarlane, Malcolm.)

MCFADYEN, JOSEPH. *The Repository of Scots and Irish Airs*, Strathspeys, Reels, & c. Part of the Slow Tunes adapted for two Violins and a Bass, others with variations. The whole with improved Bass for the Harpsichord or Pianoforte . . . J. McFadyen, Glasgow (Oblong 4 to. Slow Airs 64 pp., Strathspeys etc. 64 pp.) [1802].

MCGIBBON, WILLIAM. *M'Gibbon's Collection of Scots Tunes* for a Violin or German Flute with a Bass. Robt. Bremner. Edinburgh [1768].

   A Collection of Scots Tunes, some with variations for a violin, by William

McGibbon [Book i], Edinburgh, printed by Richard Cooper [1742]. Book ii in 1746, Book iii in 1755, both undated.

MCGLASHAN, Alexander. *A Collection of Reels*, consisting chiefly of Strathspeys, Athole Reels . . . by Alexander McGlashan. Edinburgh, [1786].

    A Collection of Scots Measures, Hornpipes, Jigs, Allemands, Cotillons. And the fashionable Country Dances with a Bass for the Violoncello or Harpsichord. By Alexander M'Glashan. N. Stewart, Edinburgh [1781]

    A Collection of Strathspey Reels. With a Bass for the Violoncello or Harpsichord by Alexander M'Glashan. Neil Stewart, Edinburgh, [1780].

MACGLASHAN, JOHN. *A Collection of Strathspey Reels*, for the Pianoforte, Violin, or German Flute. John MacGlashan, Edinburgh, 1798.

MACINTOSH, ABRM. *Thirty New Strathspey Reels & c.* With a Bass for the Violoncello or Harpsichord. Composed by Abrm. MacIntosh. Edinburgh 1792. Second Collection, Edinburgh, 1796. Third Collection n.d.

MACINTOSH, ROBERT. *Airs, Minuets, Gavotts and Reels*. Mostly for Two Violins and a Bass for the Violoncello or Harpsichord composed by Robert MacIntosh of Inver. Edinburgh [1783].

    Sixty-Eight new Reels, Strathspeys and Quick steps . . . Composed by Robert MacIntosh. Edinburgh [1793].

    A 3d. Book of Sixty-eight New Reels and Strathspeys. Also above forty old Famous Reels. For the Violin and Piano Forte with A Bass for the Violoncello or Harpsichord. Compiled and Composed by Robert MacKintosh. (Ded. to Mrs. Oswald of Auchencruive) Edinburgh, 1796.

    A Fourth Book of New Strathspey Reels, also some Famous old Reels, for the Pianoforte or Harp. Compiled and Composed by Robert Mackintosh. (Dedicated to the Duchess of Manchester), London [1804].

MACINTYRE, D. *A Collection of Slow Airs, Reels and Strathspeys*. Composed by D. MacIntyre, Teacher of Scotch Dancing—London. London, 1795.

MACKAY, ALEXANDER. A Collection of Reels, Strathspeys, and Slow Tunes, arranged for the Pianoforte. Chiefly composed by Alexr. Mackay, Musician, Islay. J. McFadyen, Glasgow [1802].

MACKENZIE, ALEX. *The National Dance Music of Scotland* ded. to The Queen, arranged for Pianoforte by Alexander Mackenzie. Conductor of Music of Theatre Royal, Royal Caledonian Hunt Meetings and Edinburgh Assemblies. Edinburgh [1845]. (Re-edited by his son, Sir A. C. Mackenzie, 1891.)

MCKERCHER, DUNCAN. *Collections* [Scottish dance music] I and II. Duncan McKercher. Edinburgh [1830–50].

MCLAREN, DANIEL. *A Collection of Strathspey Reels & c.* With a Bass for the Violoncello or Harpsichord. Daniel McLaren. Edinburgh, 1794.

MCLEAN, CHARLES. *A Collection of Favourite Scots Tunes,* with Variations for the Violin and a Bass for the Violoncello and Harpsichord, by the late Mr. Charles McLean and other eminent masters . . . N. Stewart, Edinburgh [*c.* 1772].

MACPHERSON, JOHN. *A Selection of Irish and Scots Tunes*, consisting of Airs, Marches, Strathspeys, Country Dances, & c. Adapted for the Pianoforte, Violin, and

German Flute. By John Macpherson, Mulhollan. John Hamilton, Edinburgh [1804].

MANSON, JAMES. *Hamilton's Universal Tune-Book;* A Collection of the Melodies of all nations adapted for Violin, Flute, Clarionet, etc., Edited by James Manson, Glasgow, 1853.

MARSHALL, WILLIAM. *A Collection of Strathspey Reels.* With a Bass for the Violoncello or Harpsichord. Composed by Wm. Marshall. Neil Stewart, First and Second Book, Edinburgh, 1781.

   Marshall's Scottish Airs & c. Edinburgh, 1822; vol. ii, Edinburgh [1847].

MASON, M. H. *Nursery Rhymes and Country Songs.* Miss M. H. Mason (Metzler & Co., 1878). Reprint 1908.

MILNE, Peter. *Selections of Strathspeys, Reels & c.* Peter Milne. Ran to five editions. Keith [1870].

MITCHELL, JOSEPH. *The Highland Fair: or, Union of the Clans,* an Opera written by Mr. Mitchell. J. Watts, London, 1731.

MOFFAT, ALFRED. *Minstrelsy of Scotland.* Alfred Moffat. London, 1795.

MORISON, JOHN. *A Collection of New Strathspey Reels, With a few favourite Marches.* For the Piano-Forte, Violin and Violoncello. John Morison, Peterhead. Edinburgh [1797]. Second Collection [1815].

MORRISON, WILLIAM. *A Collection of Highland Music* consisting of Strathspeys, Reels, Marches, Waltzes, and Slow Airs, with Variations, original and selected, for the Pianoforte, Violin, and Violoncello ... by William Morrison ... J. Young & Co., Inverness ... [1812].

NAPIER, WILLIAM. *A Selection of the most Favourite Scots Songs Chiefly Pastoral.* Adapted for the Harpsichord, with an Accompaniment for a Violin. By Eminent Master, etc. 3 vols. William Napier, London [1790, 1792, 1794].

   Napier's Selection of Dances and Strathspeys, with new and appropriate Basses, adapted for the Pianoforte, Harp & c.... Wm. Napier, Music Seller, and Musician in Ordinary to his Majesty, Lisle Street, Leicester Square [d. 1812]. n.d.

OSWALD, JAMES. *The Caledonian Pocket Companion.* By James Oswald. 12 books. J. Simpson, and J. Oswald, London [1743–45–51–2–3–4–5–6–8, vols. x, xi and xii, 1759].

   A Collection of the Best old Scotch and English Songs set for the Voice with Accompaniments and Thorough-Bass for the Harpsichord, J. Oswald, London, n.d.

   A Collection of Curious Scots Tunes for a Violin, German Flute or Harpsichord. By James Oswald, London [1742]. A Second Collection, same year.

   A Collection of 43 Scots Tunes with Variations. Particularly Adapted for the Violin and Harpsichord. By James Oswald. J. Bland, London, n.d.

   A Curious Collection of Scots Tunes for a Violin, Bass Viol, or German Flute, with a Thorough Bass for the Harpsichord, etc. By James Oswald, Musician in Edinburgh [1740].

PATERSON, JAMES. *A Collection of Strathspeys, Reels, etc.* by James Paterson. Glasgow, 1867.

PEACOCK, FRANCIS. *Fifty Favourite Scotch Airs.* For a Violin, German Flute, and

Violoncello. With a Thorough Bass for the Harpsichord, etc. By Francis Peacock. London [1762].

PEACOCK, J. *A Favourite Collection of Tunes with Variations Adapted for the Northumberland Small Pipes, Violin or Flute.* J. Peacock, 'Newcastle, Printed by W. Wright at His Music Shop, High Bridge'. n.d.

PETRIE, GEORGE. *The Petrie Collection of the Ancient Music of Ireland.* Arranged for the Piano-Forte. Edited by George Petrie, LL.D., R.H.A., V.P.R.I.A., etc. M. H. Gill, Dublin, 1855.

PETRIE, ROBERT. *A Collection of Strathspey Reels & Country Dances & c.* with a Bass for the Violincello or Harpsichord. Dedicated to Mrs. Farquharson of Monaltrie By Robert Petrie at Kirkmichael, Pertshire. Edinburgh [1790]. Second Collection dedicated to Mrs Garden of Troup [1795]; Third Collection dedicated to Francis Garden, Esqur. Junior of Troup [1800]. Fourth Collection [1805].

PLAYFORD, HENRY. *A Collection of Original Scotch Tunes,* (Full of the Highland Humours) for the Violin: Being the First of this Kind yet Printed: Most of them being in the Compass of the Flute. Henry Playford, London, 1700.

PLAYFORD, JOHN. *Apollo's Banquet:* containing Instructions, and Variety of New Tunes, Ayres, Jiggs, and several New Scotch Tunes for the Treble-Violin. To which is added, The Tunes of the new French Dances, now used at Court and in Dancing Schools. The 5th Edition, with new Additions. John Playford, London, 1687. (First ed. 1663, sixth ed. 1690.)

A Booke of New Lessons for the Gittern: Containing many New and Pleasant Tunes, both Easie and Delightfull for all Young Practitioners. John Playford, London, 1652.

Choice Ayres & Songs to sing to the Theorbo Lute or Bass Viol. Book 1 first edition 1673. Book 1, 1676. Book 2, 1679. Book 3, 1681. Book 4, 1683. Book 5, 1684. John Playford, London.

The English Dancing Master, 1651—*The Dancing Master,* or Directions for Dancing Country Dances, with the Tunes to each Dance, etc., London, 1652, 1665, 1670, 1686. By John Playford, London: and later editions by his son and successors in 1690, 1695, 1698, 1701, 1703, 1706, 1709, 1713, 1716, 1721 and *c.* 1728.

Musick's Delight on the Cithren, Restored and Refined to a more Easie and Pleasant Manner of Playing than formerly: etc. John Playford, London, 1666.

Musick's Hand-maide presenting New and Pleasant Lessons for the Virginals. John Playford, London, 1663 and 1678.

Musick's Recreation on the Viol, Lyra-Way. Being a new Collection of Lessons Lyra-way, etc. John Playford, London, 1669; another edition, John Playford, London 1682.

PORTEOUS, JAMES. *A Collection of Reels and Strathspeys, & c.* . . . James Porteous, Edinburgh, n.d.

PRINGLE, JOHN. A Collection of Reels, Strathspeys, and Jigs, with a Bass for the Violoncello or Pianoforte . . . by John Pringle . . . Edinburgh, printed for the author, to be had of him, no. 16 Rose Street . . . [1801].

PURDIE, R. *Celtic Melodies*—Being a Collection of Original Slow Highland Airs,

Pipe Reels, and Cainntearachd never before published. Selected and arranged by a Highlander (MS. with notes). Pub. R. Purdie, Edinburgh, 1823.

RAMSAY, ALLAN. *Musick for the Scots Songs in the Tea-Table Miscellany*. Allan Ramsay, Edinburgh [*c.* 1724].

    Scots Songs. By Allan Ramsay. The Author, Edinburgh, 1720.

    The Tea-Table Miscellany: or a Collection of Scots Songs, etc. The Tenth Edition. Being the Whole that are contain'd in the Three Volumes just published. By Allan Ramsay. George Risk, Dublin, 1734. Title of Third Volume, 'A Collection of Celebrated Songs'.

REINAGLE, ALEXANDER. *A Collection of the most Favourite Scots Tunes*. With Variations for the Harpsichord by A. Reinagle. James Aird, Glasgow [1782].

RIDDELL, JOHN. *A Collection of Scots Reels or Country Dances and Minuets with Two Particular Slow Tunes*, with a Bass for the Violin, Violoncello or Harpsichord. Composed by John Riddell, Edinburgh, 1766.

    A Collection of Scots Reels or Country Dances, and Minuets . . . Composed by John Riddell in Ayr . . . Robert Bremner, Edinburgh [1766]. A Second edition 'Greatly Improved', Glasgow, *c.* 1782.

RIDDELL, ROBERT. *A Collection of Scotch, Galwegian, and Border Tunes* for the Violin and Pianoforte . . . Selected by Robert Riddell of Glenriddell. Edinburgh [1794].

RITSON, JOSEPH (*See also* Johnson, James) *Scottish Songs* in Two Volumes (Ritson). J. Johnson, London, 1794.

ROBERTS, J. *The Quaker's Opera*. J. Roberts, London, 1728.

ROBERTSON, DANIEL. A Collection of Reels, Strathspeys, Jigs, Waltzes, & c., for the Pianoforte, Harpsichord, and Violin, with a bass for Violoncello. Composed by Daniel Robertson. Edinburgh, n.d.

ROBERTSON, JAMES STEWART. *The Atholl Collection of the Dance Music of Scotland*. James Stewart Robertson. Edinburgh, 1884.

ROCHE, F. *A Collection of Irish Airs and Marches and Dance Tunes*. Compiled and arranged for Violin, Mandoline, Flute or Pipes. 3 vols. Dublin, 1911. 2nd ed. 1927.

ROSS, ROBERT. *A Choice Collection of Scots Reels or Country Dances & Strathspeys*. With a Bass for the Violoncello or Harpsichord. Robert Ross. Edinburgh [1780].

RUTHERFORD, DAVID. *Twenty Four Country Dances* for the year 1750. Dav. Rutherford, London.

SHEPHERD, WILLIAM. *A Collection of Strathspey Reels & c.* With a Bass for the Violoncello or Harpsichord. Composed by William Shepherd. Edinburgh, 1793.

SHIELD, WILLIAM. *Rudiments of Thorough Bass for Young Harmonists* [*c.* 1815] ('London, printed for the author, and sold by J. Robinson, no. 5, Paternoster Row.') William Shield (1748–1829).

SIME, D. *The Edinburgh Musical Miscellany*. A Collection of the Most Approved Scotch, English and Irish Songs; set to Music. Selected by D. Sime, Edinburgh, 1792. Vol. ii, 1793.

SIMPSON, JOHN. *Callione or English Harmony*. A Collection of the most Celebrated English and Scots Songs. 2 vols. John Simpson, London, n.d.

SKINNER, JAMES SCOTT. *Twelve New Strathspeys and Reels* by James Scott Skinner, Edinburgh [1865].

Thirty New Strathspeys and Reels by James Scott Skinner, Edinburgh [1868]. Second edition 1874.

Miller o' Hirn Collection of Scotch Music. Composed by J. Scott Skinner, Elgin, 1881.

Elgin Collection of Scotch Music. Composed by J. Scott Skinner. Elgin, 1884.

Logie Collection of Original Music for Voice, Violin and Pianofore, Composed by J. Scott Skinner, Keith, 1888.

The Harp and the Claymore. J. Scott Skinner, . . . 1904.

SMITH, ROBERT A. *Scottish Minstrel.* Robert A. Smith. Edinburgh, 1821–4.

STEWART, CHAS. *A Collection of Strathspey Reels Gigg's & c.* With a Bass for the Violoncello or Harpsichord. Chas. Stewart Musician to Mr Strange. N.B. A few New Hornpipes Minuets and Cotilions by the most Esteemed Composers. Edinburgh, 1799.

STEWART, CHARLES. *The Killin Collection of Gaelic Songs.* With music and translations. Charles Stewart, Edinburgh, 1884.

STEWART, NEIL. *A Collection of the Newest and Best Reels or Country Dances.* Adapted for the Violin or German Flute with a Bass for the Violoncello or Harpsichord— Edinburgh, 1761, (Published in 9 Numbers of 8 pages—1, 2—1761; 3–6, 1762; 7–9 uncertain.) Neil Stewart, Edinburgh [1761].

Thirty Scots Songs Adapted for a Voice and Harpsichord. The Words by Allan Ramsey. N. Stewart & Co., Edinburgh, n.d.

A Collection of Favourite Scots Tunes, with variations for the Violin and a Bass for the Violoncello and Harpsichord, by the late Mr Charles McLean and other eminent masters . . . N. Stewart, Edinburgh, [*c.* 1772].

A Collection of Scots Songs Adapted for a Voice or Harpsichord. Neil Stewart, Edinburgh [1772].

STOCKOE, JOHN (*See* Bruce, J. Collingwood, and Stockoe, John).

SURENNE, JOHN. *Dance Music of Scotland.* John Surenne (Edinburgh, 1851).

Songs of Scotland. John T. Surenne. Edinburgh, 1852.

THOMPSONS. *Compleat Collections of 200 Country Dances.* 4 volumes published by the Thompsons London [1758 to 1780].

The Hibernian Muse, a Collection of Irish Airs. Thompsons, London, n.d.

THOMSON, ANDREW. *Selections from the Melodies of Scotland.* Andrew Thomson. London, 1851.

THOMSON, GEORGE. *A Select Collection of Original Scottish Airs* for the Voice, with Introductory & Concluding Symphonies and Accompaniments for the Piano-. forte, Violin and Violoncello. By Pleyel, Kozeluch & Haydn. 6 vols. George Thomson, Edinburgh [1793, –98, –99, 1805, –18].

The Select Melodies of Scotland, interspersed with those of Ireland and Wales, united to the Songs of Robert Burns, Sir Walter Scott, and other distinguished Poets: With Symphonies and accompaniments for the Pianoforte by Pleyel, Kozeluch, Haydn, and Beethoven . . . George Thomson Lond. 5 vols. (1822–3). Vol. 6, 1825.

THOMSON, JOHN . . . (*See* Dun, Finlay and Thomson, John).

THOMSON, W. *Orpheus Caledonius,* or a Collection of the Best Scotch Songs set to Musick by W. Thomson. London, n.d. [1725].

Orpheus Caledonius: or, A Collection of Scots Songs. Set to Musick. By W. Thomson. 2 vols. (second edition). London, 1733.

THUMOTH, BURK. *Twelve Scotch and Twelve Irish Airs* with Variations Set for the German Flute, Violin or Harpsichord, by Mr Burk Thumoth. (J. Simpson) London, [*c.* 1760].

TONSON, F. *Wit and Mirth: or Pills to Purge Melancholy*: Being a Collection of the best Merry Ballads and Songs, Old and New. T. D'Urfey. 6 vols. 1719–20 (reprint). J. Tonson, London.

TOPCLIFF, ROBERT. *A Selection of the Most Popular Melodies of the Tyne and The Wear.* Consisting of 24 Original Airs peculiar to The Counties of Durham and Northumberland . . . Robert Topcliff. O'London. Published by R. Topcliff, No. 8 Staple Inn Buildings, Holborn, and to be had at all the principal Music Shops'.) [1815].

TURNBULL, JOHN. *Garland of Scotia.* John Turnbull (ed.) Glasgow, 1841.

URBANI, PETER. *A Selection of Scots Songs* Harmonized and Improved, with Simple and Adapted Graces, etc., by Peter Urbani. Edinburgh, [1793].

URFEY, T. D'. *See* Durfey, T.

URQUAHART, ALEXANDER. *Aria di Camera,* being a Choice Collection of Scotch, Irish & Welsh Airs for the Violin and German Flute. By the following Masters. Mr. Alexander Urquahart of Edinburgh, Mr. Derm. O'Connar of Limrick, Mr Hugh Edwards of Carmarthen, Dan. Wright & Dan. Wright Junr., London, *c.* 1730.

VOCAL MAGAZINE, THE, *The Vocal Magazine,* containing a Selection of the Most Esteemed English Scots, and Irish Songs, Ancient and Modern: Adapted for the Harpsichord or Violin. Edinburgh, 1797. Vol. ii, 1798; Vol. iii, 1799.

VOX BOREALIS. *Vox Borealis, or the Northern Discoverie.* London, 1641.

WALKER, ALEXANDER. *A Collection of original Scottish Strathspeys and Reels,* dedicated to Sir Charles Forbes of Newe by Alexander Walker, 1866.

WALKER, JAMES. *A Collection of New Scots Reels, Strathspeys, Jigs &c.* with a Bass for the Violoncello or Harpsichord. James Walker, Dysart. Edinburgh, 1797. *A Second Collection of Reels, Strathspeys, Jigs &c.* Edinburgh, 1800.

WALSH, J. *The British Musical Miscellany*; or, the Delightful Grove: Being a Collection of Celebrated English and Scotch Songs, By the Best Masters, Set for the Violin, German Flute, the Common Flute, and Harpsichord. 6 vols. J. Walsh, London [1734].

Caledonian Country Dances. J. Walsh, 4 Books or Volume I. *c.* 1744. Vol. II consisted probably of other 4 books, *c.* 1768.

Country Dances Selected as Perform'd at Court and all Publick Assemblies and Entertainments, etc. J. Walsh, London [*c.* 1760].

WATLEN, JOHN. *The Celebrated Circus Tunes Performed at Edinburgh this Season.* With the Addition of some New Reels and Strathspeys set for the Pianoforte or Violin and Bass. By John Watlen. Edinburgh, 1791. Book 2, Edinburgh, 1798.

A Complete Collection of Scots Songs by John Watlen. Edinburgh, 1796.

WATTS, JOHN. *The Beggar's Opera*. Written by Mr. Gay. John Watts, London, 1728.

Momus Turn'd Fabulist; or, Volcan's Wedding, J. Watts, London, 1729.

The Musical Miscellany; Being a Collection of Choice Songs set to the Violin and Flute. By the most Eminent Masters. John Watts, London, 1729.

Patie and Peggy; or the Fair Foundling, a Scotch Ballad Opera. J. Watts, London, 1731.

The Jovial Crew, a Comic Opera. J. Watts, London, 1731.

The Chamber Maid: a Ballad Opera. J. Watts, London, 1780.

WHITE, The Misses. *A Collection of Entirely Original Strathspey Reels, Marches, Quick Steps & c.* for the Piano Forte, Violin, German Flute, & c. By Ladies resident in a remote part of the Highlands of Scotland [The Misses White]. N.B. Corrected by Nath. Gow. Edinburgh, 1798.

WHYTE, HENRY (Fionn). *The Celtic Lyre*. A Collection of Gaelic Songs, with English Translations. Music in both notations. Henry (Fionn) Whyte. Edinburgh, 1898.

WHYTE, WILLIAM. *A Collection of Scotch Airs* edited by Dr Haydn with lyrics by Sir Walter Scott. William Shyte, Edinburgh [1806].

WILSON, JOHN. *Songs of Scotland*. John Wilson. London, 1842.

WOOD, T. *The Cobler's Opera*. T. Wood, London, 1729.

YOUNG, JOHN. *A Collection of Original Scotch Tunes for the Violin*. The whole Pleasant and Comicall being full of the Highland Humour. John Young, London, n.d.

3. The Publications of Niel Gow and Niel Gow and Sons

Four collections were published under the name of Niel Gow between 1782 and 1808. The Second Editions of these, the *Fifth* and *Sixth Collections* and the four *Repositories* were by Niel Gow and Sons. In 1819, a selection of the tunes composed by the Gows, taken from the first three collections, was published under the title of *The Beauties of Niel Gow*. In this the dances are arranged as Medleys, i.e. strathspey alternating with reel, or reel alternating with jig. The remaining collections were published by Nathaniel Gow himself.

A Collection of Strathspey Reels, with a Bass for the Violoncello or Harpsichord, most humbly dedicated to Her Grace, the Duchess of Athole. By Niel Gow at Dunkeld [1784]. Second edition, Niel Gow and Sons, Edinburgh, 1801.

A Second Collection of Strathspey Reels Etc. Dedicated (by permission) to the Noblemen and Gentlemen of the Caledonian Hunt. Niel Gow, at Dunkeld [1788]. Second edition Niel Gow and Sons, Edinburgh, 1803.

A Third Collection of Strathspey Reels for the Pianoforte, Violin, And Violoncello. Dedicated to the Most Noble, the Marchioness of Tweeddale. By Niel Gow at Dunkeld [1792]. Second edition, Niel Gow and Sons, Edinburgh, 1807.

A Fourth Collection of Strathspey Reels, Etc, for the Pianoforte, Violin, and Violoncello, dedicated to the Right Honourable, the Earl of Eglintoun, by Niel Gow, at Dunkeld [1800]. Second edition Niel Gow and Sons, printed by Gow and Sutherland, Edinburgh [1808].

Part First of the Complete Repository of Original Scots Slow Strathspeys and Dances for the Harp, Pianoforte, Violin and Violoncello, etc. Humbly dedicated to Her Grace, the Dutchess of Gordon by Niel Gow and Sons, Edinburgh, 1799. (N.B. 80 of the tunes will suit the German Flute—and the whole may be adapted for Military Bands.)

A Fifth Collection of Strathspeys, Reels etc. for the Pianoforte, Harp, Violin and Violoncello. Dedicated to the Right Honourable, the Countess of Dalhousie by Niel Gow and Sons, Edinburgh [1809].

A Sixth Collection of Strathspeys, Reels etc. Dedicated to the Marchioness of Huntley. The author at Dunkeld, Gow and Shepherd and Nathaniel Gow and Sons, Edinburgh, 1822.

Part Second of the Complete Repository of Original Scots Tunes, Strathspeys, Jigs and Dances for the Harp, Pianoforte, Violin and Violoncello etc. Humbly dedicated to Her Grace, the Dutchess of Buccleugh by Niel Gow and Sons, Edinburgh [1802].

Part Third of the Complete Repository of Original Scots Slow Strathspeys and Dances. Dedicated to the Right Honourable, the Countess of Loudoun and Moira, by Niel Gow and Sons, Edinburgh [1806].

Part Fourth of the Complete Repository of Original Scots Slow Tunes, Strathspeys and Dances. Dedicated to the Nobility and Gentry of Scotland. Gow and Shepherd, Edinburgh [1871].

The Beauties of Niel Gow, being a selection of the most favourite tunes from his First, Second and Third Collections of Strathspeys, Reels and Jigs, chiefly comprising the Compositions of Niel Gow and Sons (the dances arranged as Medleys), all of which are adapted for the Harp, Pianoforte, Violin and Violoncello. Respectfully dedicated to the Noblemen and Gentlemen of the Caledonian Hunt, by Nathaniel Gow, Edinburgh, 1819.
Part 1st pp. 38; part 2nd pp. 38; part 3rd pp. 38—all folio.

The Vocal Melodies of Scotland. Dedicated to His Grace, the Duke of Buccleugh and Queensberry. Arranged for the Pianoforte, or Harp, Violin and Violoncello, by Nathaniel Gow, Edinburgh [1820]. In three parts, 36 pages each consisting of genuine Scotch tunes with their Original Variations, with Basses throughout for the Pianoforte, or Harp, Violin and Violoncello. Dedicated to Sir Walter Scott, Bart., by Nathaniel Gow, Edinburgh, 1823.

A Select Collection of Original Dances, Waltzes, Marches, Minuets and Airs. Respectfully dedicated to the Most Noble, the Marchioness of Queensberry. Many of which are composed, and the whole arranged for the Pianoforte and Harp, by Nathaniel Gow, Edinburgh, n.d.

A Collection of Airs, Reels and Strathspeys, being The Posthumous Compositions of the Late Niel Gow, Junior, dedicated to the Right Honourable, the Earl of Dalhousie, by his much obliged servant, Nathaniel Gow, Edinburgh, 1849.

A Collection of Strathspey Reels—containing the most approved Old and the most fashionable

New Reels, some of which are composed, and others with additions, by Nathaniel Gow, London and Edinburgh [1797].

New Strathspey Reels for Pianoforte, Violin and Violincello. Composed by a Gentleman . . . Nathaniel Gow, Edinburgh [1795].

A Collection of Much Admired Marches, Quick Steps, Airs, etc. Composed by a Lady . . . Nathaniel Gow, Edinburgh [1800].

A Collection of Entirely Original Strathspey Reels, Marches, Quick Steps, etc . . . by Ladies resident in a remote part of the Highlands of Scotland . . . Corrected by Nathaniel Gow, Edinburgh [1802].

A Complete Collection of Originall German Valtz . . . Dedicated to Lady Charlotte Campbell by Nathaniel Gow, Edinburgh [*c*. 1820].

A Complete Repository of Old and New Scotch Strathspey's, Reels and Jigs; Printed and sold by Gow and Shepherd, No. 40 Princes Street, Edinburgh [*c*. 1820] (pp. 48). Book Second, same title page, Edinburgh [*c*. 1820] (pp. 50).

4. Analytical Table of Collections to 1784

The *Glen Collection of Scottish Dance Music*, 1891 and 1895, provided an analytical table of 'all the known collections of Scottish Dance Music published in Scotland to the year 1784', compiled by John Glen.

'The Following Table has been prepared in order to trace the Collection in which any given tune first appeared. The tune appears in the Table under its earliest name with the Collection in which it is found. In those cases where it appeared in a subsequent Collection, under a different name, a cross reference is given.'

The spelling and arrangement are exactly reproduced. The numbers are page numbers in the collections.

Abercarney's Reel (*M‘Glashan*, 25)

A' Body looes me (*Stewart*, 18)

Acharnac (*Cumming*, 2). See Lady Mary Menzies.

Ale Wife and her Barrel, The (*Stewart*, 52)

Always Pleased (*M‘Glashan*, 2)

Anderson's Farewell (*Ross*, 31)

Anderson's Rant (*Marshall*, 7)

Anthony Murray (*M‘Glashan*, 15)

Appin House (*M‘Glashan*, 21)

Argyll's Bouling Green (*Bremner*, 70)

Arndilly's Reel (*Cumming*, 8). See Canty Body.

Arne's Reel (*Stewart*, 60)

Arthur's Seat (*Marshall*, 1)

As Black as a Coal (*Bremner*, 60)

Athol Cummers (*Bremner*, 78)

Athole House (*Dow*, 1)

Atholian Hills (*Dow*, 12)

Auld Stuart's Back again, The (*Stewart*, 23)

Auld Wife ayont the Fire (*Bremner*, 90; *Stewart*, 12)

Back of the Change House, The (*Bremner*, 93)

Balgeny's Bouling Green (*Bremner*, 39; *Riddell*, 46)

Balendaloch's Drem (*Bremner*, 33)

Ballnadallach (*Stewart*, 55)

Barley Cakes (*Bremner*, 68)

Barns of Clyde, The (*Campbell*, 77)

Because he was a bonny lad (*Bremner*, 14)

Beggar's Bennison (*Cumming*, 14)

Bernard's Well (*Stewart*, 25)

Big Bow Wow (*Ross*, 32)

Birks of Abergeldy, The (*Bremner*, 35)

Birks of Invergary, The (*Ross*, 4)

Bishop, The (*Cumming*, 11)

Black at the Bane (*M'Glashan*, 25)

Black Dance, The (*Campbell*, 58)

Blackmoor's Jig, The (*Ross*, 35)

Blair Drummond (*Bremner*, 87)

Blue Britches (*Bremner*, 67)

Bonintown Well (*Bremner*, 96)

Bonnet Makers of Dundee, The (*Bremner*, 46)

Bonnie Annie (*Dow*, 18)

Bonny Banks of Clyde, The (*Riddell*, 54)

Bonny Black Ladie, The (*Stewart*, 70)

Bonny Braes of Skelmorly, The (*Riddell*, 44)

Bonny Green of Glasgow, The (*Riddell*, 36)

Bonny Lass of Fannhiven, The (*Bremner*, 20)

Bonny Lass of Fisherrow, The (*Stewart*, 65; *Dow*, 2)

Bonny Lass of Luss, The (*Bremner*, 51)

Bonny Lass to marry me, A (*Bremner*, 24)

Bonny Lass will you lie in a Barrack (*Campbell*, 80)

Bonny Wi Thing (*Bremner*, 40)

Borlum's Reel (*M'Glashan*, 23)

Braes of Angus (*Aird*, No. 154). See Bridge of Anas.

Braes of Auchtertyre, The (*Stewart*, 45; *Campbell*, 4)

Braes of Balquheder, The (*Bremner*, 37)

Braes of Glendochert, The (*M'Glashan*, 5)

Braes of Glenorchy, The (*M'Glashan*, 12)

Braes of Mor, The (*Bremner*, 34)

Braes of Tullymet, The (*Stewart*, 64)

Breas of Athol. The (*Bremner*, 78)

Bride, The (*Cumming*, 9)

Bride is a bonny thing, The (*Bremner*, 34)

Bridge of Anas, The (*Bremner*, 58). See Braes of Angus.

Bridge of Forth, The (*Campbell*, 65)

Bridge of Foss, The (*Ross*, 1)

Bridge of Nairn, The (*Bremner* 2nd, 109). See Old Man ill never die, The.

Bridge of Perth, The (*Dow*, 9)

British Hero, The (*Stewart*, 30)

British Tarrs, The (*Dow*, 10)

Brose and Butter (*Bremner*, 32)

Brown's Reel (*Stewart*, 41)

Buchanan's Reel (*Campbell*, 61)

Bung your Eye (*Ross*, 1)

Burn of Catnie, The (*Bremner*, 53)

Cadgers of the Cannongate, The (*Bremner*, 51)

Caledonian Hunt, The (*Ross*, 6)

Cambdelmore (*Bremner*, 92)

Cameronian's Rant (*Bremner*, 82)

Campbells are coming O ho, The (*Bremner*, 83)

Campbell's Reel, The (*Campbell*, 50)

Camron has got his Wife again (*Bremner*, 4)

Cantie Crecket (*Stewart*, 16)

Canty Body (*M'Glashan*, 27)

Caper Fey (*Bremner* 2nd, 102)

Captain Cuningham of Auchinskeigh (*Riddell*, 40)

Captain Cuningham of Corsehill (*Riddell*, 13)

Captain Keller (*Stewart*, 47)

Captain Lockhart of the Tartar (*Bremner*, 27)

Captain M'Duff (*Stewart*, 68)

Captain M'Duff (*Dow*, 6)

Captain M'Duffs Delight (*M'Intosh*, 31)

Captain MacKenzie (*Stewart*, 36)

Captain M'Kenzie (*Ross*, 2)

Captain Ross (*Bremner*, 8)

Captain Sinclair (*Dow*, 13)

Carle he came o'er the Craft, The (*Bremner*, 30)

Carle's Rant, The. See Port a Bhodich.

Dutchess of Gordon (*Riddell*, 17)

Dutchess of Gordon (*Cumming*, 4)

Dutchess of Gordon (*Dow*, 1)

Dutchess of Gordon (*Marshall*, 11). Renamed Linlithgow Loch.

Dutchess of Hamilton (*Riddell*, 9)

Dutchess of Hamilton (*Dow*, 11)

Dutchess of Hamilton (*Cumming*, 3). See Ruffian's Rant.

Earl Marshal (*Bremner*, 73)

Earl of Glencairn (*M'Glashan*, 6). Now known as The Black Watch's Farewell.

Earl of Seaforth, The (*M'Glashan*, 19)

Eight Men of Mudardt (*Bremner*, 88); (*Stewart*, 23)

Elsie Marly (*Bremner*, 26)

Eppie M'Knab (*Bremner* 2nd, 111)

Ewie wi' the crooked horn (*Ross*, 16). See Carron's.

Fair Field House (*Riddell*, 11)

Feg for a kiss, A (*Bremner*, 74)

File Bek is ay ready, The (*Bremner*, 77)

Fill the Stoup (*Ross*, 36)

Finlayston House (*Riddell*, 55)

Fir Tree, The (*Bremner*, 38)

Fordell House (*Ross*, 22)

Fouller's Rant (*M'Glashan*, 3)

Frolik, The (*Campbell*, 14)

Fyket, The (*Bremner*, 6)

Gallochy's Farewell (*Marshall*, 2)

George Square (*Marshall*, 2)

General Grant (*Cumming*, 11)

Gig (*Campbell*, 71)

Gidd (*Campbell*, 28)

Gillie Callum. See Keellum Kallum.

Glasgow Bells (*Campbell*, 32)

Glasgow College (*Campbell*, 74)

Glasgow Flourish (*Campbell*, 65)

Glasgow Ladys (*Campbell*, 3)

Glasgow Lasses (*Stewart*, 49)

Glenfiddich (*Marshall*, 4)

Glengarry's Reel (*Cumming*, 18)

Glenlyon's Reel (*Stewart*, 18)

Glenmorisone (*Cumming*, 12)

Gordon Castle (*M'Glashan*, 26). See Balnadalloch.

Grant's Rant, The (*Bremner*, 64). See Green grows the Rashes.

Green grows the Rashes (*Stewart*, 13)

Greig's Pipes (*Stewart*, 44; *Campbell*, 11

Grogg (*Ross*, 2)

Grove, The (*Ross*, 5)

Haddington Assembly, The (*Dow*, 6)

Haddington Lassies (*Ross*, 25)

Had the Lass till I winn at her (*Bremner*, 12)

Hallow Fair (*Stewart*, 21)

Harlequin Tune (*Stewart*, 53)

Harlequin Tune (*Stewart*, 56)

Haugh's of Cromdale (*Cumming*, 15) See Merry Maids Meeting

He hirpl'd till her (*Bremner*, 12)

Hey to Couper (*Bremner*, 89)

Hey my Nanny (*Bremner*, 46)

Highland Dress, The (*Stewart*, 61)

Highland Hills, The (*Campbell*, 20) Now known as The Bob of Fettercairn

Highland Laddie, The (*Bremner*, 47)

Highlandman kiss'd his mother, The (*Bremner*, 10)

Highland Plaid, The (*M'Glashan*, 30)

Highland Skip, The (*Dow*, 22)

Highland Watch's Farewell to Ireland (*Stewart*, 27)

Highway to Bourtrie Hill, The (*Riddell*, 42)

Highway to Coilsfield, The (*Riddell*, 16)

Highway to Colain, The (*Riddell*, 18)

Highway to Cragie House, The (*Riddell*, 31)

Highway to Edinburgh, The (*Campbell*, 75)

Highway to Eglintoune, The (*Riddell*, 27)

Highway to Greenvale, The (*Riddell*, 35)

Highway to London, The (*Campbell*, 76)

Highway to Newfield, The (*Riddell*, 11)

Hoble About (*Bremner*, 59)

Lady Eglintoune (*Riddell*, 41)

Lady Elenora Home (*Dow*, 5)

Lady Elenora Home (*Stewart*, 57; *M'Intosh*, 34)

Lady Elgin (*Bremner*, 62)

Lady Elizabeth Crichton (*Ross*, 22)

Lady Emellia Ker (*Stewart*, 72)

Lady Forbes (*Dow*, 2)

Lady Frances Scot (*Dow*, 26)

Lady George Beauclark (*Bremner*, 33)

Lady Grant of Dalvey (*Cumming*, 6)

Lady Grant of Grant (*Cumming*, 2). See Athol Cummers.

Lady Grant of Munymusk (*Cumming*, 6)

Lady Hariot Hope (*Bremner*, 10)

Lady Helen Dalrymple's New Reel (*Riddell*, 23)

Lady Helen Douglas (*Stewart*, 69)

Lady Jean Hume (*Bremner*, 50)

Lady Jean Murray's Rant (*Bremner*, 35)

Lady Louisa Gordon (*Marshall*, 7)

Lady M'Intosh (*Bremner*, 52). Now known as A man's a man for a' that.

Lady M'Intoshe (*Stewart*, 20). See Knit the Pocky.

Lady Madaline Gordon (*Marshall*, 6)

Lady Margaret Macdonald (*Stewart*, 34)

Lady Mary Lindsay (*Riddell*, 33)

Lady Mary Menzies (*Bremner*, 82)

Lady Maxwell (*Campbell*, 25)

Lady Maxwell of Monreath (*Riddell*, 32)

Lady Nelly Wemyss's Reel (*Bremner*, 13)

Lady Susan Gordon (*Marshall*, 5)

Lady Wallace (*Riddell*, 16)

Lady Wallace (*M'Intosh*, 12)

Lady Whiteford (*Riddell*, 38)

Lady's Breast Knot, The (*Bremner*, 31)

Larickille (*M'Glashan*, 8)

Lass among the Actnach (*M'Glashan*, 27)

Lassies likes nea Brandy (*Bremner*, 83)

Lassies of Irvin (*Campbell*, 4)

Lassies of Stewarttown (*Stewart*, 46)

Lassies of the Ferry (*Stewart*, 33). Now known as Hech how Johnnie Lad.

Lassie wi the yellow coatie (*Bremner*, 76)

Last Pint Ale (*Bremner*, 37)

Lawland Lads wi Highland Kilts (*Ross*, 18). See Never out of Humour.

Lenox Love to Blantyre (*Bremner*, 17)

Lethens (*Cumming*, 19). See Bonnie Annie.

Let's to the Ard (*Bremner*, 62)

Lick the ladle Sandie (*Stewart*, 21). See Lassies likes nea Brandy.

Light and Airy (*Ross*, 13)

Links of Leith (*Bremner*, 57)

Little Men of the Mearns (*M'Glashan*, 20)

Lochgery's Rant (*M'Glashan*, 13)

Lochiel's Rant (*Bremner*, 44)

Loch-Ness (*Bremner*, 29)

Lord Albremarle (*Stewart*, 32)

Lord Alexander Gordon (*Marshall*, 3)

Lord Binny (*Dow*, 11)

Lord Cassil (*Riddell*, 14)

Lord Cassill (*Stewart*, 26; *Riddell*, 51)

Lord Dumfries's Bowling Green (*Riddell*, 15)

Lord Dumfries's Bridge (*Riddell*, 35)

Lord Eglinton (*Bremner*, 95)

Lord Eglintoune (*Riddell*, 33)

Lord Fife (*Cumming*, 16)

Lord Finlater (*Cumming*, 8). See Lord Macdonald.

Lord Frederick and his Fencibles (*Campbell*, 51)

Lord Garlie (*Riddell*, 18)

Lord George Gordon (*Marshall*, 1)

Lord Kelly (*Bremner*, 57)

Lord Kinaird (*Bremner*, 81)

Lord Kilmaur (*Riddell*, 12)

Lord Lewis Gordon (*M'Glashan*, 1)

Lord Lovate (*Cumming*, 5)

Lord Macdonald (*M'Glashan*, 19)

Lord Seaforth (*Cumming*, 8). See Highland Plaid.

Lothian Lassies (*Ross*, 17)

Lurg's Reel (*Cumming*, 15)

M'Kinnon's Reel (*Ross*, 36)

Maclachlan's Reell (*Cumming*, 16)
M'Lachlan's Rant (*Stewart*, 29)
Macleod's Reel (*M'Glashan*, 8)
Macpherson's Rant (*Cumming*, 12)
Maggy's weam is fu I true (*Bremner*, 85)
Major Montgomery (*Campbell*, 68)
Maltman comes a Monday, The (*Bremner*, 47)
Marchmont house (*Bremner*, 23)
Marquis of Huntly (*Marshall*, 6)
Marquis of Huntly's Farewell (*Marshall*, 1)
Mary Gray (*Bremner*, 81)
Mr Alexander Montgomerie (*Riddell*, 59)
Mr Crawfurd of Ardmillan (*Riddell*, 12)
Mr Johnson (*Marshall*, 1)
Mr Riedhead (*Stewart*, 1)
Mr Robert Kenedy (*Bremner*, 5)
Mr Sharp (*Campbell*, 67)
Mason Laddie (*Ross*, 9). See Braes of Glenorchy.
Merrily danced the Quaker (*Bremner*, 53)
Merry Dancers, The (*Bremner*, 94)
Merry Lads of Air (*Bremner*, 15; *Riddell*, 10)
Merry Lads of Banff (*Ross*, 14)
Merry Maids (*M'Glashan*, 31)
Milk Maids of Blantyre, The (*Bremner*, 2)
Miller's Daughter, The (*Stewart*, 45)
Miller's Daughter, The (*M'Glashan*, 5). See The Miller's Wedding
Miller's Wedding, The (*Bremner*, 41)
Miss Abercromby (*Marshall*, 5)
Miss Adam (*Dow*, 33)
Miss Admiral Gordon (*Marshall*, 3). Now known as Of a' the airts the wind can blaw.
Miss Agnes Ross (*Marshall*, 12)
Miss Anne Carre (*Stewart*, 57; *M'Intosh*, 35)
Miss Annie Livingston (*Stewart*, 47)
Miss Ann Stewart (*Marshall*, 4)
Miss Baby Montgomery (*Stewart*, 53)

Miss Balfour (*Stewart*, 71)
Miss Barbara Stewart (*Marshall*, 8)
Miss Bell Kennedy (*Riddell*, 58)
Miss Betty Campbell (*Stewart*, 62; *M'Intosh*, 34)
Miss Betty Cathcart (*Riddell*, 49)
Miss Betty M'Donald (*Bremner* 2nd, 99)
Miss Betty Plummer (*Stewart*, 64)
Miss Betty Shaw (*Stewart*, 62)
Miss Blair (*Bremner*, 5)
Miss Bruce (*Stewart*, 70)
Miss Bruce of Kinross (*Stewart*, 33)
Miss Burnet (*Marshall*, 3)
Miss Burnet of Monboddo (*M'Intosh*, 31)
Miss Cahoon (*Bremner* 2nd, 98)
Miss Chalmers (*Ross*, 24)
Miss Chamers (*Stewart*, 27)
Miss Charter (*Dow*, 7)
Miss Dallas (*Marshall*, 1)
Miss Dalrymple (*Dow*, 7)
Miss Dinwiddie (*Campbell*, 78)
Miss Douglas (*Stewart*, 55)
Miss Dundas (*Dow*, 14)
Miss Dunlop (*Campbell*, 9)
Miss Edmondston (*Stewart*, 41)
Miss Eleanora Hamilton (*Riddell*, 52)
Miss Eleanor Ker (*Riddell*, 50)
Miss Elliot (*Stewart*, 63; *M'Intosh*, 33)
Miss Erskine of Alva (*Dow*, 4)
Miss Erskine of Barjarg (*Riddell*, 53)
Miss Ewing (*Campbell*, 67)
Miss Farquharson (*Bremner*, 19). Now known as My love she's but a Lassie yet.
Miss Ferguson of Kilkerran (*Riddell*, 40)
Miss Flora McDonald (*Bremner*, 21)
Miss Fraser (*Bremner*, 18)
Miss French (*Campbell*, 66)
Miss Gardiner (*Dow*, 36)
Miss Gordon (*Stewart*, 37)
Miss Gordon of Bellie (*Marshall*, 10)
Miss Gordon of Cairnfield (*Marshall*, 4)
Miss Gordon of Glastirum (*Marshall*, 6)
Miss Gordon of Lesmore (*Ross*, 9)

Miss Grace Stewart (*Stewart*, 54; *M'Intosh*, 35)

Miss Grant (*Dow*, 1, 4)

Miss Grant of Grant (*M'Intosh*, 34)

Miss Grant of Grant (*Cumming*, 16). See Braes of Tullymet.

Miss Grant of Knockando (*Marshall*, 1)

Miss Grizie Kennedy (*Riddell*, 53)

Miss Halket (*Marshal*, 3)

Miss Hamilton of Sundrum (*Riddell*, 51)

Miss Hariot MacDonald (*Dow*, 18)

Miss Hay (*Stewart*, 5)

Miss Henderson of Fordel (*Dow*, 9)

Miss Henny Mitchelston (*Stewart*, 49)

Miss Hopkins (*Marshall*, 11)

Miss Jackson (*Stewart*, 67)

Miss Jeanie Mercer (*Stewart*, 34)

Miss Jean Stewart (*Marshall*, 2)

Miss Jean Scott (*Stewart*, 59; *M'Intosh*, 33)

Miss Jenny Ross (*Marshall*, 10)

Miss Jeanny Williamson (*Marshall*, 7)

Miss Jenny Duff (*Riddell*, 26)

Miss Jenny Wedderburn (*Ross*, 13). See Burn of Carnie.

Miss Jessy Campbell (*Campbell*, 59)

Miss Jessy Dalrymple (*Stewart*, 51; *M'Intosh*, 35)

Miss Jessy Millar (*Campbell*, 2)

Miss Johnston of Hilton (*Dow*, 24)

Miss Johnston of Hilton (*Dow*, 14)

Miss Katty Gordon of Earlston (*Riddell*, 24)

Miss Katty Maxwell (*Riddell*, 30)

Miss Katty Trotter (*Stewart*, 59; *M'Intosh*, 31)

Miss Ketty Allan (*Marshall*, 3)

Miss Lillie Ritchie (*Riddell*, 36)

Miss Lindsay (*Dow*, 36)

Miss Louisa Campbell's Delight (*M'Glashan*, 2). See Lady Mary Menzies.

Miss Lucy Campbell (*Stewart*, 51)

Miss McKenzie of Coul (*Ross*, 27)

Miss Maclean of Duart (*Dow*, 19)

Miss M'Niell (*Ross*, 23)

Miss M'Queen (*Marshall*, 5)

Miss M'Queir (*Riddell*, 24)

Miss Mary Grant (*Cumming*, 20)

Miss May Hay (*Dow*, 20)

Miss Meynell (*Ross*, 12)

Miss Molly Daker (*Stewart*, 65)

Miss Molly Grant (*M'Intosh*, 33)

Miss Morison (*Stewart*, 50)

Miss Murray (*Bremner*, 11)

Miss Murray (*Campbell*, 30)

Miss Nancy Kennedy (*Riddell*, 48)

Miss Napier (*Dow*, 3)

Miss Nelly Ferguson (*Riddell*, 43)

Miss Nelly Kennedy (*Riddell*, 37)

Miss Oswald of Dunakeer (*Dow*, 3)

Miss Park (*Campbell*, 57)

Miss Peggy Montgomerie (*Riddell*, 54)

Miss Penny M'Kinnon (*Ross*, 30)

Miss Polly Skiner (*Bremner*, 2)

Miss Polly Welsh (*Stewart*, 56)

Miss Pringle (*Stewart*, 58; *M'Intosh*, 32)

Miss Proud (*Stewart*, 48)

Miss Ramsay (*Bremner*, 3)

Miss Ross (*Marshall*, 11)

Miss Sally Eglison (*Marshall*, 2)

Miss Steuart of Urrard (*Dow*, 16)

Miss Stewart of Grandtully (*Dow*, 2)

Miss Swinton (*Stewart*, 52)

Miss Vearie Hay (*Dow*, 8)

Miss Wallace (*Campbell*, 26)

Miss Watson (*Marshall*, 4)

Miss Wedderburn (*Campbell*, 75)

Miss Wedderburn (*Marshall*, 4)

Miss Whitefoord (*Stewart*, 69)

Miss Whiteford (*Riddell*, 57)

Miss Whiteford (*Ross*, 15)

Mrs Arnot (*Riddell*, 60)

Mrs Crawfurd of Ardmillan (*Riddell*, 20)

Mrs Crawfurd of Donside (*Riddell*, 25)

Mrs Cuningham of Corsehill (*Riddell*, 20)

Ring, The (*Stewart*, 32)
Rise lazy lubber (*Cumming*, 8)
Road to Berwick, The (*Marshall*, 3)
Robin shore in herst (*Bremner* 2nd, 103)
Ross House (*Stewart*, 20)
Rothemurches Rant (*Bremner*, 42)
Royal Edinburgh Volunteers (*Campbell*, 49)
Royal Glasgow Volunteers (*Campbell*, 49)
Ruffians Rant, The (*Bremner*, 43). Now known as Roy's Wife.
Runaway, The (*Ross*, 27)
Run down the Town in haste (*Marshall*, 2)
Sailor Lassie, The (*Bremner* 2nd, 107)
Sailor Laddie (*Stewart*, 15). See Sodger Laddie.
Sailor's Wife, The (*Ross*, 24)
Sally Kelly (*Ross*, 40)
Scots Bonnet (*Bremner*, 28)
Seme rune Rallanach (*Cumming*, 2). See Fouller's Rant.
Shamboe Breeches (*Stewart*, 35)
Shaun Truish Willichan (*Bremner*, 71)
Shoe Maker's Daughter (*Stewart*, 72)
Shogallie's Reel (*Cumming*, 20)
Short Apron (*Bremner*, 9)
Sir Adam Ferguson (*Riddell*, 14)
Sir Alexander M'Donald (*Bremner*, 22)
Sir Allan M'Lean (*Ross*, 37)
Sir Archibald Grant of Monemusk (*Dow*, 5)
Sir Harry Innes (*Cumming*, 18)
Sir James Colquhoun (*Cumming*, 9). See Earl of Glencairn.
Sir John Cathcart (*Riddell*, 27)
Sir John Maxwell (*Campbell*, 74)
Sir John Malcolm (*Bremner*, 96)
Sir John Stewart of Grandtully (*Dow*, 15)
Sir John Stuart of Garntullie's Rant (*Stewart*, 29)
Sleepu Maggy (*Bremner*, 48)

Smiling Kattie (*Ross*, 11)
Sodger Laddie (*Bremner*, 22)
Soldier's Joy (*Campbell*, 56)
Space and compass (*Ross*, 4)
Spark's Rant (*Stewart*, 22)
Spell, The (*Bremner*, 73)
Spoigan (*Ross*, 8)
Sport, The (*Cumming*, 10)
Steer the gil (*Bremner*, 13)
Strathdown (*Marshall*, 10)
Straglass House (*Bremner* 2nd, 100)
Strathspey Reel, A (*Stewart*, 50)
Struan Robertson's Rant (*Stewart*, 19)
Struen Robertson's Rant (*Bremner*, 17)
Stuart's Rant, The (*Bremner*, 45)
Stumpie (*Aird* II., No. 44)
Sugarcandy (*Bremner*, 91)
Suttor's Daughter (*M'Glashan*, 6). Wilt thou be my dearie, is derived from this set. See Shoe Maker's Daughter.
Swallow, The (*Stewart*, 36)
Sweet Molly (*Stewart*, 11). See Hoptoun House.
Symon Brodie (*Campbell*, 76)
Tadie's Wattle (*Aird* II., no. 11). Now known as Torryburn.
Tail Toddle (*Aird* II., no. 97)
Taymouth (*Dow*, 12)
There's nae harm done goodwife (*Marshall*, 7)
There's nae luck (*Aird*, no. 198). Now known as Janny Cameron.
This is not my ain House (*Aird* II., no. 176)
Thomas and Sally (*Stewart*, 66)
Thomson's got a dirk (*Cumming*, 8). See Canty Body.
Three Graces, The (*Campbell*, 63)
Thro' the Moor she ran (*Ross*, 20)
Tibby Fouller o' the Glen (*M'Glashan*, 3)
Trip to London, A (*Bremner*, 18)
Troon House (*Riddell*, 56)
Tulloch Gorm (*Bremner*, 16)
Up & war them a' Willie (*Bremner*, 60)

Dance tunes, songs and poems are named in the Index of Tunes. This index includes composers, editors and compilers whose collections are listed in Appendices B2–B4.

INDEX OF TUNES

Tunes, dances, songs and poems named in the text and the Appendices (with certain exceptions) are included, those also represented by a music example having italic numerals. Excluded are the tunes in John Glen's 'Analytical Table of Collections' (Appendix B4), which is arranged alphabetically and cross-referenced, and the airs and marches and minuets of the Gillespie MS. (Appendix A5).

Variants of titles, as distinct from alternatives, are not included unless they differ greatly from the accepted style.